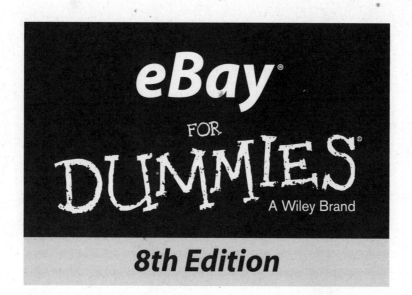

eBay®

FOR

DUMMIES®

A Wiley Brand

8th Edition

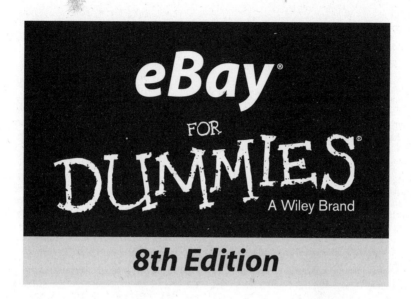

8th Edition

by Marsha Collier

eBay® For Dummies, 8th Edition

Published by: **John Wiley & Sons, Inc.,** 111 River Street, Hoboken, NJ 07030-5774, www.wiley.com

Copyright © 2014 by John Wiley & Sons, Inc., Hoboken, New Jersey

Published simultaneously in Canada

For general information on our other products and services, please contact our Customer Care Department within the U.S. at 877-762-2974, outside the U.S. at 317-572-3993, or fax 317-572-4002. For technical support, please visit www.wiley.com/techsupport.

Wiley publishes in a variety of print and electronic formats and by print-on-demand. Some material included with standard print versions of this book may not be included in e-books or in print-on-demand. If this book refers to media such as a CD or DVD that is not included in the version you purchased, you may download this material at http://booksupport.wiley.com. For more information about Wiley products, visit www.wiley.com.

Library of Congress Control Number: 2013954171

ISBN: 978-1-118-74886-2 (pbk); ISBN 978-1-118-74890-9 (ebk);
ISBN 978-1-118-74875-6 (ebk)

Manufactured in the United States of America

10 9 8 7 6 5 4 3 2 1

About the Author

Marsha Collier is the top-selling eBay author. Her name crops up a lot in the same breath as *e-commerce* and *customer service*. No surprise there. She's the author of the *For Dummies* series on eBay (*eBay For Dummies*, *Starting an eBay Business For Dummies*, *eBay Business All-In-One For Dummies*), plus many other related, best-selling titles. She is one of the foremost e-commerce experts and educators in the world. Her books are published worldwide (special editions for the U.K., Germany, India, France, Canada, Australia, Russia, China — and an edition in Spanish. As of 2007, there were a million books of her books in print, her first was published in 1997 and has been on the many top Best Seller lists.

Marsha intermixes her writing about eBay with her role as experienced spokesperson. While traveling across the United States and around the world, she makes regular appearances on television, radio, and in print to discuss online commerce and customer service.

Marsha earned her eBay stripes as a longtime seller on the site. She began her eBay selling career in 1996 to earn extra money for her daughter's education (and eventually paid for university with her eBay earnings). She grew her business to a full-time venture and was one of the first eBay PowerSellers. Nowadays, you can find everything from autographed copies of her books to photography tools, pet toys, and DVDs in her eBay Store ("Marsha Collier's Fabulous Finds" at http://stores.ebay.com/Marsha-Colliers-Fabulous-Finds) and on her website. (http://www.coolebaytools.com). Marsha also co-hosts Computer and Technology Radio on WSradio at http://wsradio.com/wsradio/show_details/52.

In 2004, Marsha began a blog, Marsha Collier's Musings (http://mcollier.blogspot.com) to talk about timely topics she thinks her readers will enjoy. An early innovator in social media, Marsha penned several books, two of her favorites are *The Ultimate Online Customer Service Guide* and *Social Media Commerce For Dummies*. Her online brand has grown as she shares thoughts on how businesses can make the most of the Internet. She has recently been awarded several honors:

- 2013 Huffington Post #2 of the Top 100 Customer Service Pros on Twitter

- 2013 Forbes Top 20 Women Social Media Influencers

- 2013 Forbes Top 50 Social Media Power Influencers

- Edelman Tweetlevel: Top Media 100 Users by Influence

- 2012 Forbes Top 50 Social Media Power Influencers

- 2012 Small Business Book Awards: Startup Book Category, *Starting an eBay Business For Dummies*

- 2012 The 100 Most Powerful Women On Twitter

- 2011 Forbes Top 10 Women Social Media Influencers

Marsha currently resides in Los Angeles, CA. You can contact Marsha via her website, coolebaytools.com.

Publisher's Acknowledgments

Executive Editor: Steven Hayes

Senior Project Editor: Nicole Sholly

Senior Copy Editor: Barry Childs-Helton

Technical Editor: Patti Louise Ruby

Editorial Assistant: Anne Sullivan

Sr. Editorial Assistant: Cherie Case

Project Coordinator: Rebekah Brownson

Cover Image: ©iStockphoto.com/mbortolino

Contents at a Glance

Table of Contents

Introduction

I just can't believe it; this is the *eighth* edition of *eBay For Dummies*. When I wrote the original edition in 1999, I had no idea that this book would become the top-selling book for those wanting to learn about eBay.

Over a million people have learned how to succeed at an eBay business by reading my books. In your hand you have the book that will get *you* on the road to your own online business. Heed my words and you'll be getting the no-nonsense facts about eBay from an active user.

I'm a longtime eBay shopper as well as a Top Rated Seller. My original career was in retail marketing, and for over 14 years I've been making money on the site. (I even put my daughter through college on my profits!) I work from home and apply my background successfully to all facets of the site.

My enthusiasm and excitement for shopping and selling on the eBay Marketplace seems to have spread to so many corners of the world. eBay users (like you and me) total close to 120 million active users worldwide — that's quite a community. It's a community of buyers who have time to scour the site for items to buy — and of sellers who forage for wholesale items to sell online and make a few dollars (or a full-time living). This makes eBay a massive e-commerce marketplace — and the best part is that eBay is available to anyone who wants to take the time to learn how it works.

My books are written sequentially, and this is the one to start with if you're a beginner. *eBay For Dummies* will give you the solid foundation you need to go on to my other, more advanced books on eBay selling.

The venue is constantly evolving; familiar links may move, but the basics are there to be found. It isn't too hard to master, but just as with any tool, when you know the ins and outs, you're ahead of the game. You can then get the deals when you shop, and make the most money when you sell. You've come to the right place to find out all about eBay. This book is designed to help you understand the basics about buying and selling on eBay, the most successful e-commerce community. You need a firm grasp of the basics before you can succeed in any endeavor. Here are all the tools you need to get moving on eBay, whether you're new to the Internet or a seasoned veteran. You see how to turn your everyday household clutter into cold, hard cash — and how to look for items that you can sell on eBay.

If you're an online shopper, I show you how to figure out how much you should spend and how to get great deals. How much money you earn (or spend) depends entirely on how *often* and how *smartly* you conduct your eBay transactions. *You* decide how often you want to run auctions and place bids; I'm here to help with the *smart* part by sharing tips drawn from what I've learned over my past ten years on eBay.

A website as complex as eBay has many nooks and crannies that may confuse users. Think of this book as a detailed road map that can help you navigate eBay, getting just as much or as little as you want from it. Unlike an actual road map, however, you won't get frustrated folding it back to its original shape. Just close the book and come back any time you need a question answered.

After you figure out the nuts and bolts, you can start buying and selling stuff. This book is full of terrific buying and selling strategies that help you get the most out of your transactions. With this book and a little elbow grease, you can join the ranks of the millions of people who use their home computers to make friends, find great deals, have a lot of fun, and make a profit. When you get the hang of eBay and feel that it's time to graduate (no cap and gown required) from this book, look for my *Starting an eBay Business For Dummies* — it'll take you to the next plateau.

About This Book

Remember those open-book tests that teachers sprang on you in high school? Well, sometimes you may feel like eBay pop-quizzes you while you're on the site. Think of *eBay For Dummies,* 8th Edition, as your open-book-test cheat sheet with all the answers. You don't have to memorize anything; just keep this book handy to help you get over the confusing parts of eBay. Over the years, some of the top sellers and buyers on the eBay site have visited with me when I'm at a book signing or teaching an eBay seminar just to show me their dog-eared, highlighted, marred copy of an earlier edition of *eBay For Dummies* that got them started. This book will do the same for you.

With all that in mind, I've divided this book into pertinent sections to help you find your answers fast. I'll show you how to

- ✔ Get online and register on eBay.
- ✔ Navigate eBay to do just about anything you can think of — search for items for sale, set up listings, monitor your transactions, and join the community circuit.
- ✔ Bid on and *win* eBay auctions and find low prices at fixed-price sales.

- Choose an item to sell, pick the right time for your listing, market it so that a bunch of people see it, and make a nice profit.

- Communicate well and close deals without problems, whether you're a buyer or a seller.

- Handle problems with finesse, should they crop up.

- Become a part of a unique community of people who like to collect, buy, and sell items of just about every type!

Do not adjust your eyes. To protect the privacy of eBay users, screen images (commonly called *screen shots*) in this book blur user IDs to protect the innocent (or not-so . . .).

Foolish Assumptions

You may have picked up this book because you heard that people are making huge money selling on eBay and you want to find out what's going on. Or you heard about the brand-name bargains and wacky stuff you can find in the world's largest shopping emporium. If either of these assumptions is true, this is the right book for you.

Here are some other foolish assumptions I've made about you:

- You have, or would like to have, access to a computer and the Internet so that you can do business on eBay.

- You have an interest in collecting, selling, or buying, and you want to find out more about doing that online.

- You want tips and strategies that can save you money when you buy and make you money when you sell. (You too? I can relate. We already have a lot in common.)

- You're concerned about maintaining your privacy and staying away from people who try to ruin everyone's good time.

Icons Used in This Book

These are facts that you just *have* to know! Just picture me jumping up and down, just waiting to interrupt your reading with a little extra bonus tidbit. Time is money on eBay. When you see this shortcut or timesaver come your way, read the information and think about all the greenbacks you just saved.

Think of this icon as a sticky note for your brain. If you forget one of the pearls of wisdom revealed to you, you can go back and reread it. If you *still* can't remember something here, go ahead and bookmark the page — I won't tell. Even better: Use a yellow highlighter on the print edition.

Don't feel my pain. I've done plenty of things wrong on eBay — and really want to save you from my mistakes. I put these warnings out there bright and bold so that you don't have a bad experience. Don't skip these warnings unless you're enthusiastic about masochism.

When you see this icon, you know you're in for the real deal. I created this icon especially for you to give you the war stories and success stories from eBay veterans that can help you strategize, make money, and avoid the perils of a poorly written item description. ("Learn from their experiences" is my motto.)

You also see a sidebar now and then — text on a gray background to make the topic stand out. Sometimes these decorative items have important short facts that I want you to know, or contain some useful technical stuff (or an interesting aside).

Beyond the Book

Like everything else in the world, eBay changes. Some of the screen grabs in this book may look slightly different from what you see on your computer. That's just eBay tweaking and improving things on the site. My job is to arm you with everything you need to know to begin conducting transactions. If you hit rough waters, just look up your issue in the table of contents or index of this book. I either help you solve it or let you know where to go on eBay for some expert advice.

Although eBay makes its complex website as easy to navigate as possible, you may still need to refer to this book for help. Don't get frustrated if you have to keep reviewing topics before you feel completely comfortable trading on eBay.

After all, Albert Einstein once said, "Don't commit to memory something you can look up." (Although I forget when he said that . . . .)

Where to Go from Here

It's time to open the book and dive in. For updates on this book and to contact me, visit my website

```
http://www.coolebaytools.com
```

You'll find articles about things going on at eBay, online business, and social media. For time-sensitive and possibly silly posts, I also have a blog at

`http://mcollier.blogspot.com`

If you'd like to ask me questions through social media, you can find me on the following networks:

- **Twitter:** @MarshaCollier

  `https://twitter.com/MarshaCollier`
- **Facebook:** Marsha Collier

  `www.facebook.com/MarshaCollierFanPage`
- **Google+:** Marsha Collier

  Circle me and join me for a hangout?

  `https://plus.google.com/101540468776840533944`
- **YouTube:** DealingDiva *(don't judge - I opened that account a long time ago).*

  I often post videos to answer questions I receive.

  `www.youtube.com/user/dealingdiva`

You can e-mail me directly from the Contact page on my website. I read all e-mails, and try to answer as many as I can. But please remember that I'm just me. No giant staff, no big office. I write books, research new products to help online citizens, consult with people just like you, run an eBay business, and try to have a life.

You can also call in and speak to me live on my radio show at 877-474-3302. Every Saturday from noon to 1 p.m. Pacific time, I cohost the *Computer and Technology Show* with Marc Cohen. (We can even help you with your tech issues). The show is also archived online at `www.computerandtechnologyradio.com` and on iTunes `https://itunes.apple.com/us/podcast/computer-technology-radio/id575805424`

Thank you for buying this book. Please let me know about your eBay successes.

Part I
Getting a Feel for eBay

In this part...

- ✓ Getting the basics on using eBay
- ✓ Reviewing the registration process
- ✓ Organizing eBay transactions and interactions through your My eBay page
- ✓ Navigating the site from the home page

Chapter 1

Why Being on eBay Is So Much Fun

eBay has emerged as *the* marketplace of the 21st century. Way back in 2003, *Wired* magazine predicted that eBay's promise is that "retailing will become the national pastime." Promise fulfilled: In 2012, e-commerce sales topped $1 trillion. The founder had a pretty great idea back in 1995 (read about some eBay history in the "eBay's humble beginnings" sidebar, later in this chapter), and the world has taken to shopping and selling online. eBay is a safe and fun place to shop for everything from collectibles to brand-new clothing, all from the comfort of your home.

eBay is now also a marketplace for new merchandise. It's no longer just the destination for locating unusual collectibles and hard-to-find china patterns. These days major brands have signed up — and you can purchase new and useful items, such as alarm systems, tablets, lightbulbs, clothing, cars, homes — just about anything you can think of.

Take a look around your house. Nice shoes (that you never wore). Spiffy artwork (that you're bored with). Great-looking clock (souvenir that doesn't match your décor). Not to mention all the other cool stuff you own. All these great fashions, household appliances, and collectibles are fabulous to own, but when was the last time your clock turned a profit? When you connect to eBay, your PC or mobile device can magically turn into a money machine. Just visit eBay and marvel at all the items that are just a few mouse clicks away from being bought and sold.

In this chapter, I tell you what eBay is and how it works. eBay is today's gas-free alternative to driving and spending hours wandering through boutiques, antiques shops, or outlet malls looking for the perfect gift or tchotchke. The site can also be your personal shopper for gifts and day-to-day items.

Not only can you buy and sell stuff in the privacy of your home, but through your connections on eBay, you can also meet people who share your interests. Those who use the eBay site are a friendly bunch, and soon you'll be buying, selling, swapping stories, and trading advice with the best of them via various social media outlets.

To get to eBay, you need to access the Internet. To access the Internet, you need a Windows PC, a Mac, or a tablet with the eBay Mobile app. (Inexpensive laptops can be found for as little as $299.)

What Is eBay, and How Does It Work?

The Internet spawned all kinds of online marketplaces (known as *e-commerce sites* to Wall Street types), and eBay is the superstar. The reason it remains the leader is simple: It's the place where buyers look to do business with both big brands and small homespun businesses.

eBay itself *doesn't* sell a thing. Instead, the site is a platform for selling and does what all good markets do: It creates a comfy environment that brings together buyers and sellers. You can think of eBay as the person who set you up on your last blind date — except the results are often a lot better. Your matchmaking friend doesn't perform a marriage ceremony but does get you in the same room with your potential soulmate. eBay puts buyers and sellers in an e-commerce environment and lets them conduct their business safely within the rules that eBay has established.

All you need to do to join eBay is fill out a few forms online and click. Congratulations — you're a member with no fees or secret handshakes (you don't pay a fee until you sell something). After you register, you can buy and sell anything that falls within the eBay rules and regulations. (Chapter 2 eases you through the registration process.)

eBay's humble beginnings

The long-standing urban legend says eBay all started with a Pez dispenser. But as romantic as the story is (of the young man who designed the site for his fiancée to trade Pez dispensers), the story is, sadly, public-relations spin. The founder, Pierre Omidyar, had the right vision at the right time, and the first item he sold on the site, originally named AuctionWeb, was a broken laser pointer. Day by day, new

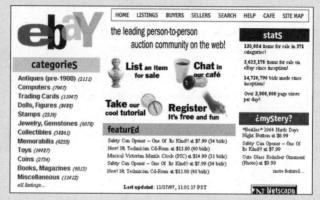

people (including me in 1996) were drawn to the site from Internet chatter. The site eventually grew (in January 1997 hosting 2 million auctions) where it began to strain Pierre's ISP server. The ISP charged him more, so he started charging a small listing fee for sellers, just so he could break even. Legend has it that the day $10,000 in fees arrived in Pierre's mailbox, he quit his day job and embarked on building an Internet legend.

eBay's AuctionWeb was born on Labor Day 1995. The name eBay is taken from Echo Bay, the name Pierre originally wanted for his company. Upon checking with the State of California, he found that the name was taken by another company, so he shortened the name to eBay — and the rest, as they say, is history.

The eBay home page, shown in Figure 1-1, is your first step to finding all the cool stuff you can see and do on eBay. You can conduct searches, learn about current promotions, and get an instant link to the My eBay page, which helps you keep track of every item you have up for sale or have a bid on. You can read more about the eBay home page in Chapter 3 and find out more about My eBay in Chapter 4.

Yikes! What happened? You say the eBay home page on your computer looks nothing like the one in Figure 1-1? Don't rub your eyes — even squinting hard won't help; eBay has a different version of the home page for those who have never registered on eBay — and customizes the page even if you're not signed in. If *you* have never registered on eBay, someone else who uses the computer may have done so already. Know that whatever version of the eBay home page you view, it has the same basic elements.

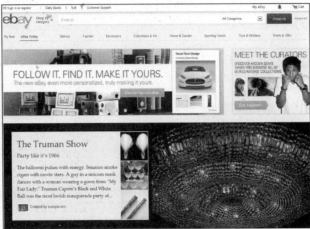

Figure 1-1:
The eBay
home page,
your starting
point for
bargains
and for
making
some
serious
cash.

All About Auctions

When it comes to auctions, the value of an item is determined by how much someone is willing to spend to buy it. That's what makes auctions exciting. eBay offers several flavors of auctions, but for the most part, they all work the same way. An *auction* is a unique sales event where the final selling price of the item for sale is not known. As a result, an element of surprise is involved — not only for the bidder (who may end up with a great deal) but also for the seller (who may end up making a killing). Here's how an auction works from a seller's perspective and a bidder's perspective:

✔ **Seller:** A seller may pay a fee, fill out an electronic form, and set up the auction, listing a *minimum bid* he or she is willing to accept for the item. Think of an auctioneer at Sotheby's saying, "The bidding for this diamond necklace begins at $5,000." You might *want* to bid $4,000, but the bid won't be accepted. Sellers can also set a *reserve price* — sort of a financial safety net that protects them from losing money on the deal. I explain how this stuff works later in this section.

✔ **Bidder:** Bidders in auctions duke it out over a period of time (the minimum is one day, but most auctions last five days, a week, or even longer) until one comes out victorious. Usually the highest bidder wins. The tricky thing about participating in an auction (and the most exciting aspect) is that no one knows the final price an item goes for until the last second — when, often, the most action occurs.

eBay auctions

Unlike "traditional" live auctions that end with the familiar phrase "Going once, going twice, sold!" eBay auctions are controlled by the clock. The seller pays a fee and lists the item on the site for a predetermined period of time; the highest bidder when the clock runs out takes home the prize.

Reserve-price auctions

Unlike a minimum bid, which is required in any eBay auction, a *reserve price* protects sellers from having to sell an item for less than the minimum amount they want for it. You may be surprised to see a 2011 Cadillac CTS-V up for auction on eBay with a minimum bid of only a dollar. It's a fair bet that the seller has put a reserve price on this car to protect himself from losing money. The reserve price allows sellers to set lower minimum bids, and lower minimum bids attract bidders. Unfortunately, if a seller makes the reserve price too high and it isn't met by the end of the auction, no one wins.

eBay charges a fee for sellers to run these types of auctions. Nobody knows (except the seller and the eBay servers) what the reserve price is until the reserve is met, but you *can* tell from the auction page whether you're dealing with a reserve-price auction. Reserve-price auctions are in the listings alongside the other items, so you have to click to find out whether it has a reserve. If bids have been made on an item, a message also appears on the page telling you if the reserve price hasn't been met. You can find out more about bidding on reserve-price auctions in Chapter 6 and setting up a reserve-price auction in Chapter 9.

Restricted-access auctions

If you're over 18 years of age and interested in bidding on items of an adult nature, eBay has an Adult Only category, which has restricted access. Although you can peruse the other eBay categories without having to submit credit card information, you must have a credit card number on file on eBay to view and bid on items in this category. Restricted-access auctions are run like the typical timed auctions. To bid on adult items, first you need to agree to the conditions listed on a terms-of-use page after you enter your User ID and password. That page pops up automatically when you attempt to access this category. The Adult Only category also hosts fixed-price sale listings.

Charity auctions: All for a good cause

A *charity auction* is a high-profile fund-raising auction run by eBay Giving Works, where the proceeds go to a selected charity. Most people don't wake up in the morning wanting to own the shoes that Ron Howard wore when he put his footprints in cement at Mann's Chinese Theater in Hollywood, but one-of-a-kind items like that often are auctioned off in charity auctions. (In fact, someone did want those shoes badly enough to buy them for a lot of money on eBay.) Charity auctions became popular after the NBC *Today Show* sold an autographed jacket on eBay for over $11,000 with the proceeds going to Toys for Tots. Charity auctions are run like most other auctions on eBay, but because they're immensely popular, bidding can be fierce, and the dollar amounts can go sky-high.

Many ultra-famous celebrities use eBay to help out their favorite charities. Billionaire Warren Buffett, for example, has auctioned a private lunch yearly — for the past 14 years — to support one of his favorite charities, the Glide Foundation. In 2013, lunch with the Berkshire Hathaway Chairman went for $1,000,100; the record high winning bid occurred in 2012 for $3,456,789. I suggest that you visit these auctions and bid whenever you can. Charity auctions are a win-win situation for everyone. (You can read more about celebrity auctions in Chapter 18.)

If you aren't interested in seeing or bidding on items of an adult nature, or if you're worried that your children may be able to gain access to graphic adult material, eBay has solved that problem by excluding adult-content items from easily accessible areas. Children under the age of 18 aren't allowed to register on eBay anyway, and should be under an adult's supervision if they do wander onto any part of the site — especially when they log in under an adult's account.

Private (shhh-it's-a-secret) listings

Some sellers choose to hold *private listings* (whether auctions or fixed-price sales) because they know that some buyers may be embarrassed to be seen bidding on a box of racy neckties in front of the rest of the eBay community. Others may go the private route because they're selling big-ticket items and don't want to disclose their bidders' financial status.

Private auctions are run like typical timed auctions, except each bidder's identity is kept secret. At the end of the auction, eBay provides contact info to the seller and to the high bidder, and that's it.

You can send questions to the seller in a private auction through eBay messages, but you can't check out your competition because the item page will never show the high bidder's User ID.

"Buy It Now" on eBay

You don't have to participate in an auction on eBay to buy something. If you want to make a purchase — if it's something you *must* have — you can usually find the item and buy it immediately. Of course, using Buy It Now (*BIN* in eBay-speak) doesn't come with the thrill of an auction, but purchasing an item at a fraction of the retail price — without leaving your chair or waiting for an auction to end — has its own warm and fuzzy kind of excitement. If you seek this kind of instant gratification on eBay, click the *Buy It Now* tab when browsing categories or performing searches.

You may visit an eBay auction only to see an option to Buy It Now. It's not an error! The seller has decided on a price at which to sell the item. By clicking Buy It Now, you can do an end run around the auction process and buy the item outright. If you bid on an auction that shows the Buy It Now option, the Buy it Now option will disappear unless the seller has placed a reserve price that hasn't been met.

eBay Stores

Visiting eBay Stores is as easy as clicking the Visit Store link on any item page. Thousands of eBay sellers have set up these online stores with merchandise meant for you to Buy It Now — and when you find a seller you like, you can visit the store with a click of your mouse. Sellers who open an eBay Store have to meet a certain level of experience on eBay, and when you buy from an eBay Store, you're protected by the same Buyer Protection policy that covers you in any eBay transaction.

Buy It Now and fixed-price sales

More and more sellers are selling items with a Buy It Now option or at a fixed price. These features enable you to buy an item as soon as you see one at a price that suits you. (For more on how these sales work, check out Chapter 6.)

Want to Make Some Cash?

If you're a seller, creating a listing page on eBay is as simple as filling out an online form. You type the name of your item and a short description, add a crisp digital picture, set your price, and voilà — it's selling time. (Okay, it's a tad more involved than that, but not much.)

eBay allows any seller without an eBay Store to post 50 free auction or fixed-price listings per calendar month (store owners get 150–2,500 free listings per month). Once you exceed the number of free listings, you are charged a fee for the privilege of listing an item for sale — $0.05 (media) to $0.30. You don't pay an additional penny unless your item sells.

When you list your item, millions of people (eBay has over 100 million registered users) from all over the world can take a gander at it and place bids. With a little luck, a bidding war may break out in your auction and drive the bids up high enough for you to turn a nice profit. After the auction, the buyer sends you the payment either through a payment service or PayPal. Then you ship the item. Abracadabra! You just turned your item (everyday clutter, no doubt) into cash. You can run as many listings as you want (no duplicates, please), all at the same time. To get info on deciding what to sell and when, leaf through Chapter 9; to find out how to set up an auction, jump to Chapter 10 — and to get the lowdown on advanced selling techniques, visit Chapter 14. When you're ready to go pro? Check out the appendix.

Get a Deal and Get It Fast!

If you're a collector or you just like to shop for bargains on everyday goods, you can browse 24 hours a day through the items up for sale in eBay's tens of thousands of categories, which range from Antiques to Writing Instruments. Find the item you want, do a little research on what you're buying and who's selling it, place your bid, and keep an eye on it until the auction closes. When I write or update any of my eBay titles (like this one or *Starting an eBay Business For Dummies*), I have a great time browsing the different categories and buying a little something here and there — it's amazing just how varied the selection is. I even bought parts for my vacuum cleaner!

Take a look at Chapter 5 for the 411 on searching for items on which to bid. When you see an item you like, you can set up a bidding strategy and let the games begin. Chapter 6 gives you bidding strategies that can make you the winner. After you win your first auction, look for expert advice about completing the transaction in Chapter 8.

You can bid as many times as you want on an item, and you can bid on as many auctions as you want. Just keep in mind that each bid is a binding contract that you are required to pay should you win.

Research for Fun and Profit

eBay's awesome search engine allows you to browse through countless *categories* and items up for sale. As a buyer, you can do lots of comparison shopping on that special something you just can't live without — or just browse around until something catches your eye. If you're a seller, the search engine allows you to keep your eye on the competition and get an idea of how hot your item is. That way, you can set a competitive price. To find out more about using search options and categories, check out Chapters 3 and 5.

The search engine also lets you find out what other people are bidding on. From there, you can read up on a seller's *feedback ratings* (eBay's ingenious reputation system) to get a sense of the seller's reliability — *before* you deal with him or her.

eBay's Role in the Action

Throughout the process, eBay's servers keep tabs on what's going on. When an auction or sale is over, eBay takes a small percentage of the final selling price and instructs the seller and buyer to contact each other through e-mail. At this point, eBay's job is pretty much over, and eBay steps aside unless a problem arises.

Most of the time, everything works great, everybody's happy, and eBay never has to step back into the picture. But if you happen to run into trouble in paradise, eBay can help you settle the problem, whether you're the buyer or the seller.

eBay regulates members with a detailed system of checks and balances known as *feedback,* which is described in Chapter 4. The grand plan is that the community polices itself. Don't get me wrong — eBay does jump in when shady activity comes to light. But the people who keep eBay most safe are the community members, the buyers and sellers who have a common stake in conducting business honestly and fairly. Every time you sell something or buy an item, eBay members have a chance to leave a comment about you. You should do the same for them. If they're happy, the feedback for the seller is positive; otherwise the feedback is negative. Either way, your feedback sticks to you like glue.

Building a great reputation with positive feedback ensures a long and profitable eBay career. Negative feedback has an effect like multiple convictions for grand theft auto — it's a real turnoff for most folks and can make it hard to do future business on eBay.

If your feedback rating becomes a –4 (negative 4), eBay suspends your buying and selling privileges. You can find out more about how eBay protects you as a buyer or a seller in Chapter 16.

Buyers can leave positive or negative feedback for a seller, but sellers can only click "positive." Sellers still do have the option to leave a descriptive comment so that problematic buyers don't get off scot-free.

Features and Fun Stuff

So eBay is all about making money, right? Not exactly. The folks at eBay aren't kidding when they call it a community — a place where people with similar interests can compare notes, argue, buy, sell, and meet each other. Yes, people have married after meeting on eBay. (Take a guess how their friends bought the wedding gifts!)

The Security Center is the catchall resource for information and services about making deals on eBay safer — and for information on what to do if something goes sour. I don't like to think about it, but sometimes — despite your best efforts to be a good eBay member — buyers or sellers don't keep their word. In a very small percentage of cases, unscrupulous louts try to pull scams. You may buy an item that isn't as it was described, or the winner of your auction may not send payment. Sometimes even honest members get into disputes. Trust & Safety is an excellent resource when you need questions answered or you need a professional to come in and handle an out-of-hand situation. Chapter 16 tells you all about the Security Center.

Extra Apps You're Gonna Want

At some point in your eBay career, you'll become comfortable with all the computer-related hoops you have to jump through to make the eBay magic happen. At that time, you may be ready to invest in a few extra apps or devices that can make your eBay experience even better. Digital cameras and online fee apps can help make your time on eBay a more lucrative and fun adventure. You find out how to use digital technology for your sales in more detail in Chapter 18.

Chapter 2

Ready, Set, Go! Signing Up on eBay

In This Chapter

▶ Using eBay's forms

▶ Getting personal about privacy

▶ Identifying with User IDs and passwords

▶ Learning the ropes (eBay rules and regs)

You've no doubt figured out that you sign on to eBay electronically, which means that you don't *really* sign on the dotted line as folks did in days of old. Nowadays, the art of scrawling your signature has become as outdated as vinyl records (although you can still get very collectible vinyl records on eBay if you're feeling nostalgic).

Compared to finding a parking space at the shopping center during the holidays, signing up for eBay is a snap. The toughest thing you have to do is type your e-mail address correctly (and, if you're like me, that's often a challenge).

In this chapter, you find out everything you need to know about registering on eBay. You get tips on what information you have to disclose and what you should keep to yourself. Don't worry — this is an open-book test. You don't need to memorize state capitals, the periodic table, or even multiplication tables. (Whew.)

Registering on eBay

You don't have to wear one of those tacky "Hello, My Name Is" stickers on your shirt after you sign on, but eBay does need to know some things about you before it grants you membership. You and millions of other folks will be roaming around eBay's online treasure trove; eBay needs to know who's who. So, keeping that in mind, sign in, please!

The only hard-and-fast rule on eBay is that you must be 18 years of age or older. Don't worry, the Age Police won't come to your house to card you; they have other ways to discreetly ensure that you're at least 18 years old. (**Hint:** Credit cards do more than satisfy account charges.) If you're having a momentary brain cramp and you've forgotten your age — but if you can remember reading *Harry Potter* books right after the first movie of the series came out, or seeing *Star Wars Episode 2: Attack of the Clones* in the theater, or wearing out a VHS tape of the original *Toy Story* while growing up, you're in. Head to the eBay home page and register. The entire process takes only a few minutes.

Registering Is Free

Before you can sign up for some fun on eBay, you have to be connected to the World Wide Web. This is the time to fire up your computer and connect to the Internet. After you open your Internet browser, you're ready to sign up.

Just type www.ebay.com in the address box of your browser and press Enter; this will take you to the eBay home page. Right there, in the upper-left corner, is the Register link (look for a button or link indicating Register somewhere on the page, as shown in Figure 2-1). Click the word Register and let the sign-up process begin.

Click here to sign up for eBay.

Figure 2-1:
Click the
Register
button, and
soon you'll
be dealing
online like
a pro!

The eBay home page changes all the time. If you don't see a Register button, look around the page — a Register button or link will be there somewhere.

Here's an overview of how easy it is to register:

1. **Enter the basic required info.**

2. **Read and accept the User Agreement and Privacy Policy.**

3. **Confirm your e-mail address.**

4. **Breeze through (or past) any optional information.**

The following sections fill you in on all the details.

Thanks to a bunch of really smart tech types, you access the Registration pages securely, through an *SSL* (Secure Sockets Layer) encrypted connection to eBay. You can tell you're on an SSL connection because the normal *http* at the beginning of the web address (also called the URL) is now *https*. I could tell you how SSL works, but instead I'll just give you the bottom line: It *does* work, so trust me and use it. The more precautions eBay (and you) take, the harder it is for some hypercaffeinated high-school kid to get into your files.

When you're at the Registration form, you go through a four-step process.

Like, what's your sign? Filling in required information

After you click the Register button, you're taken to the heart of the eBay Registration pages. You may register as a business or as an individual; I registered as an individual (you can change your registration to a business on eBay later). So if you don't quite have a business up and running, register simply as an individual. To get started, follow these steps:

1. **At the top of the first registration page, after eBay shows the steps of the registration process, fill in some required information.**

   Here's what eBay wants to know about you:

   - Your full name (eBay keeps this information on file in case the company or a member who is a transaction partner needs to contact you).

   - Your e-mail address (`yourname@myISP.com`).

   If you have an existing business and you want to register on eBay with your business name, it's a good idea to click the link that says *start a business account,* as shown in Figure 2-2. That way you start out on the right foot with a legitimate business registration. eBay will still need your personal information because you represent your business on eBay.

Click here to register a business account.

ebay Get started with eBay

Create your personal account or start a business account.

First name   Last name

Email

eBay user ID ❷

Password

Confirm password

By clicking "Submit" I agree that:
- I have read and accepted the User Agreement and Privacy Policy.
- I may receive communications from eBay and can change my notification preferences in My eBay.
- I am at least 18 years old.

Submit

Figure 2-2:
Register as
a business
account,
rather
than with
a personal
one, if your
business is
already set
up to go.

If you register with an anonymous e-mail service such as Yahoo! Mail, Gmail, or Hotmail, you may be taken to a page that requires additional information for authentication. You must provide valid credit card information for identification purposes. Your information is protected by eBay's Privacy Policy, and your credit card won't be charged.

After you input your personal information, you're ready to create your eBay persona.

2. Scroll down the page to select your new eBay User ID.

See "A Not-So-Quick Word about Choosing a User ID," later in this chapter, for some tips on selecting your User ID.

Because many of the "good" User IDs are taken, eBay checks the availability of your preferred ID. (Figure 2-3 shows eBay's suggestions when a User ID is already taken.) If your chosen name is taken, try again. (Lather, rinse, repeat.) Finding an awesome User ID can be as difficult as finding an untaken vanity plate at the California DMV.

Figure 2-3:
Type your
proposed
User ID
and check
whether it's
available.

eBay user ID ⊘

queen-of-shopping

Sorry, that user ID is not available. Please try again.

- Use at least 6 characters (letters, numbers,
  periods, underscores, dashes only).
- To protect your privacy, do not use your
  email address or full name for your user ID.

Suggestions:
queenofshopping-2013
queenofshopping-us
2013queenofshopping
13queenofshopping
queenofshopping-us

By clicking "Submit" I agree that:

- I have read and accepted the User Agreement and Privacy Policy
- I may receive communications from eBay and can change my notification preferences in My eBay.

3. **Choose a password, enter it in the Password text box, and then type it a second time in the Confirm password box to confirm it.**

   For more information on choosing a password, see "A Quick Word about Passwords," later in this chapter.

4. **Indicate that you agree to eBay's User Agreement and Privacy Policy and click Continue.**

   You can find more information on this agreement later in the chapter.

   Depending on the phase of the moon, eBay may have the questions in this step-by-step registration in a slightly different order. Just follow these steps and keep clicking Continue at the bottom of each screen until you're finished.

5. **Create your unique secret question and input the answer.**

   The secret question you select here is used by eBay to identify you if you ever have problems signing in.

   I recommend not using any fact that is generally known about you by your friends or in social media.

6. **Now eBay will want your contact information.**

   Input your address and primary telephone number. eBay keeps this information on file for future communication.

   At different points in the registration process, eBay may send you an e-mail or send a text to (or call) your phone to give you a confirmation code. Just type the code you receive from them onto the next page. This is eBay's way of verifying your information each step of the way. More of the verification process further on.

7. **If eBay requires your credit card information (for identification that confirms you're a real person), it will ask on the next screen.**

8. **Type your date of birth.**

If eBay finds a glitch in your registration, such as an incorrect area code or ZIP code, you see a warning message. This is one of eBay's security measures that ward off fraudulent registrations. Use the Back button to correct the information. If you put in a wrong e-mail address, for example, eBay has no way of contacting you — so you don't hear a peep from eBay regarding your registration until you go through the entire process all over again.

9. **Click the Continue button and check your e-mail!**

eBay will send you an e-mail containing a clickable link. Clicking the link from the e-mail opens a window in your Internet browser. Ba-da-boom! You're registered!

10. **Sign up for a PayPal account.**

To transact business on eBay, you will need a PayPal account. You will be presented with a link to sign up. If you don't have one, now is the time to sign up. PayPal is safe, and all your information is kept confidentially — with the same level of safety you expect from a financial organization.

Do you solemnly swear to . . . ?

During the registration you'll be asked to check the boxes that say you agree to the eBay User Agreement and Privacy Policy. At this point, you take an oath to keep eBay safe for democracy and commerce. You promise to play well with others, not to cheat, and to follow the Golden Rule. No, you're not auditioning for a superhero club, but don't ever forget that eBay takes this stuff very seriously — and most eBay members do, too. You can be kicked off eBay or worse. (Can you say "federal investigation"?)

Be sure to read the User Agreement thoroughly when you register. So that you don't have to put down this riveting book to read the legalese right this minute, I provide the nuts and bolts here:

✔ You understand that every transaction is a legally binding contract. (Click the User Agreement link at the bottom of any eBay page for the current eBay Rules and Regulations.)

✔ You agree that you can pay for the items you buy and the eBay fees that you incur. (Chapter 8 fills you in on how eBay takes its cut of the auction action.)

✔ You understand that you're responsible for paying any taxes.

✔ You're aware that if you sell prohibited items, eBay can forward your personal information to law enforcement for further investigation. (Chapter 9 explains what you can and can't sell on eBay — and what eBay does to sellers of prohibited items.)

✔ eBay makes clear that it is just a *venue,* which means it's a place where people with similar interests can meet, greet, and do business.

A little about User Agreements and Privacy Policies

As you spend more and more time on the Internet, you'll be required to click many boxes that say you agree to a User Agreement or Terms of Service. These documents can be pages long — and involve a lot of making sure that you agree to do the right thing. The bottom line is, if you don't agree, you can't use the site (or the app).

Privacy Policies are a bit more important. You should always know how much of the information you give will be kept confidential — and how much of that info can be given away. Many sites share your personal data — and you often have the option of "opting out" of data sharing. I always recommend reading the privacy provisions carefully before you click.

When everything goes well, the eBay website is like a school gym that opens for Saturday swap meets. At the gym, if you don't play by the rules, you can get tossed out. But if you don't play by the rules on eBay, the venue gets un-gymlike in a hurry. eBay has the right to get state and federal officials to track you down and prosecute you.

If you're a stickler for fine print, click the links provided on the Registration page for all the *Ps* and *Qs* of the latest policies. The User Agreement is vital to your success on eBay.

Before you can proceed, you must click the check box, indicating that you really, *really* understand what it means to be an eBay user. Because I know that you, as a law-abiding eBay member, will have no problem following the rules, go ahead and click the I Agree to These Terms button at the bottom of the page. You're transported to a screen that tells you eBay is sending you an e-mail. You're almost done.

It must be true if you have it in writing

After you accept the User Agreement and Privacy Policy, eBay takes less than a minute to e-mail you an activation notice. When you receive the eBay registration activation e-mail, don't delete it.

With your confirmation code from the e-mail in hand, head back to the secure eBay Registration page by clicking the link supplied in your e-mail. If your e-mail doesn't support links, go to this address:

```
https://scgi.ebay.com/ws/eBayISAPI.dll?RegisterConfirmCode
&RegisterConfirmCode&registerconfirmcode=
```

After you reconnect with eBay and it knows your e-mail address is genuine, you'll be heartily congratulated with an eBay e-mail. It's time to start shopping!

If you don't receive your eBay registration confirmation e-mail within 24 hours, there was most likely an error in your e-mail address. At this point, the customer-support folks can help you complete the registration process. Try visiting the Contact Us area from the Customer Support link at the top of the page and indicate that you're a guest.

If, for some reason (even a late night watching the *Breaking Bad* marathon is a perfectly acceptable excuse), you incorrectly type the wrong e-mail address, you have to start the registration process all over again with a different User ID (eBay holds the previous ID for 30 days). If you run into a snag, you can click the Live Help link on the page as in Figure 2-4. At the bottom of the pop-up will be a Call Us button to reach Live Help from 5:00 a.m. to 10:00 p.m. Pacific time, seven days a week.

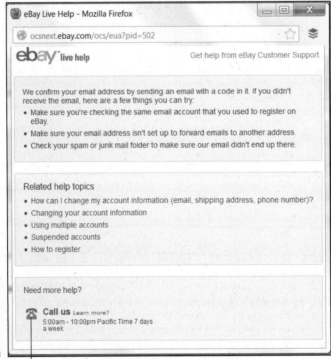

Figure 2-4:
The eBay
Live Help
page.

Even without registering, you can
still get help from eBay.

If somebody you're in a transaction with requests your info, you get an e-mail from eBay giving you the name, phone number, city, and state of the person making the request. Keep your own information up to date. If you don't, you risk penalties. See Chapter 15 for details.

A Quick Word about Passwords

Choosing a good password is not as easy (but is twice as important) as it may seem. Whoever has your password can (in effect) "be you" on eBay — running sales, bidding on auctions, and leaving possibly litigious feedback for others. Basically, such an impostor can ruin your eBay career and possibly cause you serious financial grief.

As with any online password, you should follow these rules to protect your privacy:

- ✔ Don't choose an obvious password, such as your birthday, your first name, or (especially!) your Social Security number. (**Hint:** If it's too easy to remember, it's probably easy to crack.)

- ✔ Make things tough on the bad guys — combine numbers and letters (use uppercase and lowercase) or create nonsensical words.

- ✔ Don't give out your password to anyone — it's like giving away the keys to the front door of your house.

- ✔ If you ever suspect that someone has your password, immediately change it by going to the following address:

  `https://scgi.ebay.com/ws/eBayISAPI.dll?FYPShow`

- ✔ Change your password every few months just to be on the safe side.

- ✔ Don't use the same password for eBay and PayPal.

A Not-So-Quick Word about Choosing a User ID

eBay gives you the option of picking your User ID. Making up a User ID is my favorite part. If you've never liked your real name (or never had a nickname), here's your chance to correct that situation. Have fun. Consider choosing an ID that tells a little about you. Of course, if your interests change, you may regret having too narrow a User ID.

You can call yourself just about anything; you can be silly or creative or boring. But remember, this ID is how other eBay users will know you. So here are some common-sense rules:

- Don't use a name that would embarrass your mother.
- Don't use a name with a negative connotation, such as *scam-guy*.
- Don't use a name that's too weird. If people don't trust you, they won't buy from you.
- eBay doesn't allow spaces in User IDs, so make sure that the ID makes sense when putting two or more words together.

If you're dying to have several short words as your User ID, you can use underscores or hyphens to separate them, as in *super-shop-a-holic*. If you sign in to eBay once a day on your computer, typing underscores or dashes won't slow you down.

You can change your User ID once every 30 days if you want to, but I don't recommend it. People come to know you by your User ID. If you change your ID, your past does play tagalong and attaches itself to the new ID. But if you change your User ID too many times, people may think you're trying to hide something.

Nevertheless, to change your User ID, click the My eBay link at the top of most eBay pages. From your My eBay login page, click the Account tab, then scroll to the Personal Information link. Click the Edit link next to User ID under Account Information. Follow essentially the same steps you used when selecting your initial ID — and you have a new eBay identity.

eBay also has some User ID rules to live by:

- No offensive names (like &*#@@guy).
- No names with *eBay* in them. (It makes you look like you work for eBay, and eBay takes a dim view of that.)
- No names with & (even if you *do* have both looks&brains).
- No names with @ (like @Aboy).
- No symbols such as the greater than or less than symbols (> <) or consecutive underscores _ _.
- No IDs that begin with an *e* followed by numbers, an underscore, a dash, a period, or a dot.
- No names of one letter (such as Q).

When you choose your User ID, make sure that it isn't a good clue for your password. For example, if you use *Natasha* as your User ID, don't choose *Boris* as your password. Even Bullwinkle could figure that one out.

AUCTION ANECDOTE

The craze that began with AW

Back in 1994, when eBay founder Pierre Omidyar had the idea to start a web auction, he named his first venture Auction Web. The following figure shows a vintage Auction Web Internet auction that I won in February 1997. There were some great deals even in those days!

TIP

Hey, AOL users, this one's for you: Make sure that your Mail Controls are set to receive e-mails from eBay. If you have Internet e-mail blocked, you need to update your AOL Mail Controls. To do so, enter the AOL keyword **Mail Controls**.

Your License to Deal (Almost)

You are now officially a *newbie,* or eBay rookie. The only problem is that you're still at the window-shopping level. If you're ready to go from window-shopper to item seller, just zip through a few more forms, and before you know it, you can start running your own auctions on eBay.

TIP

Until you've been a member of eBay for 30 days, a picture of a beaming, golden, cartoonlike icon shows up next to your User ID on the site. This doesn't mean that you've been converted into a golden robot; the icon merely indicates to other eBay users that you are new to eBay.

Chapter 3

Finding Your Way Around eBay

*T*he famous writer Thomas Wolfe *was* wrong; you *can* go home again. At least on eBay. Try to visit the eBay home page on a regular basis; it's a place to keep up with eBay's newest offerings. Month after month, millions of people (just like us) land on eBay's home page without wearing out the welcome mat (probably because they are wearing their robes and slippers). The eBay home page is the front door to the most popular marketplace on the Internet.

Everything you need to know about navigating eBay begins right here. In this chapter, I give you the grand tour of the areas you can reach right from the home page with the help of links.

What Is the Home Page?

The eBay *home page* is shown in Figure 3-1 and includes the following key areas:

   ✔ Navigation links at the top of the page with six eBay links that can direct you straight to important eBay areas. (These links repeat on every page).

   ✔ A search box that helps you find items by title keywords as well as a link to eBay's Advanced Search page.

   ✔ A string of links to the top level of the product listing category structure.

Figure 3-1:
The home
page —
starting
point for fun,
profit, and
values.

 Do not adjust your computer monitor. You're not going crazy. Today you may notice that a link that was on the eBay home page a minute ago is gone. That's normal. The links on the eBay home page change often to reflect what's going on — not just on the site, but in the world as well.

Sign In, Please

Sign In is possibly the most powerful of all the links on the eBay pages, and it will be your first stop if you plan on doing any business on the site. Click the Sign In link in the upper-left corner of the page and you will arrive at the official Sign In page (shown in Figure 3-2).

Figure 3-2:
The eBay
Sign In
page.

When you go to the Sign In page and then sign in, you don't have to enter your User ID again that day. You can set your preferences to take you directly to your My eBay Summary page. This little timesaver is essential for every eBay user. (See Chapter 4 for info on My eBay.)

You can search for items on eBay without signing in, but what fun is that? If you haven't registered with eBay, you're pretty much out of luck if you find a great deal on a lamp that's just what you've been looking for — and the auction closes in five minutes!

If you're the only one who uses your computer, be sure to select the box that says *Stay Signed In*. This way, you're always signed in to eBay within the browser every time you go to the site. The Sign In process places a *cookie* (a technical thingy — see Chapter 15 for details) on your computer that remains a part of your computer for the rest of the day. If you don't select the box, you will be signed in on your computer just for this session.

After you've registered and have done some business on the site, eBay will prompt you to sign in before you proceed anywhere on the site. If (say) you're on a friend's computer, or have just updated your browser, here's how to get to the eBay Sign In page and sign in:

1. **Click the Sign In link at the eBay home page.**

   In the address bar, you'll notice the URL of the new page that appears is a Secure Sign In page. The change from `http` to `https` indicates that your personal information is secure. (See Chapter 2 for details about SSL.)

2. **Enter your User ID and password.**

3. **Select the Stay Signed In box if you're not at a public computer. If you are using someone else's computer, remember to sign out when you leave.**

You're now signed in to eBay and can transact on the site with ease. When you sign in, you should be brought to your My eBay page. If not, enter your My eBay page by clicking the My eBay link that appears at the top of any eBay page. (See Chapter 4 for more on My eBay.)

Follow the Links

As mentioned, the *navigation links* at the top of the eBay home page list six top-level eBay links that take you directly to different eBay areas through drop-down menus. You can also click the Cart link to view your cart before payment. Using the navigation area is a one-stop click zone. You can find this area at the top of every page you visit on eBay. No matter where you are on the site, you go straight to a related page when you click one of the six navigation links.

Think of links as expressways to specific destinations. Click a link just once, and the next thing you know, you're right where you want to be. You don't even have to answer that proverbial annoying question, "When are we gonna get there?" from the noisy kids in the backseat.

Here, without further ado, are the six upper-level navigation links and where they take you:

- **Daily Deals:** Featured items and deals that are good for the day in many categories.

- **My eBay:** Clicking the top-level link, My eBay, may bring you to different places depending on how long you've been on eBay. If you are new to the site, it will bring you to your personal My eBay transactions page. This is where you will keep track of all your buying and selling activities and account information. Figure 3-3 shows a My eBay All Selling page.

  If you've been selling on the site for a while, and are subscribed to the Selling Manager or Selling Manager Pro products, clicking this link will take you to those pages. (The complete details on this area can be found in Chapter 4.)

  By mousing over (and not clicking) the My eBay link, you make a drop-down menu appear with additional links:

  - **Summary:** Clicking here takes you to your eBay Summary page. Your Summary page (see Figure 3-4) is very similar to the My eBay page; your Watch List and purchases are featured at the top.

  - **Bids/Offers:** Clicking here takes you to a page that tracks any bids you've placed on items up for auction. It also shows any listing in which you've placed an offer. (Find how to make an offer on a fixed-price item in Chapter 7.)

Figure 3-3:
My eBay is
a simplified
page that
shows your
transactions
on eBay.

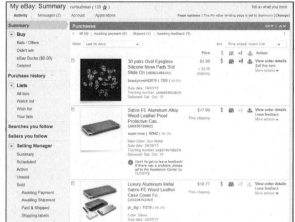

Figure 3-4:
The My
eBay
Summary
page is
eerily simi-
lar to the My
eBay page.

• **Watch List:** On every eBay item, there is a link to watch an item. It gives you an opportunity to bookmark an item for possible future purchase, or to keep an eye on bidding in an auction. Any item you've marked as such will be listed on this page. (More on your Watch List in Chapter 4.)

• **All Lists:** This page duplicates the listing of items you are watching, along with any other lists you've set up.

• **Purchase History:** If you've been buying items on eBay, the site has kept an online record of every purchase you make there. Going to this page allows you to view all your purchases as far back as three years ago.

• **Selling:** Here you'll find an interactive list of all the items you currently have up for sale on eBay.

• **Followed Searches:** If (like me) you have many different things you search for, eBay gives you a tool to save a certain search you make. (Chapter 5 gives you the info on this.) On this page you can view or edit or add product searches.

• **Messages:** Click this link and you'll be brought to the eBay message area (also accessible from the tabs at the top of your My eBay page). When someone wants to contact you in relation to an eBay item, their messages will appear here. You'll also find messages from eBay — which it also sends to your registered eBay e-mail address.

   This is eBay's private e-mail system, where you reply without exposing your personal e-mail address. During a transaction is the only time e-mail addresses are exchanged.

✔ **Sell:** Takes you to the start of the Sell Your Item form, which you must fill out to start your sale. I explain how to navigate this form in Chapter 10.

✔ **Community:** The drop-down menu you'll find here gives you four options. Clicking the various options takes you to pages where you can find the latest eBay news and announcements (eBay changes things twice a year and posts notices so sellers can keep up to date), ask questions of fellow sellers in the eBay community, try new features, and find out more about eBay. (Chapter 17 will give you ideas on how to use these resources.)

✔ **Customer Support:** A quick and valuable support page appears when you click the Customer Support link. Here you can find answers to many of your questions, as well as keep apprised of eBay's rules and regulations that govern trading on the site. You will also find a link to the Resolution Center where you can solve many a problem with a trading partner. I explain its uses in Chapter 4.

✔ **Notification Bell:** If you have eBay messages or a notification from eBay, you'll be able to see them here.

Also at the top of the eBay home page, you find several powerful links that are just as important as the links on the navigation bar:

✔ **eBay Logo:** Click the eBay logo and it takes you right back to the home page. Use this link from any other page when you need to get back to the home page right away.

✔ **Sign In or Register:** When you're signed in to eBay, you will see a greeting (mine says "Hi Marsha!"). Click the down arrow next to your name to sign in or out. If you haven't registered on eBay, turn to Chapter 2 to get the quick and painless facts about the easy eBay registration process.

Exploring Your Home Page Search Options

An ancient expression says, "Every journey begins with the first eBay search." Okay, I updated the quote just a tad, but they are wise words nonetheless. You can start a search from the home page in one of two ways:

✔ **Use the search box.** It's right there at the top of the home page, with the Search button next to it. It's a fast way of finding item listings.

✔ **Use the Advanced link next to the search box on the home page.** This link takes you to the Advanced Search page, where you can do all kinds of specialized searches.

Both options can give you the same results. The instructions I offer in the next two sections about using these search methods are just the tip of the eBay iceberg. For the inside track on how to finesse the eBay search engine to root out just what you're looking for, visit Chapter 5.

Seeking items through the search box

To launch a title search from the home page, follow these steps:

1. **In the search box, type no more than a few keywords that describe the item you're looking for.**

   Refer to Figure 3-1 to see the search box.

2. **Click the Search button.**

   The results of your search appear onscreen in a matter of seconds.

You can type just about anything in this box and get some information. Say you're looking for *Star Trek* memorabilia. If so, you're not alone. The television show (now known as *Star Trek: The Original Series*) premiered on September 8, 1966, and even though it was canceled in 1969 because of low ratings, *Star Trek* became one of the most successful science-fiction franchises in history — a new movie, *Star Trek Into Darkness,* came out in 2013! If you like *Star Trek* as much as I do, you can use the search box on the eBay home page to find all sorts of *Star Trek* stuff. I just ran a search and found 188,961 items — in hundreds of categories — with *Star Trek* in their titles (your results will probably vary).

 To find an item that sold on eBay in the past, perform your search from the search box. On the results page, scroll down and on the left, you have the ability to refine your search. Under the Show Only heading, you can select Completed Listings, which shows all the items that have gone through the sales cycle and have expired unbought or have been purchased. Select the Sold Listings box to see a list of items of this type that have been sold in as long as the last 90 (or so) days, as well as what they sold for. You can use this type of search to strategize your asking price before you put an item up for sale (or to determine how much you'll have to pay to purchase an item).

Try the Advanced link next to the search box to narrow your search. This link takes you to the Advanced Search: Find Items page, which is explained in the following section.

When you search for popular items on eBay (and a classic example is *Star Trek* memorabilia), you may get inundated with thousands of listings that match your search criteria. Even if you're traveling at warp speed, you could spend hours checking each auction individually. ("Scotty, we need more power *now!*") If you're pressed for time like the rest of us, eBay has not-so-mysterious ways to narrow your search so finding a specific item is much more manageable. Turn to Chapter 5 for insider techniques that can help you slim those searches and beef up those results.

Going where the Advanced Search box takes you

One of the most important buttons on the eBay page is the Advanced link next to the search box. When you click here, you're whisked away to the Advanced Search: Find Items page, which promptly presents you with several search options. Each option enables you to search for information in a different way. Here's how the search options on the menu can work for you:

- ✔ **Find Items:** Search by keywords, item number, in eBay Motors, or by an individual seller or bidder. Type the keywords that describe an item (for example, **Superman lunch box** or **antique pocket watch**) and click Search, and you can see how many are available on eBay. The site gives you the option to search by one of the main categories — but to get the largest number of items, use All Categories and then narrow your search from the results.

  Sellers on eBay are notorious for listing in the wrong category (especially when they're rushed and upload lots of listings quickly). A search for all matching keywords will bring some of those hidden nuggets to the surface. Just peruse the pictures on the Search results page.

  Another handy way to search is by *item number*. Every item that's up for sale on eBay is assigned an item number, which is displayed next to the item name on its page. To find an item by number, just type the number in the box, click Search, and away you go. (To find out more about how individual sales pages work on eBay, spin through Chapter 6.)

- ✔ **Advanced Search drop-down menu:** By clicking this link, you can define your search without using a bunch of code. It works pretty much the same as the basic Search method, but you can exclude more features from your search.

  You can also search by location to find items for sale in and around your neighborhood. Figure 3-5 shows some of the Advanced Search options.

Figure 3-5:
The
Advanced
Search
page and its
options.

The In This Category search filter is a snappy function that helps you figure out which subcategories have the item you want — or, if you want to sell, helps you decide where to list your item for sale. What you get is not only a regular search in a selected category, but also a column on the left side of the page that tells you which subcategories (within the top-level category you selected) list your item — as well as how many of the item you'll see listed in each subcategory.

Although Chapter 5 tells you all you need to know about searching eBay, the following list explains some other searches you can perform from the Search page. In a nutshell, here's what they do:

- ✔ **By Seller:** Every person on eBay has a personal User ID (the name you use to conduct transactions). Use a By Seller search if you liked the merchandise from a seller's auction and want to see what else the seller has for sale. Type the seller's User ID, and you get a list of every item that person has up for sale.

- ✔ **By Item Number:** Every item has a number (you can find it just below the Description tab on the item page) which uniquely identifies a listing. You can type in an item number you've saved there. (You can also type in an item number in the regular search box to find a listing as well).

- ✔ **Items in Stores:** Here's something I bet you didn't know. When you use eBay's advanced search, it searches eBay Stores for matching items. Since eBay Store items show up in the regular search, I can't imagine why you'd need to use this option.

    If you're looking for a particular eBay Store, eBay provides a search box that allows you to search for a store by name (or part of the name).

Home Links, the Next Generation

If you look carefully, you can see that the home page has several other links that give you express service to key parts of the site after you've registered on the site. These results are based on your searching history, what you've bought, and what eBay might think you're interested in.

If you've been browsing around the site and then return to the home page, you see several boxes with images of items you've looked at in past history. You'll see items you have indicated that you want to watch on your My eBay page, your recently viewed items, and your recent searches.

eBay also gives you recommendations on popular products that are similar to things you've searched for. There's also information on what items are *trending* (growing in popularity) on the site.

You may notice that some graphic links on the home page change from day to day — or even hour to hour.

Maneuvering through Categories

So how does eBay keep track of the millions of items that are up for sale at any given moment? The brilliant folks who developed this system decided to group items into a nice, neat little storage system called *categories*. The home page lists most of the main (top-level) categories, but currently eBay must list tens of thousands of subcategories — ranging from Antiques to Writing Instruments. And don't ask how many sub-subcategories (categories within categories) eBay has — I can't count that high.

Well, okay, I *could* list all the categories and subcategories currently available on eBay — if you wouldn't mind squinting at a dozen pages of really small, eye-burning text. But a category browse is an adventure that's unique for each individual, and I wouldn't think of depriving you of it. Suffice to say that if you like to hunt for that perfect *something,* you're in browsing heaven now.

Here's how to navigate around the categories:

1. **Click the category that interests you, such as Collectibles & Art.**

   You're transported to the category's page. You see categories and sub-categories listed next to each heading. Happy hunting. (You can also mouse over the category link to see a drop-down menu showing just the top categories).

If you really and truly want to see a list of all the categories and subcategories once you've clicked through to the top category, click the arrow to the right of the subcategories to view sub-subcategories in the flyout menu, as shown in Figure 3-6.

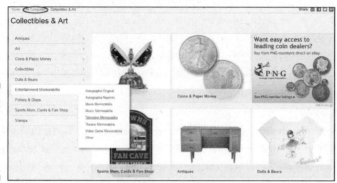

Figure 3-6:
Delving deeper into eBay's subcategories.

To see all the eBay categories, click the link to All Categories just above the category title on the page (also shown in Figure 3-6). Alternatively, you can go to www.ebay.com/sch/allcategories/all-categories.

2. **When you mouse over the major categories, a flyout menu appears, showing top categories that may interest you. Click a subcategory, and keep digging through the sub-subcategories until you find what you want.**

    For example, if you're looking for items honoring your favorite television show, click the Collectibles and Art category on the home page, and on the resulting page, select Entertainment Memorabilia, and additional categories will appear. When you click it, you will arrive at a page similar to Figure 3-7. On the left of the page, there are even more subcategories of the category.

    If you mouse over the Television Memorabilia subcategory heading, the menu will show up with links to various sub-subcategories that include Ads, Flyers, Clippings, Photos, Posters, Press Kits, Props, Scripts, Wardrobe, and Other. Farther down the page, below the menus, you also find links to the most popular searches in the category.

    Scroll to the bottom of the page and you see a complete listing of all the subcategories. Click any link here to see the listings in the categories. From the listings page (among other things), you can click the boxes at the top to narrow your search to Auctions or Buy It Now items.

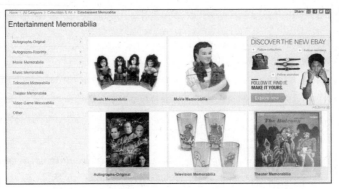

Figure 3-7:
Landing on
the Enter-
tainment
Memorabilia
main
category
page.

3. **When you find an item that interests you, click the item, and the full
   listings page pops up on your screen.**

   Congratulations — you've just navigated through several million items
   to find that one TV-collectible item that caught your attention. (Pardon
   me while I bid on that *Big Bang Theory*/Johnny Galecki–signed picture
   for my husband.) You can instantly return to the home page by clicking
   its link at the top of the page (or return to the listings page by
   repeatedly clicking the Back button at the top of your browser).

If you are not a fan of the graphic representations on the category pages, click
the category name in the upper-right corner (see Figure 3-8) next to the words
Prefer Search Results and you will see a full listing, just as if you had arrived
there from a search.

Figure 3-8:
The
Television
Memorabilia
page with
the option
to view in
list (search)
style.

Near the bottom of every search style page, you can see a line of numbers.
The numbers are page numbers, and you can use them to fast-forward
through all the items in that subcategory (next to the numbers you can also
select how many items you want to see on the pages). So, if you feel like

browsing around page 8 without going through eight pages individually, just click number 8: You're presented with the items on that page (their listings, actually). Happy browsing.

If you're a bargain hunter by habit, you may find some pretty weird stuff while browsing the categories and subcategories of items on eBay — some of it super-cheap and some of it (maybe) just cheap. There's even a **Weird Stuff** category that breaks down into subcategories of **Slightly Unusual, Totally Bizarre,** and **Really Weird**! I just checked that category and saw a sale for the contents of some guy's junk drawer. Only $2.00 and $20 shipping, but I'm moving along. I have enough of my own junk around without importing fresh stuff.

Remember, that (as with any marketplace) you're responsible for finding out as much as possible about an item before you buy — and definitely before you bid. So, if you're the type who sometimes can't resist a good deal, ask yourself what you plan to *do* with the pile of garbage you can get for 15 cents — and ask yourself *now,* before it arrives on your doorstep. Chapters 6 and 7 offer more information on savvy bidding.

Bottoming Out

At the very bottom of the home page is an easy-to-miss tab entitled Legal & More. Clicking the tab takes you to an unassuming group of links that provide more ways to get to some seriously handy pages. I list some of my favorites in this section:

- **Tools & apps:** Several links are important here.

    Mobile Apps: Click here to download eBay's mobile app.

    Security Center: This link takes you to a page where concerns about fraud and safety are addressed. It's such an important eBay tool that I dedicate an entire chapter to this program. Before buying or selling, it's a good idea to check out Chapter 16.

    Site Map: My favorite way to find what I want on eBay, using this very handy road map of links.

    Downloads: Here's where you can download some of eBay's handy browser extensions. They add on to your browser to keep eBay notifications as part of your browser. They link to eBay-supplied selling-assistance software. (See Chapter 20 for more on these programs.)

    Developers: So are you a geek too? If you are, you can enter eBay's Developer program and get access to the eBay API for fun and profit.

✔ **Gift Center:** Send someone an eBay gift certificate or card for any special occasion. You can print it yourself, or eBay will send it to any address you provide. The gift certificate is good for any item on the site for the value you specify, and you can pay for it immediately with PayPal. If the person you give the gift certificate to bids higher than the value of the gift certificate, he or she can make up the difference by using another payment option.

✔ **About eBay:** Click this link to find out about eBay, the company, and to get its press releases, company overview, and stock information. You can also find out about eBay community activities and charities — and even apply for a job at eBay.

- **Policies:** This is a good place to visit to brush up on the site's policies and guidelines.

- **Government Relations:** Here's where your eBay membership can make a real difference. Join eBay's Main Street Member Program and become involved with important legislation that may affect your online future. If you sign up, you'll receive important updates.

✔ **Community:** Visit the Announcements Board (linked here) when you want to know about any late-breaking news.

✔ **eBay Sites:** Click United States, and a menu will appear with links to eBay's international auction sites — 32 total, in addition to the U.S. (see Figure 3-9). Click one of these links and you jet off (virtually) to eBay sites in these countries. The international sites are in the countries' native languages. It might be a good place to practice your third-year French — or maybe not!

Figure 3-9: eBay is a world-wide phenomenon. Isn't it fun to be part of it?

After you leave eBay USA, you're subject to the contractual and privacy laws of the country you're visiting.

Chapter 4

Your Very Own, Private eBay

In This Chapter

▶ Making the My eBay page your control panel

▶ Keeping tabs on all transactions: buying and selling

▶ Organizing your data

▶ Rolling with your feedback

*I*t may seem that eBay is this huge company that doesn't even know you exist, but they do. They know all about you, and they give you a space to easily manage your eBay business. eBay's My eBay page is viewed only by you and is the space for all your activities on eBay — sort of a "This is your eBay life." I think it's the greatest organizational tool around, and I want to talk to somebody about getting one for organizing my life outside of eBay.

In this chapter, you find out how you can use the My eBay page to keep tabs on what you're buying and selling, find out how much money you've spent, and add categories to your personalized list so you can get to any favorite eBay place with just a click of your mouse. You gain knowledge of the ins and outs of feedback — what it is, why it can give you a secure feeling that you're in charge, and how to manage it so all that cyber-positive reinforcement doesn't go to your head.

I do want to preface this chapter by warning you that the My eBay page has become the hub for the zillions of features that eBay offers. As a beginner on the site, you'll be doing yourself a favor if you stick to the basics of the buying, selling, feedback, and account settings. eBay's offerings are helpful, but they can do a heck of a job confusing you when you're just starting out. Ease into the extra options slowly.

Getting to Your My eBay Page

Using your My eBay page makes keeping track of your eBay life a whole lot easier. And getting there is easy enough. After you enter eBay, sign in through the Sign In link (described in Chapter 3). After you sign in to eBay, you can access your My eBay page by clicking the My eBay link in the navigation area (see Figure 4-1) at the top of almost every eBay page.

Click here

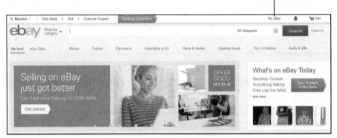

Figure 4-1:
The My eBay link in the navigation bar.

If you forget your eBay User ID or password when you're signing in, click the Forgot Your User ID or Forgot Your Password link. For your User ID, you can then type your e-mail address, and eBay will send you an e-mail with your User ID. Your User ID appears in any search results, posts, or pages. For the password, you have to answer your secret question (the one you filled in when you registered). If you don't remember that, eBay will send you a password-reset e-mail if you input your correct contact information with telephone number.

Houston, we don't have a problem

Here's an item I wish I'd bought: a very clean 8-x-10-inch color Neil Armstrong–signed official NASA portrait w/COA (Certificate of Authenticity). In his last years, Armstrong, the first human on the moon, was reclusive, and his autographs are difficult to obtain in any form. Many forgeries and reproductions are being offered, so buyer beware. This portrait came with a lifetime COA. The starting price was $10, and the portrait sold on eBay in 1999 for $520!

Many believe that Neil Armstrong's autograph will be among the most important of the 20th century. Just think about it. He was the first human to step onto another celestial body.

This feat will never happen again, and the first people on other planets may not land there in our lifetimes. When I updated this book for the third edition, this same portrait was selling for $650. When I checked this out for the 4th edition in 2004, the picture sold for $1,925. A quick scan in 2005 showed that such a signed picture just closed at $2,025, and for $3,500 in 2009.

Armstrong original signed photos are still selling (one just — Best Offer Accepted — was listed for $5,995), but you'll not find a signed photo up for sale for less than $3,000. Why, oh why, didn't I follow my own advice and buy one in 1999?

After you click the My eBay link, you arrive at your My eBay Summary page. As you can see by my busy page in Figure 4-2, you can access just about anything for your shopping pleasure right here. There will be some handy reminders on the top of this page. All pertinent buying reminders also show up here. In the links on the left, you also find a Summary page that covers your selling business (should you have one). Bottom line? These reminders help keep your business under control.

Figure 4-2:
Your My
eBay
Summary
page, the
hub for
your eBay
activities.

The My eBay menus in the navigation area on the left side of the page take you to the main areas of My eBay. Also, look at the left side of the My eBay Summary page in Figure 4-2. Under the Summary heading are many convenient links that take you to different areas of your eBay business. Table 4-1 gives you the scoop on the major links on the page.

Table 4-1	The Major Links on Your My eBay Page
Click Here	*To See This on Your My eBay Page*
Buy	Every listing that you're currently bidding on, have marked to watch, and made a Best Offer on, as well as the items you didn't win.
Sell	Every listing for items you're currently selling. Also, there are links to any listings you've scheduled to start at a later date. Most important, you have links to lists of items you've sold (and not sold).
Purchase History	Here you find the receipts and records for the items you have purchased on eBay. From here you can also contact the seller and if you have a problem you can't work out, file a report with eBay.
Lists	This area links to your Watch List, collections of Searches and Sellers you follow, as well as any custom lists you make.

In the bottom-left section, under the Shortcuts heading, are important links to activities and information.

Don't confuse the My eBay page with the About Me page. The About Me page is a personal web page that you can create to let the world know about you and your eBay dealings. (You don't have to have an About Me page if you don't want to — but they are free for the taking and are fun to share.) I tell you how to get your own About Me page in Chapter 14.

Keeping Track of Your Personal Business

Your My eBay page has three or four tabs: Activity, Messages, Account, and Applications (if you have been active on the site for a while). They're on the top of the page below the My eBay heading. If you mouse over the Account tab, you see a drop-down menu like the one in Figure 4-3. Clicking Account brings you to a Summary page that has snippets of each topic in the My Account section. It's convenient to use the drop-down menu options so you can immediately access the place you want to explore.

Figure 4-3: Access individual areas of your account in this menu.

In this chapter, I will not list every option available to you — only the ones I feel you should double-check at first.

What's that thingy?

For the first 30 days after you register or change your User ID (which you can do anytime, as Chapter 2 explains), eBay gives you an icon that stays next to your User ID every time it appears on eBay (when you bid, run an auction, or post a message on any of the boards).

So why the icon? eBay calls the graphic of a beaming critter the "Changed ID" icon. It's sort of a friendly heads-up to others that you are a new user. (If you've changed your User ID, the icon consists of two of the little guys with an arrow connecting them.) You still have all the privileges that everybody else has on eBay while you're breaking in your new identity. The icons are nothing personal — just business as usual.

Checking your account information

The Account drop-down menu has options to take you to two very important areas of My eBay: Personal Information and Addresses. This is where you update your contact information. Initially, all this data comes from your registration. But it's policy on eBay that every user files his or her current contact information — so if you move or change phone numbers, e-mail addresses, or banks, you need to input that information here.

It's also where you can change your User ID (if you ever decide that Charlie18907 doesn't properly reflect your personality). Also, your instant-messenger name can be inserted here so you can get IM alerts (at Yahoo! Messenger or AOL service). When you use the eBay Mobile app, notifications will be sent directly to your smartphone. You can also change your password and all your other registered information in this area.

On eBay you can change your User ID at any time (every 30 days), and your feedback rating will follow.

Choosing your communication preferences

Because we live in a world where everyone has his or her own way of doing business, eBay allows you to set a multitude of preferences for your eBay account. One of the links leads to the Communication Preferences page. The Preferences settings are all important to your eBay tasks. You have to decide which activities you want activated for your eBay account (you can always change these later). The most convenient thing is to select all the options that make sense to you. You can set many Notification preferences:

✔ **Notification Delivery:** This is where you let eBay know which method of notification works best for you. You can also indicate whether you want HTML or text-based e-mails.

✔ **Buying Notifications:** Be careful here. If you indicate that you *want* all this e-mail and you plan to be active on the site, prepare to be deluged. Select wisely! But remember, you can always make changes. You can get real-time notifications on your shopping for the following:

- Watched Item (also daily, weekly, or monthly) e-mail

- Watched Items that were relisted by the seller

- Confirmations for your bids

- E-mails when you're outbid in an auction

- Winning Buyer e-mails

- Losing Bidder e-mails

As you can see, this is way too many e-mails, especially if you do a lot of buying and selling. They will send you e-mails for even more than I mention here. For sanity's sake, narrow your selections to the minimum.

✔ **Selling Notifications:** If you're selling on the site, most of these notifications will be useful. You can indicate you want to receive the following e-mails (among others):

- Notification that you've saved a draft on the Sell an Item form

- E-mail confirmation each time you list an item for sale

- Yay! The end-of-listing e-mail when your item has sold

- Boo. The e-mail you get when your item doesn't sell

- Notification when your buyer performs Checkout

These are all important, especially when you're a new seller. When you become more active as a seller, you might want to whittle these down a bit — but not too much! Information is power.

✔ **Other Transactions and Notices:** Again, up to you. These can be overwhelming. eBay gives you the option to receive e-mails in the following areas:

- Member-to-member communications

- Receive Second Chance offers

- Reminders to leave feedback

- Account preference changes

Without enumerating everything else (I can see you're about to doze off), you can also opt into (or opt out of) eBay surveys, promotions, telephone updates, and direct USPS mail from eBay.

Next on the Preferences hit parade are your *actual* site preferences — how you'd like to conduct business on the site. These are settings for the more-advanced seller. You can make most of these decisions on the Sell an Item page. If you have time, though, click through each of the individual links to show the options and be sure that the default settings work for you.

When you finally get your My eBay page set up the way you like it, save yourself a lot of work and time by using your browser to bookmark your My eBay page as a favorite. Doing so saves you a lot of keystrokes later. If you want to send a shortcut to your desktop, in Internet Explorer choose File⇨Send⇨Shortcut to Desktop. This way, you can open your browser directly onto your My eBay page. Some eBay members make their My eBay pages into their browser home pages so that their My eBay pages appear the minute they log on. That's true dedication.

Your Feedback link

A convenient link to Feedback is part of the menu. In the Feedback area, you see all the items that need your feedback attention, and you can see the recent feedback that has been left for you. Save yourself a trip; you can leave feedback more conveniently from the item page, your Sell page, or your Buy page.

Account links

Not surprisingly, the My Account option leads you to more links for your PayPal and eBay Seller accounts. After you start selling, your Accounts pages become powerful. Figure 4-4 shows you the Seller Account summary section of my My eBay page. There's also a drop-down menu so you can view past or current invoices. You can look up every detail of your account history, as well as make changes to your personal preferences (such as how and when you want to pay fees).

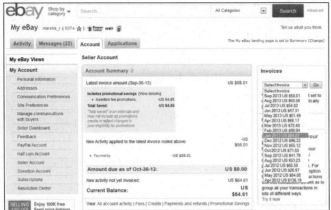

Figure 4-4:
The Seller
Account
section of
my My eBay
page.

Before you jump into the money game, you may want to review the links that
eBay gives you for managing your money:

- ✔ **Seller Account:** Click here to get a complete explanation of your eBay
  account — charges, credits, and your current balance since your last
  invoice.

- ✔ **View Invoices:** Click the drop-down menu to see your most recent
  invoice and details of the transactions. You can also arrange to
  download PDF copies of your invoices.

- ✔ **PayPal Account:** A quick click here, and you're taken to the PayPal home
  page. Check out Chapter 6 for more on the PayPal payment service.

When you give eBay your credit card information, eBay attempts to
authorize your card immediately. Your credit card company's response,
either Declined or Approved, appears on your Seller Account Payment
Methods area.

- ✔ **Automatic Payment Method:** Although you need to post a credit card
  for ID purposes to sell on eBay, you can pay your eBay bill in one of
  three ways. They like to deduct it directly from your registered checking
  account, but I prefer the ways listed next. You can change your method
  of payment at any time. See Table 4-2 to find out when the different
  payments are charged to your account.

  - • **Credit Card on File:** You can place your credit card on file with
    eBay so that eBay can place your selling charges on your credit
    card each month. I've been using this format since I became an
    eBay user and find that it works out very well.

> • **PayPal:** You can make single payments directly through your PayPal account. If you have a cash balance in your account, you can have it applied to your eBay bill; if not, you can pay the amount through the credit card you registered on PayPal.

Table 4-2	eBay's Automatic Seller Fees Payments		
Billing Cycle	*Payment Due by*	*Deducted from Checking Account*	*Credit Card Charged*
15th of month	15th of next month	5th of the next month	5–7 days after receipt of invoice
Last day of month	The last day of next month	20th of next month	5–7 days after receipt of invoice

Understanding Your Seller Dashboard

If you look at the links in the box on the left of your Account Summary page, you see a group of links to quickly zip to specific areas as well as navigating by using the tab with its drop-down menu. One of the most important is the link to the Seller Dashboard, which is where eBay calculates your ratings on the site. An explanation of the Detailed Seller Ratings (DSRs) is in Chapter 8. Figure 4-5 shows you a shot of my Seller Dashboard.

Figure 4-5:
Viewing my current Seller Dashboard.

This is an important place to go on a regular basis because eBay evaluates your status on the site daily. Your status affects your placement in searches and whether you get a discount on your fees (based on your customer satisfaction ratings) if you're a Top Rated Seller.

Using the Resolution Center

If you sell an item and the buyer backs out (a rare but disheartening situation), you can at least get a refund on some of the fees that eBay charges you as a seller. These are the Final Value Fees, and they're based on the selling price of the item. In the Resolution Center, you can keep track of the disputes in progress and send or receive messages from the other party regarding payment.

Before you can collect a Final Value Fee refund, the following conditions must apply:

- After your listing is over, you have to allow a buyer at least two business days to respond to you. If the buyer doesn't respond, you can send an e-mail politely reminding him or her of the commitment that a buyer makes to buy.

- If at least four days have elapsed since the end of the transaction and you have the feeling that you're not going to see your money, you *must* open an Unpaid Item Case. After you file this notice, eBay sends you a copy, and the bidder gets an ominous e-mail with a reminder to complete the transaction or to respond with a reason.

- The buyer may have a very good reason (say, someone didn't read this book and clicked Buy It Now on your item six times), and you are allowed to mutually agree not to go through with the transaction. The buyer must respond when eBay e-mails the buyer for confirmation.

You have up to 32 days from the end of the listing (or immediately if the buyer is no longer a registered user) to file an Unpaid Item Case — and you can't get a Final Value Fee credit without filing this alert.

- The buyer has up to four days to send payment after you file the Unpaid Item Case, or contact you to "work out" payment arrangements. You should try to send a message through the Dispute Console to resolve the situation during this time.

- If you do not receive a payment, you'll have to manually close the case to receive your credit. In this case, you must address the issue in the Resolution Center within 36 days or you're out of luck.

If you began the process and filed for a Final Value Fee credit — but then manage to work things out with the buyer — eBay removes the complaint from the buyer's account after the buyer pays through eBay's approved payment methods. Buyers with too many of these warnings, however, can be suspended from using the eBay site.

Organizing in the Lists Section

Part of the fun of eBay is searching for stuff that you'd never in a million years think of looking for. Wacky stuff aside, most eBay users spend their time hunting for specific items — say, Barbie dolls, designer dresses, plumbing supplies, or smartphone accessories. That's why eBay came up with the Lists area of your My eBay page. Whenever you view your My eBay Lists links, you see a list of your watched items, favorite searches, and sellers. But because eBay isn't psychic, you have to tell it what you want listed.

If you shop eBay at all like I do, you'll be looking for similar things and sellers over and over. The My eBay Lists area allows you to make note of your favorite searches and sellers. You can perform these searches and visit these stores with a click of your mouse.

Searches you follow

You have the opportunity to list a bunch of searches here. When you want to repeat one of these searches, just click the Search name to search for the item. eBay will even e-mail you your searches when new items are listed. (For more on that advanced function, check out Chapter 18.)

To add a search to your favorites, first perform the search. (For details on how to perform a search, see Chapter 5.) When the search appears on your screen, click the Follow This Search link, as shown at the top of the search results.

The search is now transported to your My eBay Lists, Searches You Follow area for that particular search. You will be notified by e-mail when new items are listed, unless you click the link that pops up (Figure 4-6) that reads Don't Send Me E-mail Alerts.

If you change your mind and no longer want to follow the search, click the Following This Search link and a red x will appear. Clicking there will remove the search from your list.

Figure 4-6:
Adding a
Favorite
Search
to your
Following
list.

The search is saved to your Searches You Follow (Lists) on My eBay and on your Profile page as Interests.

Sellers you follow

When you find a seller whose merchandise and prices are right up your alley and you'd like to occasionally check out the seller's auctions, you can list the seller in the Sellers You Follow area:

When you've shopped eBay and found a seller that you're happy with (or just like their items), click the + sign next to Follow This Seller on the listing page. The seller is saved to your Sellers You Follow (Lists) page and on your Profile page.

Keeping your follows on the "down low"

If you follow some sellers or searches because you source merchandise from them, or use them for researching products (or you don't want the fact that you are following public), you can remedy the situation.

1. Go to your Profile page by clicking your eBay User ID on any page.

2. Scroll down to the Following section.

3. Click the cog icon on the right next to the word Settings.

   You will be brought to a page where you can set Privacy settings for any Interests (for Searches You Follow) or Members (for Sellers You Follow).

4. Find the Seller or Search that you wish to make private, and click the globe icon below the picture next to the word *public*.

5. A menu will drop down and (as in Figure 4-7) you can click to change your setting to private.

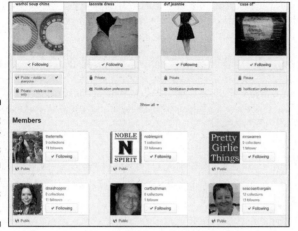

Figure 4-7: Making your Follows private from your Profile settings page.

Once you've set a Follow to private, folks can no longer see it on your Profile page, but you can still reach it from your My eBay⇨Sellers (or Searches) You Follow lists.

Sleuthing with your Watch list

The Watch List may be the most active area of the My eBay page (see Figure 4-8). This is the place for you to work on your strategy for getting bargains without showing your hand by bidding. In this area, you can watch the auction evolve and decide if you want to bid on it. When you come across a fixed-price listing that you don't want to take advantage of just now, save it

Figure 4-8: The Watch list on the My eBay page.

here for future reference. You also can list several auctions for the same item and watch them develop and then bid on the one that can give you the best deal. You can track the progress of up to 100 items in your Watch List area.

Moving listings into the Watch area is easy. When you find an item that you want to keep track of, look for the Add to Watch List link, which is located on the listing page. You can also add to your Watch List by clicking the Add to Watch List link, as shown in Figure 4-9. Just click this link to transport the item to your Watch List area.

Figure 4-9:
The drop-down list in the bidding/buying box gives you many options to save the listing for future reference.

Got the time? eBay does. Click the eBay Official Time link, which is at the bottom of virtually every eBay page. The eBay clock is so accurate that you can set your watch by it. And you may want to, especially if you want to place a last-second bid before an auction closes. After all, eBay's official time is, um, *official*.

Following the Action on Your Buying

I have the most fun on eBay when I'm shopping. Shopping on eBay is exciting, and I can find a zillion great bargains. Fortunately, eBay gives you a place to keep all your shopping information together: the Buying area.

Seeing the items you're buying

When you bid on an item, eBay automatically lists the item in the Buy > Active area of your My eBay page. If you're winning an auction, the price appears in green; if you're losing, it appears in red. After the auction's over, the listing moves to Purchase History (yea!) or Didn't Win (boo!). You can watch the progress of the auction from here and see the number of bids on the item, the high bid, and how much time is left until the end of the auction. All this information can help you decide whether you want to jump back in and make a bid.

eBay also keeps a total of all your active bids and buys to the left of your data in the Totals: Buying Total box — which I hope helps you stay within your spending limits.

Keeping track of your purchased items

When you win an auction or purchase an item with Buy It Now, it appears in the Purchase History area. From this area, you can visit the listing to print the auction page or double-check it. From the links in the Action column, you can also pay for your item through PayPal; if you've already paid, you can view the PayPal payment details. You can also click a Leave Feedback link here from the drop-down menu — after you've received the item and are satisfied with your purchase — to leave feedback.

Surveying Your Sales on Your My eBay Sell Page

Your My eBay page supplies you with the tools to keep track of items you're selling on eBay. The My eBay Sell page works much the same as the Buy page, but this time you're making the money — not spending it! Your current auctions and fixed-price listings are listed in the Active area. The auctions with bids on them appear in green, and the ones without bids (or where the reserve hasn't been met) are in red. In the left column, you have a dollar total of the current bids on your auctions, items sold, and totals of payments received.

Your Active Selling page

As with the Buy section, the Sell area keeps track of your ongoing listings on eBay. You can observe the action in real time (or at least every time you refresh the page). You can see how many bids have been placed, when an auction closes, and the time left in an auction. If you want more information about what's going on (for example, how many people are watching or bidding), just peruse your listings in this area.

Your Sold page

When the sale is final, the items go into the Sold area (shown in Figure 4-10). Here's where you can keep track of the sale. You can check whether the buyer has paid with PayPal as well as the transaction status. If the buyer has completed Checkout, you can get his or her information by clicking the Next Steps/Status link. If the buyer hasn't completed Checkout, you can click the Send Invoice button to send the buyer an invoice. Very handy!

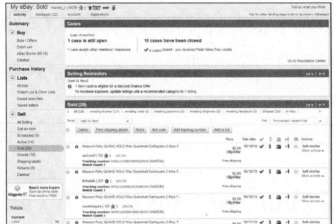

Figure 4-10:
The Sold area and all its options.

If you haven't heard from the buyer after a day after purchase, you may need to re-send your invoice. See Chapter 12 for more information on post-sale correspondence.

After the transaction is complete (which means the item has arrived and the buyer is happy with his or her purchase), you can click the handy Leave Feedback link to leave feedback about the buyer.

You can also relist the item from a quick link or place a Second Chance offer to an underbidder if you have more than one of the item. See the nearby sidebar for more on the Second Chance feature.

eBay's Selling Manager/Selling Manager Pro

If you're at the point where you're selling bunches of items on the site, you may want to subscribe to one of eBay's Selling Manager tools. These tools make your Selling area look completely different and give you the opportunity to handle more sales in a compact and convenient design. See Chapter 20 for detailed information.

Your secret seller tool — Second Chance!

The e-commerce experts at eBay have come up with another great selling tool. Say you have multiples of a single item (you *did* sell that set of Minton china one piece at a time, didn't you?) or the winning bidder backs out of the transaction without paying. Second Chance offer gives you the opportunity to offer the item to one of the underbidders (okay, the losers) at their high bid price (gee, maybe they didn't lose after all). You can also create a Second Chance if you set a reserve that wasn't met before the auction ended. The Second Chance opportunity is available for up to 60 days after the sale ends.

You can offer the item to as many of the underbidders (as you have merchandise to cover) at a time and make this personal offer good for one to seven days. Each bidder receives an e-mail regarding the offer and can access it on the site through a special link. It is visible to only you and the other bidder for the duration of the offer. The best part is that eBay doesn't charge any additional listing fees for this feature — but you are charged the Final Value Fee after the transaction is complete.

Keeping Track of Your Transactions

Yes, I bug you about saving stuff at the outset of your selling career because I care. The eBay transaction process can be daunting, and beginners can easily lose track. The best way to protect yourself is to keep good records on your own. This is your money, so keep a close eye on it.

Now don't become a packrat and overdo it. To help point you in the right direction, here's a list of important documents that I think you might want to print and file whether you're a buyer or a burgeoning seller:

- ✔ eBay invoices for your sales
- ✔ PayPal statements indicating any payment you receive that doesn't clear
- ✔ Insurance or escrow forms
- ✔ Refund and credit requests
- ✔ Receipts from purchases you make for items to sell on eBay

Always, always, *always* save every e-mail message you receive about a transaction, whether you buy or sell, until the transaction is over and feedback is left. Also save the end-of-transaction e-mails that eBay sends. For more information about e-mail from eBay and correspondence etiquette after the auction is over, see Chapters 8 and 12.

Why should you keep track of all this stuff? Here are some reasons:

- Even if you're buying and selling just a few items a month on eBay, you need to keep track of who you owe and who owes you money.

- Good e-mail correspondence is a learned art, but if you reference item numbers as you correspond, then your e-mail and eBay messages are an instant record. If you put your dates in writing — and follow up — you have a nice, neat paper trail (even if the trail is digital).

- Documenting the transaction through eBay Messages will come in handy if you ever end up in a dispute over the terms of the sale.

- If you sell specialized items, you can keep track of trends and your frequent buyers.

- Someday the IRS may come knocking on your door, especially if you buy stuff for the purpose of selling it on eBay. Scary, but true. For more on where you can get tax information, take a look at Chapter 9.

When it comes to keeping records via e-mail and documents about transactions, I say that after you receive your feedback (positive, of course), you can dump it. If you get negative feedback (how could you?), hang on to your paperwork for a little longer. Use your discretion, but generally you can toss the paperwork from a bad transaction after it has reached some sort of resolution. (You can find out more about feedback in the next section.)

Once a month, do a seller search on yourself and print your latest eBay history. Chapter 5 tells you more about doing seller searches, organizing your searches, and starting files on items you want to track.

Getting and Giving Feedback

You know how they say you are what you eat? On eBay, you are only as good as your feedback says you are. Your feedback is made up of comments — good, bad, or neutral — that people leave about you (and you leave about others). In effect, people are commenting on your overall professionalism. (Even if you're an eBay hobbyist with no thought of using it professionally, a little businesslike courtesy can ease your transactions with everyone.) These comments are the basis for your eBay reputation.

Because feedback is so important to your reputation on eBay, you don't want others leaving feedback or making bad transactions under your name. The only way to ensure that this doesn't happen is to keep your password a secret — always. If you suspect somebody may know your password, change it before that person has a chance to sign in as you and ruin your reputation. (For more on selecting and protecting your level of privacy, see Chapters 1 and 15.)

When you get your first feedback, the number that appears next to your User ID is your feedback rating, which follows you everywhere you go on eBay, even if you change your User ID or e-mail address. It sticks to you like glue. Click the number next to any User ID and get a complete look at the user's feedback profile. The thinking behind the feedback concept is that you wouldn't be caught dead in a store that has a lousy reputation, so why on earth would you want to do business on the Internet with someone who has a lousy reputation?

You're not required to leave feedback, but because it's the benchmark by which all eBay users are judged, whether you're buying or selling, you should *always* leave feedback comments. Get in the frame of mind that every time you complete a transaction — the minute the package arrives safely to your buyer (if you're a seller) or an item you've bid on and won arrives — you should go to eBay and post your feedback.

Every time you get a positive comment from a user who hasn't commented on you before within the past week, you get a point. Every time you get a negative rating, this negative cancels out one of your positives. Neutral comments rate a 0 — they have no impact either way. eBay even has what it calls the Star Chart, shown in Figure 4-11, which rewards those with good-and-getting-higher feedback ratings.

Figure 4-11:
The eBay feedback achievement Star rating.

Star	Color	Number of ratings
☆	Yellow	10 to 49
★	Blue	50 to 99
☆	Turquoise	100 to 499
☆	Purple	500 to 999
★	Red	1,000 to 4,999
☆	Green	5,000 to 9,999
☆	Yellow shooting star	10,000 to 24,999
☆	Turquoise shooting star	25,000 to 49,999
☆	Purple shooting star	50,000 to 99,999
★	Red shooting star	100,000 to 499,999
☆	Green shooting star	500,000 to 999,999
☆	Silver shooting star	1,000,000 or more (Wow!)

The flip side (or Dark Side for *Star Wars* fans) of the star system is negative numbers. Negative comments deduct from your total of positive comments, thereby lowering the number beside your User ID. *eBay riddle:* When is more than one still one? Gotcha, huh? The answer is, when you get more than one feedback message from the same person in the same week. Confused? This should help: You can sell one person 100 different items, but even if the buyer gives you a glowing review 100 times in the same week, your feedback rating doesn't increase by 100. In this case, the other 99 feedback comments appear in your feedback profile, but your rating increases only by 1.

Sellers are only allowed to leave positive feedback for buyers — I know this may not make sense, but that's the way it is. You can leave a "positive," but still be honest about your transaction in your words. eBay made this rule so sellers wouldn't leave retaliatory feedback to buyers who left them negative feedback.

Should a buyer who hasn't paid leave you a negative, eBay cooperates and removes the feedback, provided you've filed an Unpaid Item report.

If feedback is left individually and stretched out over several weeks (only one per week), the person on the other end of the transaction will get a single feedback point each time you leave a positive. I do this for my buyers who buy multiple items from me (it's easy from the My eBay page). But most buyers don't seem to know this rule so I'll get several positives — one after another — netting me only one positive. *Sigh*

Anyone with a –4 rating may have his or her eBay membership terminated. Remember, just because a user may have a 750 feedback rating, it doesn't hurt to click the number after the name to double-check the person's feedback page. Even if someone has a total of 1,000 feedback messages, 250 of them *could* be negative. Always note the feedback percentage.

You can get to your personal feedback profile page right from your My eBay page by clicking the number next to your User ID.

Feedback comes in three exciting flavors:

- **Positive feedback:** Someone once said, "All you have is your reputation." Reputation is what makes eBay function. If the transaction works well, you get positive feedback; whenever it's warranted, you should give it right back.

- **Negative feedback:** If there's a glitch (for instance, it takes six months to get your *Charlie's Angels* lunch box, or the seller substitutes a rusty Thermos for the one you bid on or you never get the item), you have the right — some would say *obligation* — to leave negative feedback.

- **Neutral feedback:** You can leave neutral feedback if you feel so-so about a specific transaction. It's the middle-of-the-road comment. Say you bought an item that had a little more wear and tear on it than the seller indicated, but you still like it and want to keep it.

How to get positive feedback

If you're selling, here's how to get a good reputation:

- Establish contact with the buyer (pronto!) after the listing ends (see Chapter 12).
- After you receive payment, send the item posthaste (see Chapter 12).
- Make sure that the item you ship is exactly in the same condition as you described it (see Chapter 10).
- Package the item carefully and ship it in an appropriate package (see Chapter 12).
- React quickly and appropriately to problems — for example, the item's lost or damaged in the mail, or the buyer is slow in paying (see Chapter 12).

If you're buying, try these good-rep tips:

- Send your payment fast (see Chapter 8).
- Keep in touch through e-mail with the seller if problems arise (see Chapter 8).
- Work with the seller to resolve any problems in a courteous manner (see Chapters 8 and 12).

How to get negative feedback

Okay, this section can be read in one of two ways: (a) as what to do if you're a glutton for punishment or (b) as a list of major blunders (with their antidotes). So here goes: If you're selling, here's what to do to tarnish your name big-time:

- Tell a major untruth in the item description. (To defend truth, justice, and legitimate creative writing, see Chapter 10.)
- Take the money but "forget" to ship the item. (Who did you say you are? See Chapter 16.)
- Package the item poorly so that it ends up smashed, squashed, or vaporized during shipping. (To avoid this pathetic fate, see Chapter 12.)

If you're buying, you can't get official negative feedback, but the sellers still have their "say." If you want to make your eBay experience a drag, here's how to make a serious mess of the feedback comments you get:

- ✔ Bid on an item, win the auction, and never respond to the seller. (Remember your manners and see Chapter 6.)

- ✔ Pick up the item in person and give the seller a personal check that bounces and never make good on the payment. (See Chapter 16 — and don't pass Go.)

- ✔ Ask the seller for a refund because you just don't like the item. (Remember how to play fair and see Chapter 8.)

The Feedback page

When you click the feedback number next to a member's User ID, you'll see all the tools you need to gauge the member. Think of your feedback profile as your eBay report card. Your goal is to get straight *As* — in this case, all positive feedback. Unlike a real report card, you don't have to bring it home to be signed.

When someone clicks the feedback number next to your User ID, they see the following information (see Figure 4-12):

- ✔ **Your User ID:** Your eBay nickname appears, followed by a number in parentheses — the net number of the positive feedback comments you've received, minus any negative feedback comments you may have (but that wouldn't happen to you).

- ✔ **Your Membership Information:** Listed here is the date you first signed up as a member of the eBay community. Below that is the country from which you're registered, your star rating (refer to Figure 4-11), and any icons leading to more areas related to you on eBay, such as your About Me page (see Chapter 14). This area also notes whether you have an eBay Store.

- ✔ **Detailed Seller Ratings:** This area sums up the ratings, from one to five, that buyers have left for you.

- ✔ **Your Recent Feedback Ratings:** This area is a scorecard of your feedback for the last 12 months. At the bottom of the feedback tote board is a summary of your bid retractions in the past six months — the times you have retracted bids during an auction.

Figure 4-12:
The
Feedback
profile —
there's one
for every
member.

Be careful when you retract a bid. All bids on eBay are binding, but under what eBay calls "exceptional circumstances," you may retract bids — very sparingly. Here are the circumstances in which it's okay to retract a bid:

✔ If you mistakenly put in the wrong bid amount — say, $100 rather than $10

✔ If the seller adds to his or her description after you place your bid, and the change considerably affects the item

✔ If you can't contact the seller (your e-mail continuously bounces back and the phone number doesn't work)

You can't retract a bid just because you found the item elsewhere cheaper, or you changed your mind, or you decided that you really can't afford the item. If that's the case, message the seller directly and ask *the seller* to please remove your bid. See Chapter 6 for more information on retracting bids.

Reading your feedback

Your eBay reputation is at the mercy of the one-liners that buyers and sellers leave for you in the form of feedback comments. Each feedback box contains these reputation-building (or reputation-trashing) ingredients:

✔ The User ID of the person who sent the feedback. The number in parentheses next to the person's name is his or her own feedback rating.

✔ The date and time the feedback was posted.

✔ The item number of the transaction that the feedback refers to.

- ✔ Seller or Buyer (only in the All Feedback area) — indicating whether you were the seller or the buyer in the transaction.
- ✔ Feedback bullets in different colors: praise (in green with a plus mark), negative (in red with a minus mark), or neutral (in gray with a white dot).
- ✔ The feedback the person left about you.

You have the last word — responding to feedback

After reading feedback you receive from others, you may feel compelled to respond. If the feedback is negative, you may want to defend yourself. If it's positive, you may want to say thank you.

To respond to feedback, follow these steps:

1. **Click the Feedback link in the drop-down menu under the Account tab on your My eBay page, and then click the Go to Feedback Forum link at the top of the page.**

   You're transported to the Feedback Forum, where you can reply to feedback comments left for you.

2. **Click the Reply to Feedback Received link on the right side of the page.**

   You will land on a page that lists all the feedback you have received.

3. **Find the feedback you want to respond to and click reply.**

   You may now type your response.

If you want to follow up to a feedback you've already left for someone, follow the preceding steps, but in Step 2, click the Follow Up to Feedback Left link on the Feedback Forum page.

 Do not confuse *replying* to feedback with *leaving* feedback. Replying does not change the other user's feedback rating; it merely adds a line below the feedback with your response.

Leaving feedback with finesse

Writing feedback well takes some practice. It isn't a matter of saying things; it's a matter of saying *only the appropriate things*. Think carefully about what you want to say because when you submit feedback, it stays with the person for the duration of his or her eBay career. I think you should always leave feedback, especially at the end of a transaction, although doing so isn't mandatory. Think of leaving feedback as voting in an election: If you don't leave feedback, you can't complain about lousy service.

eBay says to make feedback "factual and emotionless." You won't go wrong if you comment on the details (either good or bad) of the transaction. If you have any questions about what eBay says about feedback, click the Feedback link on your My eBay page and then click the Go to Feedback Forum link.

In the Feedback Forum, you can perform six feedback-related tasks:

- ✔ **See feedback about an eBay user.**

- ✔ **Leave feedback for many items at once.** Here, you see all pending feedback for all transactions within the past 90 days. You are presented with a page of all your transactions for which you haven't left feedback. Fill them in, one at a time, and with one click you can leave as many as 25 feedback comments at once.

- ✔ **Review and respond to existing feedback about you.**

- ✔ **Review the feedback you have left for others.** Here you may also leave follow-up feedback after the initial feedback, should situations change.

- ✔ **Report buyer problems.**

- ✔ **Check the Feedback FAQ to review any changes in the feedback system.**

In the real world (at least in the modern American version of it), anybody can sue anybody else for libel; this fact holds true on the Internet, too. It's a good idea to be careful not to make any comments that could be libelous. eBay is not responsible for your actions, so if you're sued because of negative feedback (or anything else you've written), you're on your own. The best way to keep yourself safe is to stick to the facts and to not get personal.

If you're angry, take a breather *before* you type your complaints and click the Leave Comment button. If you're convinced that negative feedback is necessary, try a cooling-off period before you send a comment. Wait an hour or a day and then see whether you feel the same. Nasty feedback based on emotion can make you look vindictive (even if what you're saying is true).

Safety tips for giving feedback

And speaking of safety features you should know about feedback, you may want to study up on these:

- ✔ **Remember that feedback, whether good or bad, is *sticky*.** eBay won't remove your feedback comment if you change your mind later. Be sure of your facts and carefully consider what you want to say.

- ✔ **Before you leave feedback, see what other people had to say about that person.** Is your thinking in line with the comments others have left?

✔ **You can leave feedback as long as the transaction remains on the eBay server.** This is usually within 90 days of the end of the listing. After 90 days have passed, you must have the transaction number to leave feedback.

✔ **Your comment can be a maximum of only 80 letters long, which is really short when you have a lot to say.** Before you start typing, organize your thoughts and use common abbreviations to save precious space.

✔ **Before posting negative feedback, try to resolve the problem by e-mail or telephone.** You may discover that your reaction to the transaction is based on a misunderstanding that can be easily resolved.

✔ **eBay users generally want to make each other happy, so use negative feedback *only as a last resort*.** See Chapters 8 and 10 for more details on how to avoid negative feedback.

If you do leave a negative comment that you later regret, you can't remove it. You can go back to follow up and leave an explanation or a more positive comment (but it won't change the initial feedback or rating), so think twice before you blast.

The ways to leave feedback

Several ways are available to leave feedback comments:

✔ If you're on the user's Feedback page, click the Leave Feedback link; the Leave Feedback page appears.

✔ In the Purchased Items area of your My eBay page, click the Leave Feedback link next to the listing.

✔ Go to your listing and click the Leave Feedback icon.

✔ In the Feedback Forum, click the Leave Feedback link to see a list of all your completed items from the last 90 days for which you haven't yet left feedback.

To leave feedback for a buyer, follow these steps:

1. **Enter the required information.**

   Note that your item number is usually filled in, but if you're placing feedback from the user's Feedback page, you need to have the number at hand.

2. **Type your comment.**

   Only positive feedback can be left for a buyer, so choose your words carefully.

3. **Click the Star ratings from one to five to rate the transaction.**

   I rarely give under four stars when the seller has fulfilled the transaction.

4. **Click the Leave Feedback button.**

Mincing words: The at-a-glance guide to keeping feedback short

eBay likes to keep things simple. If you want to compliment, complain, or take the middle road, you have to do it in 80 characters or less. That means your comment needs to be short and sweet (or short and sour if it's negative, or sweet and sour if you're mixing drinks or ordering Chinese food). If you have a lot to say but you're stumped about how to say it, here are a few examples for any occasion. String them together or mix and match!

Positive feedback:

✔ Very professional

✔ Quick e-mail response

✔ Fast service

✔ A+++

✔ Good communication

✔ Exactly as described

✔ Highly recommended

✔ Smooth transaction

✔ Would deal with again

✔ An asset to eBay

✔ I'll be back!

Negative feedback:

✔ Never responded

✔ Never sent item

✔ Desperately slow shipping

✔ Beware track record

✔ Not as described

Neutral feedback:

✔ Slow to ship but item as described

✔ Item not as described but seller made good

✔ Poor communication but item came OK

Part II
Buying Like an Expert

Visit www.dummies.com/extras/ebay for information about rating your seller.

In this part...

✔ Learning to search like a pro

✔ Grading a collectible's value

✔ Digging into researching, bidding, and winning auctions

✔ Knowing when to place a bid or take a pass

Chapter 5

Deal or No Deal? Buying Advice and Searching Tips

In This Chapter

▶ Getting real-world buying advice on collectibles

▶ Obtaining solid online buying advice

▶ Checking out information sources for savvy buyers

▶ Conducting a special item search on eBay

*P*icture all the stores you've ever seen in your life, located in one giant mall. You walk in and try to find the single item you're looking for. (Not an easy proposition). Consider also walking into a store with thousands of aisles of shelves with tens of millions of items on them.

Browsing the categories of listings on eBay can be just as pleasantly mind-boggling, without the prospect of sore feet. Start surfing around the site, and you instantly understand the size and scope of what's for sale there. Everything. Without question, you'll feel overwhelmed at first, but eBay comes up with lots of ways to help you find exactly what you're looking for. As soon as you figure out how to find the items you want to bid or buy on eBay, you can protect your investment-to-be by making sure that what you find is actually what you seek.

Of course, searching is easier if you have an idea of what you're looking for. In this chapter for collectors, I offer the first-time buyer some expert tips and tell you how to get expert advice from eBay and other sources. I also give you tips for using the eBay search engine from a buyer's perspective.

The best advice you can follow as you explore any free-market system is *caveat emptor* — let the buyer beware. Although nobody can guarantee that every one of your transactions will be a great deal, research items thoroughly before you bid or buy so that you don't lose too much of your hard-earned money — or too much sleep.

Online Tips for Collectors

If you're just starting out on eBay, chances are you like to shop and you also collect items that interest you. You'll find out pretty early in your eBay adventures that a lot of people online know as much about collecting as they do about bidding — and some are serious contenders.

How can you compete? Well, in addition to having a well-planned buying strategy (covered in Chapter 7), knowing your stuff gives you a winning edge. I've gathered the opinions of two collecting experts to get the info you need about online collecting basics. (If you're already an expert collector but want help finding that perfect something on eBay so you can get ready to bid, you've got it. See "Looking to Find an Item? Start Your eBay Search Engine," later in this chapter.) I also show you how one of those experts puts the information into practice, and I give you a crash course on how items for sale are (or should be) graded.

Although these tips from the experts are targeted for collectors, much of the information is sound advice for those involved in any transaction online.

The experts speak out

Bill Swoger closed his collectibles store in Burbank, California, and sold the balance of his G.I. Joe and Superman items on eBay. Lee Bernstein, a columnist who ran a collectibles business from her home base in Schererville, Indiana was the author of eBay's now-defunct Collectibles "Inside Scoop." My favorite tips, along with Bill and Lee's, follow:

- ✔ **Get all the facts before you put your money down.** Study the description carefully. It's your job to analyze the description and make your bidding decisions accordingly. Find out whether all original parts are included and whether the item has any flaws. If the description says that the Fred Flintstone figurine has a cracked back, e-mail the seller for more information on just how cracked Fred really is.

- ✔ **Don't get caught up in the emotional thrill of bidding.** First-time buyers (because they have fewer than ten transactions under their belts) tend to bid wildly, using emotions rather than brains. If you're new to eBay, you can get burned if you just bid for the thrill of victory without thinking about what you're doing.

I can't stress how important it is to determine an item's value, whether collectible or new. But because item values are such flighty things (depending as they do on supply and demand, market trends, and all sorts of other variables), I recommend that you get a general idea of the item's value and use this ballpark figure to set a maximum amount of money you're willing to bid for that item. Then *stick to* your maximum and don't even think about bidding past it. If the bidding gets too hot, there's always another auction. To find out more about bidding strategies, Chapter 7 is just the ticket.

✔ **Know what the item should cost.** Buyers used to depend on *price guides* — books on collectibles and their values — to help them bid. Bill says that price guides are becoming a thing of the past. Sure, you can find a guide that says an original-cast *Lion King* Broadway poster in excellent condition has a book price of $150, but if you do a search on eBay, you'll see that they're actually selling for less than half that amount.

When your search on eBay turns up what you're looking for, average the current prices you find. Also check the sold listings. Doing so gives you a much better idea of what you need to spend than any price guide can.

✔ **Timing is everything, and being first costs.** If you're into movie posters, for example, consider this: If you can wait three to six months after a film is released, you can get the poster for 40 to 50 percent less. The same goes for many new releases of collectibles. Sometimes you're wiser to wait and save money.

✔ **Be careful of presale items.** Sometimes you may run across vendors selling items that they don't have in stock but that they'll ship to you later. For example, before *Star Wars Episode I: The Phantom Menace* came out, some vendors ran auctions on movie posters they didn't have yet. If you had bid and won, and for some reason the vendor had a problem getting the poster, you'd have been out of luck. Don't bid on anything that can't be delivered as soon as you pay for the item. See some of eBay's presale rules later in this chapter.

✔ **Being too late can also cost.** Many collectibles become more difficult to find as time goes by. Generally, as scarcity increases, so does desirability and value. Common sense tells you that if two original and identical collectibles are offered side by side, with one in like-new condition and the other in used condition, the like-new item will have the higher value.

✔ **Check out the seller.** Check the feedback rating (the number in parentheses next to the person's User ID) a seller has before you buy. If the seller has many comments with a minute number of negative ones, chances are good that this is a reputable seller. For more on feedback, see Chapter 4.

Although eBay forbids side deals, an unsuccessful bidder may (at his or her own risk) contact a seller after an auction is over to see if the seller has more of the item in stock. If the seller is an experienced eBay user (a high feedback rating is usually a tipoff) and has more of the item in stock, he or she may consider making a perfectly eBay-legal Second Chance offer. Don't ask to buy the item off-site. eBay strictly prohibits selling items off the site. If you conduct a side deal and are reported to eBay, you can be suspended. Not only that, but buyers who are ripped off by sellers in away-from-eBay transactions shouldn't look to eBay to bail them out; if you go that route, you're on your own. The way to purchase these items is by asking the seller to post another of the item for you — or if you were an underbidder in the auction, send you a Second Chance offer. That way, you're also protected by eBay's buyer protection.

✔ **If an item comes to you not as described, contact the seller to work it out.** Use eBay messages to let the seller know exactly what you received and how it differs from the description on the listing. Give the seller a chance to make good before you go nuclear. Chapter 6 provides pointers on dealing with transactions that go sour.

Following an expert on the hunt

I know that not many of you collect G.I. Joes, but by studying what an expert looks for in this specialty collectible, you can get a good idea of what you should look for when purchasing whatever it is that you collect. Bill looks for specific traits when he buys his very collectible G.I. Joe figures. Although his checklist is specific to the G.I. Joe from 1964 to 1969, the information here can help you determine your maximum bid on other collectibles (or whether an item is even *worth* bidding on) before an auction begins.

As you find out in Chapter 7, the more you know before you place a bid, the happier you're likely to be when you win. Bill's checklist can save you considerable hassle:

✔ **Find out the item's overall condition.** For G.I. Joe, look at the painted hair and eyebrows. Expect some wear, but overall, a collectible worth bidding on should look good.

✔ **Be sure that the item's working parts are indeed working.** Most G.I. Joe action figures from this period have cracks on the legs and arms, but the joints should move, and any cracks should not be so deep that the legs and arms fall apart easily.

✔ **Ask whether the item has its original parts.** Because you can't really examine items in detail before buying, e-mail the seller with specific questions relating to original or replacement parts. Many G.I. Joe action figures are rebuilt from parts that are not from 1964 to 1969. Sometimes the figures even have two left or right hands or feet! If you make it clear to the seller before you buy that you want a toy with only original parts, you'll be able to make a good case for a refund if the item arrives as rebuilt as the Six-Million-Dollar Man. Chapter 7 has plenty of tips on how to protect yourself before you bid, and Chapter 16 has tips on what to do if the deal goes bad.

✔ **Ask whether the item has original accessories.** A G.I. Joe from 1964 to 1969 should have his original dog tags, boots, and uniform. If any of these items are missing, you will have to pay around $25 apiece to replace each missing item. If you're looking to bid on any other collectible, know in advance what accessories came as standard equipment with the item, or you'll be paying extra just to bring it back to its original version.

✔ **Know an item's value before you bid.** A 1964 to 1969 vintage G.I. Joe in decent shape, with all its parts, sells for $250 to $400 without its original box. (Mint-in-box Joes can sell for thousands of dollars.) If you're bidding on a G.I. Joe action figure on eBay and you're in this price range, you're okay. If you get the item for less than $250, congratulations — you've nabbed a bargain.

✔ **If you have any questions, ask them *before* you bid.** Check collectors' guides, research similar auctions on eBay, and visit one of eBay's category discussion boards.

Making the grade

Welcome to my version of grade school without the bad lunch. One of the keys to establishing value is knowing an item's condition, typically referred to as an item's *grade*. Table 5-1 lists the most common grading categories that collectors use. The information in this table is used with permission from (and appreciation to) Lee Bernstein.

Table 5-1	Collectibles Grading Categories	
Category (Also Known As)	**Description**	**Example**
Mint (M, Fine, Mint-In-Box [MIB], 10)	A never-used collectible in perfect condition with complete packaging (including instructions, original attachments, tags, and so on), identical to how it appeared on the shelf in the original box.	Grandma got a soup tureen as a wedding present, never opened it, and stuck it in her closet for the next 50 years.
Near Mint (NM, Near Fine, Like-New, 9)	The collectible is perfect but no longer has the original packaging or the original packaging is less than perfect. Possibly used but must appear to be new.	Grandma used the soup tureen on her 25th anniversary, washed it gently, and then put it back in the closet.

(continued)

Table 5-1 *(continued)*

Category (Also Known As)	Description	Example
Excellent (EX, 8)	Used, but barely. Excellent is just a small step under Near Mint, and many sellers mistakenly interchange the two, but "excellent" can have very minor signs of wear. The wear must be a normal, desirable part of aging or so minor that it's barely noticeable and visible only upon close inspection. Damage of any sort is "very minor." Wear or minor normal factory flaws should be noted. (Factory flaws are small blemishes common at the time of manufacture — a tiny air bubble under paint, for example.)	Grandma liked to ring in the New Year with a cup of soup for everyone.
Very Good (VG, 7)	Looks very good but has defects, such as a minor chip or light color fading.	If you weren't looking for it, you might miss that Grandma's tureen survived the '64 earthquake, as well as Uncle Bob's infamous ladle episode.
Good (G, 6)	Used with defects. More than a small amount of color loss, chips, cracks, tears, dents, abrasions, missing parts, and so on.	Grandma had the ladies in the neighborhood over for soup and bingo every month.
Poor (P or G-, 5)	Barely collectible, if at all. Severe damage or heavy use. Beyond repair.	Grandma ran a soup kitchen.

Grading is subjective. Mint to one person may be Very Good to another. Always ask a seller to define the meaning of the terms used. Also, be aware that many amateur sellers may not really know the different definitions of grading and may arbitrarily add Mint or Excellent to their item descriptions.

Finding More Research Information

Experts have been buying, selling, and trading collectible items for years. But just because you're new to eBay doesn't mean that you have to be a newbie for decades before you can start bartering with the collecting gods. I wouldn't leave you in the cold like that — and neither would eBay. You can get information on items you're interested in, as well as good collecting tips, right at the eBay website. Visit the category-specific discussion boards in the community area. You can also search the rest of the web or go the old-fashioned route and check the library (yes, libraries are still around).

Keep in mind that there are truly several prices for an item: the retail (or manufacturer's suggested retail price — MSRP) price, the book value, the secondary market price (the price charged by resellers when an item is unavailable on the primary retail market), and the eBay selling price. The only way to ascertain the price an item will go for on eBay is to research the listings of sold items. Later in this chapter, I give you the skinny on how to research completed sales.

Searching sites online

If you don't find the information you need on eBay, don't go ballistic — just go elsewhere. Even a site as vast as eBay doesn't have a monopoly on information. The Internet is filled with websites — and, for that matter, Internet *auction* sites that can give you price comparisons and information about cyberclubs.

Your home computer can connect to powerful outside *servers* (really big computers on the Internet) that have their own fast-searching systems called *search engines.* Remember, if something is out there and you need it, you can find it right from your home PC in a matter of seconds. Here are the addresses of some of the web's most highly regarded search engines or multi-search-engine sites:

- Google (www.google.com)
- Microsoft Bing (www.bing.com)
- Shopzilla (www.shopzilla.com)
- Yahoo! (www.yahoo.com)

The basic process of getting information from an Internet search engine is pretty simple:

1. **Type the address of the search-engine site in the Address box of your web browser.**

   You're taken to the website's home page.

2. **Find the text box next to the button labeled Search or something similar.**

Getting professional info from Terapeak Research

If you become an eBay fanatic someday, you may find yourself praising the genius of an amazing service offered by eBay and Terapeak. Terapeak Research allows you to research pricing further back than the 90 days of sold listings (30 days for unsold listings) that eBay search allows. If you come across a special or very old item, and there are not many on the site, you can use this tool to find how much the item has sold for in the past few months.

A little further on in the chapter is some of the research I performed on a G.I. Joe Buzz Aldrin figure. Researching the price lets me know when the item is trending and getting the highest prices.

As with third-party applications, there is a charge to use the service. But the price is right, and they offer a seven day free trial. There are several levels of search: from 7 to 90 days (and a custom search for 365 days of history). I recommend using the 30-day search because in my (not-so-) humble opinion, 90 days is an eternity in Internet time — what sold well three months ago may be worth bupkis now. But if the item is truly rare, a 90-day search will give you a better idea of long-term value. You can find its site at www.terapeak.com.

3. In the text box, type a few words indicating what interests you.

Be specific when typing search text. The more precise your entry (see search shortcuts later in this chapter), the better your chances of finding what you want. Look for tips, an Advanced Search option, or help pages on your search engine of choice for more information about how to narrow your search.

4. Click the Search (or similar) button or press Enter on your keyboard.

The search engine presents you with a list of the Internet pages that feature the requested information. The list of links includes brief descriptions and links to the first group of pages. You'll find links to additional listings at the bottom if your search finds more listings than can fit on one page. (And if you ask for something popular, like *Harry Potter,* don't be surprised to get millions of hits.)

Always approach information on the web with caution. Not everyone is the expert he or she would like to be. Your best bet is to get lots of different opinions and then boil 'em down to what makes sense to you. And remember — *caveat emptor.* (Is there an echo in here?)

Many people out here on the West Coast buy cars on eBay. (Could it be because cars are way more expensive here? Maybe.) If you're researching prices to buy a car on eBay, look in your local newspaper to get a good idea of prices in your community. Several good sites are on the Internet. My personal favorite is www.nadaguides.com. I've had many of my friends (and editors) visit the various sites, and we've settled on this one because it seems to give the most accurate and unbiased information.

Finding other sources of information

If you're interested in collecting a particular item, you can get a lot of insider collecting information without digging too deep:

- ✔ **Go to other places on the Internet.** The Internet is full of insider info. Remember to take advice with caution, however, because sometimes the "competition" likes to keep the good nuggets of info for themselves.

- ✔ **Go to the library (or buy a book)!** Books and magazines are great sources of info, especially out-of-print books. You'll no doubt find at least one book or one magazine specializing in your chosen item. For example, if old furniture is your thing, *Antiquing For Dummies,* by Ron Zoglin and Deborah Shouse, can clue you in to what antiques collectors look for.

If you find an interesting specialty magazine at the library, try entering the title in your search engine of choice. You may just find that the magazine has also gone paperless and you can read it online.

✔ **Go to someone else who's in the know.** Friends, clubs, and organizations in your area can give you a lot of info. Ask your local antiques dealer about clubs you can join and see how much info you end up with.

Looking to Find an Item? Start Your eBay Search Engine

The best part about shopping on eBay is that, aside from collectibles, you can find just about everything from that esoteric lithium battery to new designer dresses (with matching shoes) to pneumatic jackhammers. New or used, it's all here — if you can find it hiding in the millions of new daily listings. (According to rumors on the web, 89 million listings are on the site worldwide at any given time. That's a lot of virtual gavels banging!)

Finding the nuggets (deals) can be like searching for the proverbial needle in the haystack. The search secrets in this chapter will put you head and shoulders above your competition for the deals.

eBay has lots of ways for you to search for items (sample — in Chapter 3). Although eBay allows you to search by item number, let's be realistic here. Do you remember what I said a few paragraphs back about the number of active listings? I can't remember my own phone number, let alone an item number (and I never write them down correctly). Look for those numbers to get longer and longer as eBay continues to grow in popularity. These main options are the most useful for researching:

✔ Search Title Keywords (or Search Title and Description)

✔ Search Items by Seller or Bidder

✔ Search Items on eBay Motors

You can access these additional search options by clicking the Advanced Search link to the right of the Search box at the top of any eBay page. Each search option can provide a different piece of information to help you find the right item from the right seller at the right price.

If you plan to repeat specific eBay searches, I recommend that you conduct searches often by saving them in your My eBay Saved Searches area (see Chapter 4 to find out how). And when you find a particularly juicy item or subcategory, bookmark it, or if it's an item, click Watch This Item (a link on the listing), or use your My eBay page. (See Chapter 4 for more on eBay's personal shopper.)

Testing, testing . . . how long does a search take on eBay?

Having a massive search engine is a matter of necessity on eBay — millions of items are up for auction at any given time — and often, an easy, fast search makes all the difference between getting and not getting. After all, time is money, and eBay members tend to be movers and shakers who don't like standing still.

So how long do searches really take on eBay? I put it to the test. In the Search window of the eBay home page, I typed **1933 World's Fair Pennant** and let 'er rip.

The search engine went through the millions of general items and World's Fair items (860 of them in 1999, 1,200 items in 2003, 2,100 in 2006,

13,847 in 2010, and today over 23,443!) and gave me my one specific item in a blink of an eye. (Now, if the wizards at eBay could only figure out a way to find that sock that always escapes from clothes dryers, they'd really be on to something.)

Narrowing the search to the pennant, in 1999, that slightly wrinkled felt pennant got four bids and sold for $17.50; in 2003, the aging pennant sold for $43.88 with eight bids. In 2009, one went for $14.99. Things must be looking up; one just sold for $26.51 (7 bids). You can never take the temperature of the collectibles market. It can run either hot or cold!

Using the Advanced Search page

When you click the Advanced Search link to the right of the Search box, the Search page appears. It's the most basic of searches (with a few options) and the one you'll be using the most.

When you use any of the Search options on eBay, the search engine looks for every listing (auction or fixed-price) that has the words you're looking for in the title (or the description if you specify so). The title (as you may expect) is a group of *keywords:* words used to describe the item. For example, if you're looking for an antique sterling iced tea spoon, just type **sterling iced tea spoons** into the search window (see Figure 5-1). If someone is selling a sterling iced tea spoon and used exactly those words in his or her title or description, you're in Fat City.

Figure 5-1:
Using
Search to
find sterling
iced tea
spoons.

Before you click the Search button, know you can narrow your search further. If you go to Advanced Search, you have the option of choosing how you want the search engine to interpret your search entry. You can have the search engine search the title and description for

- ✔ All the words you type
- ✔ Some of the words you type
- ✔ The exact phrase in the order you wrote it

When you're familiar with the tricks listed later in this chapter, you'll be able to get most of these fancy Search results in one of the many search boxes you see littered around the eBay site.

In addition to the following, you can find other useful criteria on the Advanced Search page (more on this further on):

- ✔ **What price range you want to see:** Type the price range you're looking for, and eBay searches the specific range between that low and high price. If money is no object, leave this box blank.

- ✔ **Words to exclude:** If you want to find a sterling iced tea spoon, but you don't want it to be plated silver, exclude the word *plated* from the drop-down menu.

- ✔ **From sellers:** You can exclude (or include) particular sellers. If you like, you can just search sellers from your Saved Sellers list. (But why?)

- ✔ **Within a category:** Use this option if you want to limit your search to a particular main (or *top-level*) category, for example, instead of searching all eBay categories. But why? eBay sellers are notorious for making listing mistakes and selecting wrong categories. Wait till you see your results, and then decide whether you want to narrow things.

- ✔ **The item location:** You can narrow your search to the United States only, North America, or worldwide. Depending on your item, this search criterion can help weed out the most esoteric items. If you're looking for hefty items (like an elliptical exercise machine that will probably end up as a place to hang clothes) that would cost much too much to ship, you can specify how many miles from your ZIP code (or any ZIP) you will allow the search to extend.

- ✔ **The order in which you want your results to appear:** If you indicate Time: Ending Soonest, the search engine gives you the results so that items closing soon appear first on the list. Best Match is the eBay default, and I recommend you select a sort that better fits your needs. Time: Newly Listed lists all the newly listed items. Price: Lowest First and Price: Highest First list them just that way.

> ✔ **Whether you want search to check through item titles alone or check both item titles *and* item descriptions:** You'll get more hits on your search if you select the Include description check box, but you may also get too many items that are out of your search range. See "Shortcuts for a quick eBay search," later in this chapter, for some solid advice.

Okay, *now* click the Search button. In a few seconds, you see the fruits of all the work you've been doing (see Figure 5-2). (Wow, you're not even perspiring.)

Check this box to include the description.

Choose an option for sorting results.

Figure 5-2: Use eBay's handy refined Search to ferret out even more related listings.

 You may notice that eBay has a way to refine your search in boxes to the left of your results. Be sure to click the related specifics here because eBay's search functions can often be a bit temperamental — and you don't want to miss any great deals.

 Next to item listings you often see pictures, or *icons.* A golden yellow rising-sun picture means the listing is brand new (this icon stays on for the first 24 hours an item is listed). The gold seal with the words *Top Rated Plus* indicates an item is being sold by a seller who gives top-rated service on eBay.

 An easy way to keep track of an item you're interested in is to click the Add to Watch List link just below the current bid amount of an item page. The listing then appears on your My eBay Watch List, and you can keep your eyes on the action.

On the left side of the results page may be a list of categories that your search term is listed under, which is a great reference. Next to each category is a number in parentheses that tells you how many times your search item appears in that category. Figure 5-3 shows a sample of the category spread. To view the items appearing only in a particular category, click that category (or subcategory) title.

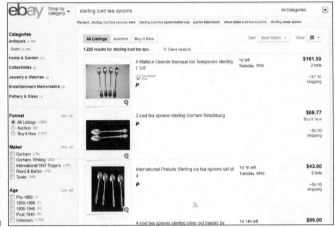

Figure 5-3: Search results showing the category breakdown on the left.

Finding Sold Items

To the left of the search results (if you scroll all the way down), you'll see options listed under Show Only so you can limit what you see to certain items. If you click Completed Listings, you're presented with every expired item (whether or not it sold) that matches your keywords. A Completed Listings search returns results of items that have already ended.

To get the real data on how much the item will sell for, select the Sold Listings box. This is my favorite search option because you can use it as a strategic bidding tool. How? If you're bidding on an item and want to know whether the prices are likely to go too high for your pocketbook, you can use this search option to compare the current price of the item to the selling price of similar items from items that have already sold.

You can use this tool also if you want to sell an item and are trying to determine what it's worth, the demand, and whether this is the right time to list the item. (Chapter 10 offers the nuts, bolts, and monkey wrenches you need to set up your auction.)

Type your keyword criteria, scroll down the page, and click the Sold Listings box. Step by step, here's how to do a Sold Items Only search:

1. **In the title search field, type the title name or the keywords of the item you want to find.**

2. **Click the Search box.**

3. **On the search results page, select the Sold Listings check box to see items that have sold (and how much they sold for) as far back as the eBay search engine will permit.**

   Currently, you can go back about three months.

4. **Once the sold listings appear, tell eBay how you want the results sorted.**

   In the Sort drop-down menu, choose one of the following options:

   - *End Date: Recent First:* Lists the most recently sold items first.

   - *Date Listed: Oldest First:* Shows items that were sold from the oldest listings to the newest.

   - *Distance: Nearest First:* Unless you're looking to see how many of your item sold close to you, this is a pretty useless sort. You want pricing info!

   - *Price+ Shipping: Lowest First:* Lists items from the lowest price attained to the highest price paid for an item.

   - *Price+ Shipping: Highest First:* Lists completed items from highest to lowest. (This is a very useful option when you're searching for a 1967 Camaro and you want to buy a car and not a Hot Wheels toy.)

   Your search results will refresh immediately.

Figure 5-4:
The convenient Show Only Sold Listings box on the search results page.

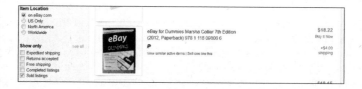

An international search

On the Advanced Search page (you get there by clicking the word *Advanced* to the right of the search box), you can select any country (from Afghanistan to Zimbabwe, no kidding!) or narrow your search to the United States or Canada, as shown in Figure 5-5. Don't forget that you have to pay for shipping, so if you don't want to pay to ship a heavy, Victorian-style fainting sofa from Hungary to Hoboken, New Jersey, stick close to home. By the same token, I'll bet Egyptian cotton is even better when it comes from Egypt. (It is — I've bought from an Egyptian seller!)

The Location Search option is pretty much an international version of Search, and it's done the same way. You have the choice of narrowing your country search to countries that offer an item, and to which countries they ship to. (Most eBay sellers will ship to the United States).

Figure 5-5:
The Interna-
tional
Search
Location
selector.

Finding a specific seller

In eBay's Advanced Search, locate the By Seller link in the links on the left, shown in Figure 5-6; the By Seller pages show you a list of all the items a seller is selling, and it's a great way for you to keep tabs on people you have successfully done business with in the past. The By Seller search is also a strategy that eBay users use to assess the reputation of a seller. You can find out more about selling strategies in Chapter 9.

Figure 5-6:
You can
search for
all items by
an individual
or search
for one item
from many
sellers.

View all items by a single seller

Select the By Seller option in the left-side Items search area in Advanced Search. Follow these steps:

1. **In the By Seller search field, type the eBay User ID of the person you want to learn more about.**

2. **If you want to see items that this seller has conducted in the past, select the Show Completed Listings box.**

   You can choose to see all fixed-price listings, as well as auctions, that have ended in the last day, last 7 days, or last 15 days.

   eBay keeps past item results active for only 30 days; if you're looking for something sold 31 days ago (or longer), sorry — no dice.

3. **In the Sort By drop-down box, select how you want the results of your search to appear onscreen.**

   If you want to see the items that are closing right away, select End Date: Recent First.

4. **Choose the number of results you want to see per page.**

   If the person you're looking up has 200 listings running, for example, you can limit the number of results to a manageable 50 listings on four separate pages.

5. **Click the Search button at the bottom of the form.**

   Figure 5-7 shows the results page of a By Seller search.

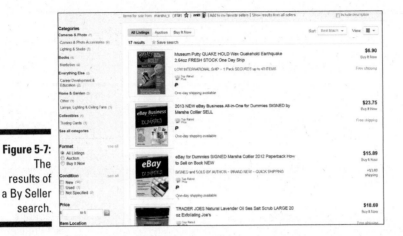

Figure 5-7:
The
results of
a By Seller
search.

Finding items by keywords for multiple sellers

If you're looking for a specific item from a group of sellers, you can enter the search information in the bottom half of the Advanced Search Find Items page. You may need to perform this type of search after you settle into shopping on eBay and have several sellers you like doing business with (or alternatively, you can exclude sellers you prefer not to do business with). With this method, you can limit the search for a particular item to just the sellers you want, rather than tens of thousands of sellers.

When you find a seller who you want to continue doing business with, you can add his or her link to your My eBay: Sellers You Follow area. Just click the Follow This Seller link on the item page. It then appears on your My eBay page, in the Sellers You Follow area. You can search their sales with a click of your mouse!

A Bidder search

The By Bidder search option is unique because sellers and buyers alike use it when an auction is going on to figure out their best strategies. After all, money is the name of the game. You can only find a Bidder search in Advanced Search by clicking Search by Seller; then the Bidder option will appear. For information on conducting a Bidder search, look at Chapter 7.

Free hanging chads . . .

eBay gives you the opportunity to have the same fine museum-quality items as the Smithsonian Institution. In November 2001, the Palm Beach County Board of County Commissioners found themselves in a bit of a pickle. Due to the infamous Presidential election of November 7, 2000 — fraught with hanging, pregnant, and dimpled chads — the announcement of the election winner was delayed for an unprecedented 37 days. As a result of this election, the Florida legislature outlawed the future use of punch-card voting systems — all Florida counties had to move to more stable, state-approved voting machines.

Palm Beach County chose to move to a touch-screen type of voting device, which cost its residents over $14 million. What to do with the old historic punch-card voting machines? Yep, donate one to the Smithsonian — and auction the rest on eBay. Palm Beach County donated machine #1 to the Auction for America; it netted $4,550.01 for the Twin Towers fund.

The rest? Well, the Palm Beach County folks should have read this book. They ran a Dutch auction for 3,055 of the basic voting packages, with a starting bid of $300. Included with the voting machine was the iniquitous "butterfly ballot" with official stylus; a brass plaque certifying that it was used in the November 7 election; a Certificate of Authenticity signed by Theresa LePore, Palm Beach County Supervisor of Elections; 25 demonstrator punch cards for playing polling place at home; a signed photograph of the folks in charge of recounting the ballots: Palm Beach County Supervisor of Elections Theresa LePore, Palm Beach County Commissioner Carol Roberts, and Judge Charles Burton; and "any chads which are in the machine from previous elections." What a package! There also were 569 Premier packages, which included an Official Ballot box, starting at $600.

In the 10-day auctions (run at the same time!), Palm Beach County sold 78 of the Premier packages and 389 of the Basic voting-machine packages. I called the County Commissioner's office to find out why my voting machine hadn't arrived and asked when the rest would be auctioned. I was assured they would be put back up on eBay auction, but at a higher starting bid.

Palm Beach County should have followed the strategies in this book, the way some smart eBay sellers did. Soon after, one of the basic packages sold after a 7-day auction for $670. Other entrepreneurial sellers have been selling voting machines from counties other than Palm Beach on eBay. Unfortunately for those who purchase them, only the Palm Beach County machines had the infamous butterfly ballot.

Shortcuts for a quick eBay search

After you become familiar with each of eBay's search options, you need a crash course in what words to type into those nice little boxes. Too little information and you may not find your item. Too much and you're overwhelmed with information. If you're really into bean-bag toys, for example, you may be looking for Ty's Tabasco the Bull. But if you just search for *Tabasco,* you'll get swamped with results ranging from hot sauce to advertisements.

Some simple tricks can help narrow your eBay search results when you're searching from pages other than the main Search page (where you don't find all the searching bells and whistles). Table 5-2 has the details.

Table 5-2   Symbols and Keywords for Conducting Searches with the eBay Search Engine

Symbol	Effect on Search	Example
No symbol, multiple words	Returns auctions with all included words in the title.	**reagan letter** might return an auction for a mailed message from the former U.S. president, or it might return an auction for a mailed message from Boris Yeltsin to Ronald Reagan.
Quotes ""	Limits the search to items with the exact phrase inside the quotes.	**"Wonder Woman"** returns items about the comic book/TV heroine. Quotes don't make the search term case-sensitive. Using either uppercase or lowercase in *any* eBay search gets you the same results.
Separating comma without spaces (a,b)	Finds items related to either the item before or after the comma.	**(gi joe,g.i. joe)** returns all G.I. Joe items, no matter which way the seller listed them.
Minus sign –	Excludes results with the word after the –.	Type **box –lunch**, and you'd better not be hungry because you may find the box, but lunch won't be included.
Minus symbol and parentheses	Searches for auctions with words before the parentheses but excludes words inside the parentheses.	**midge –(skipper,barbie)** means that auctions with the Midge doll won't have to compete for Ken's attention.
Parentheses	Searches for both versions of the word in parentheses.	**political (pin,pins)** searches for *political pin* and *political pins*.

Here are additional tips to help you narrow any eBay search:

- **Don't worry about capitalization:** You can capitalize proper names or leave them lowercase; the search engine doesn't care.

- **Don't use *and, a, an, or,* or *the*:** Called *noise words* in search lingo, these words are interpreted as part of your search. So if you want to find something from *The Sound of Music* and you type **the sound of music**, you may not get any results. Most sellers drop noise words from the beginning of an item title when they list it, just as libraries drop noise words when they alphabetize books. So make your search for **sound music**. An even more precise search would be **"sound of music"** (in quotes).

- **Search within specific categories:** This type of search narrows your results because you search only one niche of eBay — just the specific area you want. For example, if you want to find Tabasco the Bull, start at the home page and, under the Categories heading, click Toys and Bean Bag. The only problem with searching in a specific category is that sometimes an item can be in more than one place. For example, if you're searching for a Mickey Mouse infant snuggly in the Disney category, you may miss it because the item might be listed in infant wear. It's best not to limit yourself to a category because some of the best deals are miscategorized by sellers. What makes them such a good deal is that not everyone can find them. But you know better.

Finding eBay Members: The Gang's All Here

With millions of eBay users on the loose, you may think tracking folks down is hard. Nope. eBay's powerful search engine kicks into high gear to help you find other eBay members in seconds.

Here's how to find people or get info on them from eBay:

1. **From the top of most eBay pages, click the Advanced link next to the Search box.**

   This action takes you to the main Search page, where two links appear on the left side of the page, under Members.

2. **In the box on the left side of the page, click the Find a Member link.**

   This link takes you to the main Find Members page, where you can search for other members of the community. When you find the member, you can see his or her About Me page (see Chapter 14 to find out how to create your own personal eBay web page). You can also get a look at the feedback profile of a user (see Chapter 4 for details about feedback), find User ID histories of fellow eBay members (which comes in handy when you're bidding on items, as Chapter 7 avows), or get contact information when you're involved in a transaction.

If you're involved in a transaction with another eBay member and feel that you need to contact the individual by phone, click the Find Contact Information link, which is under the Advanced Search, Members heading on the left side of the screen. On that page you'll need to type the transaction number, along with the other person's User ID. eBay compares this data with yours; if you are indeed involved in a transaction with each other, eBay e-mails you the other person's phone number (along with the person's full name, city, and state). Your contact information is, in turn, sent to the other party.

Clicking the arrow in the Favorite Searches drop-down box at the top right of the page allows you to scroll through your My eBay Favorite Searches. You can tell eBay about the items you're looking for, and it does automatic searches for you. You can also have eBay e-mail you when auctions that match your descriptions crop up. (Chapter 18 gives you more info on how this works.)

Chapter 6

Get the Deal: Shopping eBay

*B*rowsing different categories of eBay, looking for nothing in particular, you spot that must-have item lurking among other Justin Timberlake paraphernalia in the Collectibles category. Sure, you *could* live without that faux-gold Justin Timberlake buckle with belt, but life would be so much sweeter *with* it. And even if it isn't in mint condition, at least it'll hold your pants up on casual Fridays.

When you bid for items on eBay, you can get that same thrill that you would get at Sotheby's or Christie's for a lot less money, and the items you win are likely to be *slightly* more practical than an old Dutch masterpiece you're afraid to leave at the framer's.

In this chapter, I give you the 411 about ways to shop on eBay, as well as a rundown of the nuts and bolts of auction bidding strategies. I also share some tried-and-true tips that'll give you a leg up on the competition. (Hey, I buy lots of stuff on eBay.)

The Item Listing Page

At any given point, you have more than a million pages of items that you can look at on eBay, making item pages the heart (better yet, the skeleton) of eBay listings. All item pages on eBay — whether auctions, fixed-price items, or Buy It Now items — look about the same. For example, Figure 6-1 shows a conventional auction page with a Buy It Now option; Figure 6-2 shows a fixed-price sale; and Figure 6-3 shows a fixed-price sale with a twist — the

Make Offer option. All item pages show the listing title at the top of the selling area, bidding or buying info in the middle, and seller info below that. Below all this is a tabbed area that displays the complete description of the item, along with a tab for shipping and payment information.

Figure 6-1:
Here's one of my typical auctions, featuring the Buy It Now button and the Place Bid button.

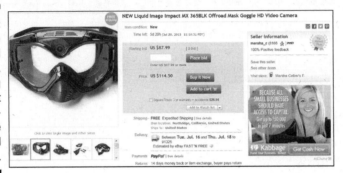

Figure 6-2:
In a fixed-price sale, you see the Buy It Now button and the opportunity to place the item in your shopping cart, but no Place Bid button.

Figure 6-3:
Some sellers offer a Make Offer option on their fixed-price sales.

The listing types have some subtle differences. Some listings feature multiple pictures at the left of the page, others only a single picture, depending on how the seller sets up the sale page. (Some sellers insert pictures within the item description.) Most listings have set item specifics in the description (as shown in Figure 6-4). This area is set up by eBay or filled in by the seller to give you a snapshot description of the item for sale. If you search for an item and end up finding it available in a fixed-price sale, you won't see the Place Bid button (refer to Figure 6-1). But overall, the look and feel of these pages will be the same.

Figure 6-4:
Item specif-
ics are filled
in by eBay
or the seller
according to
the param-
eters eBay
sets up for
them.

Item specifics			
Condition:	New: A brand-new, unused, unopened, undamaged item in its original packaging (where packaging is applicable). Packaging should be the same as what is found in a retail store, unless the item is handmade or was packaged by the manufacturer in non-retail packaging, such as an unprinted box or plastic bag. See the seller's listing for full details. See all condition definitions	Type:	Backdrop Stands
Model:	Infiniti	Backdrop Type:	Scratch-resistant, flexible, textured ABS plastic
MPN:	15-WICB	Brand:	Cloud Dome

When you come to a fixed-price listing with the Make Offer option, you can make an offer with a price that you'd like to pay for the item. (I talk about the best ways to make your offer later in this chapter.)

Here's a list of the information you see as you scroll down on a typical item page:

✔ **Item Title:** The title describes the merchandise for sale. It's generally made up of keywords (rarely a complete sentence) that identify the item.

If you're interested in a particular type of item, take note of the key words used in the title (you're likely to see them again in future titles). Doing so helps you narrow future searches.

✔ **Item Category:** Located above the item, here's a listing you can click if you want to do some comparison shopping. (Chapter 5 gives you more searching strategies.)

✔ **Current Bid:** This field in an auction indicates the dollar amount the bidding has reached, which changes throughout the auction as people place bids. If no bids have been placed on the item, this field is called *Starting Bid*.

Sometimes, next to the current dollar amount in an auction, you see the words *Reserve not met* in tasteful parentheses. This statement means that the seller has set a *reserve price* for the item — a secret price that must be reached before the seller will sell the item. If you don't see this note on a listing item page, don't be alarmed. Most auctions don't have reserve prices. Also, the moment a reserve is met, the indicator disappears.

✔ **Buy It Now:** If you want the item immediately and the price quoted in this area is okay with you, click the Buy It Now link, which takes you to a page where you can complete your purchase. This is also an option in an auction listing (refer to Figure 6-1). In this case, you can still place a bid for the lower bid price and the listing will convert to an auction format.

✔ **Add to Cart**: If you're on a mini shopping spree and planning to buy a few items, click this box and the item will be added to your eBay shopping cart.

Items placed in your shopping cart are not yours until you check out. If the seller has only one of an item in stock, another buyer can swoop in and buy it while you're browsing the site.

✔ **Quantity:** This field appears only in multiple item fixed-price sales. This is where you indicate how many of an item you wish to purchase. Next to the quantity, you will see how many are currently available and how many of the item have been sold. You can be sure that it's a fixed-price sale because you have no opportunity to bid; you can just use the Buy It Now option (or Add to Cart) for whatever quantity of the item you desire. If a seller is selling two items for the price of one, the item quantity still shows up as 1 (as in 1 set of 2 bookends).

✔ **Time Left:** The official clock keeps ticking down as time passes. When the item gets down to the last hour of an auction, eBay automatically starts an interactive clock that counts the minutes and seconds. This field tells you the time remaining in this particular auction.

Timing is the key in eBay auction bidding strategies (covered in Chapter 7). eBay's world headquarters is in California, so eBay uses Pacific standard time or Pacific daylight time as the standard, depending on the season. Not a major deal if you live on the West Coast as I do, but it can be an issue if you live anywhere else. Not to worry: My website, `www.coolebaytools.com`, has time charts that translate eBay time to time zones all over the U.S. and the world.

✔ **Item Condition:** All sellers must clearly state the condition of the item (or items) for sale. eBay varies the guidelines a seller may use in this area, depending on the category in which the item is listed. But rest assured that if an item is listed as *new*, it will be a brand-new, unused, unopened, undamaged item. If you'd like a peek at the category-specific parameters, go to `http://pages.ebay.com/help/sell/item-condition.html`.

✔ **Bids:** This field (next to the Current or Starting bid) tells you how many bids have been placed on an auction. To use the number of bids to your advantage, you have to read between the lines. You can determine just how much attention this item has received by comparing the number of bids the item has received over time. Based on the amount of bids in an item, you can create a time strategy (which I talk about later in this chapter).

If you want to see the starting bid, you have to click to see the bid history, by clicking the number of bids, as shown in Figure 6-5. By clicking there, you can also find out the number of individuals bidding and what date and time bids were placed. The dollar amount of each bid is shown in the bidding history, but bidders' maximum bids are kept secret.

Bidding is more an art than a science. Sometimes an item gets no bids because everyone's waiting until the last second to bid. You see a flurry of activity as bidders all try to outbid each other (called *sniping,* which Chapter 7 explains). But that's all part of the fun of eBay.

Figure 6-5:
Clicking the Number of Bids link before or after an auction will give you an idea of how much competition you may have for an item.

Click here to see the bid history.

✔ **Shipping:** This area gives you the shipping price to your location, The Item Location field tells you (at the very least) the country where the seller is located, and you may also see more specific info, such as the city and geographic area where the seller is. (What you see depends on how detailed the seller wants to be.) Also listed are the countries that the seller is willing to ship the item to.

Factor in the geographic location of a seller when you consider bidding on an item. If you buy from someone in your own state, you may also have to pay sales tax on your purchase. If the item is in Australia, for example, and you're in Vermont, you may decide that you don't really *need* that wrought-iron doorstop. (Remember, *you* may have to pay the shipping charges.)

✔ **Add to Watch List:** Click this link to magically add the item to the Watch section of your My eBay page. From there, you can keep an eye on the progress of the auction — without bidding. If you haven't signed in, you have to type your User ID and password before you can save the auction to your My eBay page.

Be sure to use the *Watch* feature. Organization is the name of the game on eBay, especially if you plan to bid on multiple auctions while you're running auctions of your own. I figure you're in the bidding game to win, so start keeping track of items now.

✔ **Add to Collection:** On the heels of the success of Pinterest, eBay has instituted a feature where you can build your own collections of favorite items and styles. Chapter 17 gives you more information on how to build a Collection.

✔ **Social Sharing:** You can tip off a friend on a good find via e-mail, get some advice from an antiques or collecting expert, or run the auction by a friend who's been around the eBay block a few times and ask for strategy advice. (You find this next to the Add to Watch List link with a small envelope icon.) There are also links to share the page on Facebook, Twitter, or Pinterest — but I say that if you're bidding on an auction, why invite the competition?

✔ **Print:** If you'd like to print a copy of the listing for reference, click here to get a complete printout of a listing. That way you get the entire description for your records.

✔ **Seller Information:** This area gives you links to the seller's profile (by clicking the seller's name) and to their feedback ratings (by clicking the number next to the seller's ID). By clicking these links, you can get a better idea of your trading partner. The number next to the seller's ID allows you to view his or her entire feedback history to make sure that you feel comfortable doing business with this person (as shown in Figure 6-6).

Keep in mind that no matter what the seller's rating is, your purchase is covered under eBay's Buyer Protection to be exactly as described.

You also have the opportunity to Follow the seller on your My eBay page by clicking Follow This Seller. (From there you can decide whether you want your list to be public or private). Another link takes you to a list of the other items the seller has up for sale.

Clicking through to the Feedback profile page, you get a few more options:

- *Positive Feedback Percentage:* The eBay computers cipher this figure. It's derived from all the positive and negative feedback that a user receives.

- *Contact Member:* Clicking this link connects you to eBay's message system. You can ask the seller a question regarding the item here.

- *View Items for Sale:* This link takes you to a page that lists all the seller's current auctions and fixed-price sales.

  If the seller has an eBay store, a link to it appears next. I give you a step-by-step guide on how these links work later in this chapter.

✔ **Item Number:** Just above the description area, you'll find the item number on the far right. This number identifies the item within the eBay servers. Keep track of this info for later inquiries.

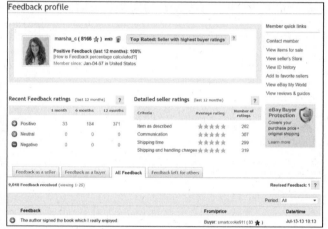

Figure 6-6: A quick glance will give you a good idea of who you're dealing with.

✔ **Description tab:** You see a tabbed bar consisting of two tabs. The opening (default) is the Description tab. The other tab is the Shipping and Payments tab. Be sure to scroll down the page and read the entire item description information carefully *before* bidding or buying.

✔ **Shipping and Payments tab:** Click this tab to see the details on shipping (shown in Figure 6-7). You see

- Who pays (most often the seller offers free shipping, but you never know).

- Whether the seller offers alternatives like expedited shipping.

- Which states have to pay sales tax (if any).

- The estimated delivery date.

- Whether the seller is willing to ship to your area. (Sometimes sellers won't ship internationally, and they'll let you know here.)

Also, be sure to check the item description for other shipping information and terms.

TIP

If the item doesn't have free or flat-rate shipping, the seller may have conveniently included eBay's shipping calculator to calculate your costs. eBay knows your ZIP code, so you're presented with the shipping cost to your location.

The seller's return policy will be listed here too, so if you want to have the option to return an item (if it doesn't fit?), you'd better check here first.

The Payment details area tells you the payment methods that the seller accepts: PayPal, Skrill, ProPay, or the seller's own merchant credit card service. Many sellers allow you to pick up the item at their location. Often you're directed to read the item description for more details. (I explain how to decipher item descriptions later in this chapter.)

Figure 6-7:
Check the
shipping
and pay-
ment boxes
below
the item
description
to find out
about addi-
tional costs,
shipping,
and taxes
that may
apply when
you buy.

Shipping and handling			
Item location: Northridge, California, United States			
Shipping to: United States			
Quantity: 1 Change country: United States ▾		ZIP Code: 91325 Get Rates	
shipping and handling	To	Service	Delivery*
Free shipping	United States	Expedited Shipping	Between Wed. Jul. 17 and Fri. Jul. 19 to 91325 per eBay FAST 'N FREE
US $27.50	United States	One-day Shipping (USPS Express Mail®)	Estimated by Wed. Jul. 17
* Estimated delivery dates include seller's handling time, and will depend on shipping service selected and receipt of cleared payment. Delivery times may vary, especially during peak periods.			
Estimated sales tax			
Seller charges sales tax for items shipped to: CA*(8.0%)			
* Tax applies to subtotal + S&H in these states only			
Return policy			
Item must be returned in the same condition that it was received. Other conditions apply.			
After receiving the item, your return within:	Refund will be given as:		Return shipping
14 days	Money back or item exchange (buyer's choice)		Buyer pays return shipping
Payment details			
Payment method	Preferred / Accepted		
PayPal VISA [cards]	PayPal Preferred		
Immediate payment required for this item			

Beating the Devil in the Details

As with any sale — whether you find it at Joe's Hardware, Bloomingdale's, or Target — carefully check out what you're buying. The item page gives you links to help you know what you're bidding on — and who you're potentially buying from. If you take advantage of these features, you won't have many problems. But if you ignore these essential tips, you may end up unhappy with what you buy, who you buy it from, and how much you spent.

Read the item description carefully

The *item description* is the most critical item on the listing page. This is where the seller gives the details about the item being sold. Read this page carefully and pay very close attention to what is, and *isn't,* written.

Don't judge a book by its cover — but do judge a seller by his or her item description. If the sentences are succinct, detailed, and well structured, you're most likely dealing with an individual who planned and executed the listing with care. It takes time and effort to post a good listing. If you see huge lapses in grammar, convoluted sentences, and misspellings, you might want to ask the seller further questions (if you really want the item from this seller, that is — there may be others available on eBay). Make sure that you feel comfortable dealing with this person or business; decide for yourself whether he or she seems to be out to sell junk for a quick buck or is selling on eBay for the long term.

If additional pictures are available, take a good look. The majority of eBay sellers spruce up their auctions with multiple photos of their items. The seller should answer a few general questions in the item description. If these questions aren't answered, that doesn't necessarily mean that the seller's disreputable — only that if you're really interested, you should e-mail through eBay messages and get those answers before you bid. In particular, ask questions like these:

- ✔ Is the item new or used?

- ✔ Is the item a first edition or a reprint? An original or a reissue? (See Chapter 5 for tips on how to assess what you're buying.)

- ✔ Is the item in its original packaging? Does it still have the original tags?

- ✔ Is the item under warranty?

eBay requires that sellers spell out exactly how the item will be shipped. Check the Shipping and Payments tab, which is next to the Description tab, to see whether an actual shipping charge applies — and if so, how much it'll cost you. Some sellers use eBay's incredibly convenient shipping calculator. Here are a few other things to consider regarding your item:

- ✔ If you're in a hurry to get the item, is the seller shipping within a day?

- ✔ If there are shipping charges, does the amount seem reasonable?

Most experienced eBay buyers know that, depending on the item, a tiny scratch here or there may be worth the risk of making a bid. But a scratch or two may affect the value *and* your bidding price. (Look at Chapter 5 for more expert advice for buying collectibles.)

- ✔ Is this item the genuine article or a reproduction — and if it's the real deal, does the seller have papers or labels certifying its authenticity?

> ✔ What size is the item, and how much does it weigh? (That life-size fiberglass whale may not *fit* in your garage. That baby grand piano might cost a lot to ship from Anchorage, so you need to factor in the cost of shipping when you consider how much you're willing to pay.)

Get the scoop on the seller

I can't tell you often enough that the single most important way you can make a transaction go well is to *know who you're dealing with*. Apparently, the eBay folks agree; they enable you to get info on the seller right from the feedback page. I recommend that you take advantage of the links offered there. (Chapter 5 demonstrates how to conduct a thorough By Seller search.)

eBay, like life, is full of shades of gray. Some sellers are unfairly hit with negative comments for something that wasn't their fault. If you suspect that a seller has received a bum rap (after you've read all his or her positive feedback), be sure to look for the seller's response. (Look at Chapter 4 for more on reading and leaving feedback.)

Although scoping out an eBay feedback profile is *just that fast, just that simple,* you still need to take the time to read the feedback. (There's that echo again. Good thing it's a wise echo.) Someone with 500 positive feedback messages may look like a good seller, but if you take a closer look, you may find that his or her ten most recent feedback messages are negative.

View the seller's other items

To find out what other sales the seller has going on eBay, all you have to do is click the corresponding link on the item page; you're taken to a list of the other item pies the seller has a finger in. If the seller has no other items up for sale and has no current feedback, you may want to do a more thorough investigation and conduct a By Seller search that will show you all of that person's completed listings in the last 30 days. (See Chapter 5 for details.)

Ask seller a question

If anything about the transaction is unclear to you, remember this one word: *ask.* Find out all the details about that item before you bid. If you wait until you've won the item before you ask questions, you may get stuck with something you don't want. Double-checking may save you woe and hassle later.

You can find out more about payment options, shipping charges, insurance, and other fun stuff in Chapters 8 and 12.

If you're bidding on a reserve-price auction, don't be afraid to message the seller and ask what the reserve is. Yeah, reserves are mostly kept secret, but there's no harm in asking — and many sellers will gladly tell you.

Spell check pays off

A savvy eBay user I know benefited from a major seller error. The seller titled his auction "Swede Star Trek Cast Jacket." My friend checked out the item description and found that it was written with bad spelling and incoherent grammar, so she e-mailed the seller for more information. The seller explained that the jacket was a suede cast jacket given as a "wrap" gift to the cast and crew of the movie *Star Trek: Generations*. He had won it in a local radio contest, and it was brand new. Because of the seller's mistake, only one bidder bid on this lovely green suede (silk-lined!) jacket, which my friend picked up for $150. Because of its *Star Trek* connection, the jacket is worth upwards of $400 to collectors. So study the item page carefully. You may get lucky and find that errors can work to your benefit. (And a word to the wise: Check your own spelling and grammar carefully when you put an item up for sale.)

To ask a seller a question, follow these steps:

1. **Scroll all the way to the bottom of the description to the *Questions and Answers about This Item* box and click the Ask a Question link.**

   You're presented with the Find Answers form.

2. **Select a topic from the list that most closely matches your query.**

   The seller may have posted common answers to questions. If you haven't found your answer, click Other and a Continue button will appear.

3. **Click Continue to get an eBay message form. Fill in the topic and the message area; then click Send Message.**

   Expect to hear back from the seller within a day. If it takes the seller more than a day to respond (unless it's over the weekend — eBay sellers often take a little rest), and you get no explanation for the delay, consider buying from someone else.

You can always change your User ID, but your past life (in the form of feedback messages) stays with you on eBay. Along with your feedback from your previous User ID, all your previous User IDs are listed as well in a User ID history search from the eBay Search page.

Factoring in the Extras

Before you think about placing a bid on an item, you should consider the financial obligation you have to make. In every case, the maximum bid you place won't be all you spend on an item. I recommend that you look closely at the payment methods that the seller is willing to accept — and also factor in shipping (if any). If you live in the same state as the seller, you may have to pay sales tax if the seller is running an official business.

Payment methods

Several payment options are available, but eBay only allows sellers to show electronic payment methods. The seller is not required to accept any other form of payment but PayPal or one of the other electronic payment options (PayPal, ProPay, Skrill, or a merchant account). These are the forms of payment available to you:

✔ **Credit card:** Paying with a credit card is a favorite payment option for many buyers, offered mainly by businesses and dealers. I like paying with credit cards because they're fast and efficient. In addition, using a credit card offers you another ally — your credit card company — if you're not completely satisfied with the transaction. Credit cards can also be used for payment through the other electronic payment options a seller may offer. I still prefer PayPal.

✔ **PayPal:** I pay for all my eBay purchases through PayPal. Owned by eBay, PayPal is the largest Internet-wide payment network. All sellers on eBay should accept PayPal and accept MasterCard, Visa, American Express, and Discover as well as electronic checks and debits. The service is integrated directly into eBay transactions, so paying for your item is a mouse click away.

After you register with PayPal to pay for an item, PayPal debits your credit card or your bank checking account (or your PayPal account — if you have earned some money from sales) and sends the payment to the seller's account. PayPal does not charge buyers to use the service. Buyers can use PayPal to pay any seller within the United States (and around the world in over 55 countries). Some international bidders can pay for their eBay items from sellers in the United States. To see a current list of PayPal's accepted currencies, go to

```
www.paypal.com/us/cgi-bin/webscr?cmd=xpt/Marketing/
seller/mc/MCIntro-outside
```

PayPal deposits the money directly into the seller's PayPal account, from which the seller can withdraw to their own bank account. The service charges the seller a small transaction fee, so the seller absorbs the cost.

Your credit card information is known only to the PayPal service. The seller never sees your credit card info. Another major advantage is that you have protection behind you when you use PayPal. And you have the right to dispute charges if the item arrives damaged or doesn't show up at all.

For more details, check out the PayPal website (www.paypal.com).

✔ **PayPal's Bill Me Later:** If you find that your credit card limit is about to hit, and you really want an item, Bill Me Later could be your answer. PayPal's Bill Me Later is like using an online credit card; just select Bill Me Later as your payment choice when you check out on eBay. Keep in mind you're opening a credit account, so they will need some personal information to approve your using their service.

Approval takes only seconds and after your account is set up, you'll see Bill Me Later as a payment option when you check out through PayPal. Clicking Bill Me Later brings up a window asking for your birth date and the last four digits of your Social Security number. After you accept the terms, approval takes just seconds; Bill Me Later is then added to your PayPal account.

✔ **Pay On Pickup:** Sometimes you may buy an item from someone in your neighborhood and may be able to arrange a direct pickup, instead of waiting for an item to be shipped. You're on your own with this type of transaction — but at least you get to meet the person you are transacting business with.

Most business on eBay is conducted in U.S. dollars. If you happen to buy an item from an international seller, you may need to convert American dollars into another currency. eBay has a currency converter, located at the following URL: pages.ebay.com/services/buyandsell/currencyconverter.html

Just select your choice of currency, type the amount, and click Perform Currency Conversion.

Using an escrow service

Even though most sales on eBay are for items that cost $100 or less, using an escrow service comes in handy on occasion — such as when you buy a big-ticket item or something extremely rare. *Escrow* is a service that allows a buyer and seller to protect a transaction by placing the money in the hands of a neutral third party until a specified set of conditions are met. Sellers note in their item descriptions whether they're willing to accept escrow. If you're nervous about sending a lot of money to someone you don't really know (like a user named Clumsy who has only two feedback comments and is shipping you bone china from Broken Hill, Australia), consider using an escrow company.

Using an escrow company is worthwhile only if the item you're bidding on is expensive, rare, fragile, or traveling a long distance. If you're spending less than $300 for the item, I recommend that you purchase insurance from your shipper instead — just in case. eBay has a partnership with Escrow.com to handle eBay escrow sales in Canada and the United States. After a transaction closes, the buyer sends the payment to the escrow company. After the escrow company receives the money, it e-mails the seller to ship the merchandise. After the buyer receives the item, he or she has an agreed-on period of time to look it over. If everything's okay, the escrow service sends the payment to the seller. If the buyer is unhappy with the item, he or she must ship it back to the seller. When the escrow service receives word from the seller that the item has been returned, the service returns the payment to the buyer (minus the escrow company's handling fee, of course).

Before you start an escrow transaction, make sure that you and the seller agree on these terms (use e-mail to sort it out). Here are three questions about escrow that you should know the answers to before you bid:

- ✔ Who pays the escrow fee? (Normally, the buyer does, though sometimes the buyer and seller split the cost.)
- ✔ How long is the inspection period? (Routinely, it's two business days after receipt of the merchandise.)
- ✔ Who pays for return shipping if the item is rejected? (The buyer usually pays.)

Shipping costs

Don't let the sale go down with the shipping. If the item is not an odd shape, excessively large, or fragile, experienced sellers calculate the shipping based on Priority Mail at the U.S. Postal Service, which is the unofficial eBay standard. Expect to pay a minimum of $5 for the first pound and another $0.50 for tracking the item.

Some sellers smartly use First Class Mail for items that weigh less than 13 ounces when packed, and sellers of media will often use the slower-delivery Media Mail for their items. These forms of shipping will save you big bucks!

It has also become somewhat routine for the seller to add a dollar or so for packing materials such as paper, bubble wrap, tape, and such. This is a fair and reasonable handling charge because the cost of these items can add up over time.

You may come across sellers trying to nickel-and-dime their way to a fortune by jacking up the prices on shipping to ridiculous proportions. If you have a question about shipping costs, ask before you bid on the item.

Before bidding on big stuff like a barber's chair or a sofa, check for something in the item description that says "Buyer Pays Actual Shipping Charges." When you see that, always message the seller prior to your bid to find out what those shipping charges would be to your home. On larger items, you may need to factor in packing and crating charges. The seller may also suggest a specific shipping company.

Placing Your Bid on an Auction

Okay, so you've found the perfect item to track (say, a really classy New Kids on the Block wristwatch), and it's in your price range. You're more than interested — you're ready to bid. If this were a live auction, some stodgy-looking guy in a gray suit would see you nod your head and start the bidding at, say, $2. Then some woman with a fierce hairdo would yank on her ear, and the NKOTB watch would jump to $3.

eBay reality is more like this: You're sitting at home in your fuzzy slippers, sipping coffee in front of the computer; all the other bidders are cruising cyberspace in their pajamas too. You just can't see 'em. (Be really thankful for the small things.)

When you're ready to jump into the eBay fray, you can find the bidding box at the top of the auction item page. If the item includes a Buy It Now option, you see that next to the bidding form.

To fill out the bidding form and place a bid, first make sure that you're registered (see Chapter 2 for details) and then follow these steps. After you make your first bid on an item, you can instantly get to auctions you're bidding on from your My eBay page. (If you need some tips on how to set up My eBay, see Chapter 4.)

1. **Enter your maximum bid in the appropriate box.**

   The bid needs to be an increment or more higher than the current minimum bid. The lowest amount you can bid is displayed just below the Place Bid box. (See the later section, "Bidding to the Max: Automatic Bidding," for more information about bidding increments.)

   You don't need to put in the dollar sign but *do* use a decimal point — unless you really *want* to pay $1,049.00 rather than $10.49. If you make a mistake with an incorrect decimal point, you can retract your bid (see "Retracting your bid," later in this chapter).

2. **Click Place Bid.**

   The Review Bid page appears on your screen, filled with a wealth of legalese. This is your last chance to change your mind: Do you really want the item, and can you really buy it? The bottom line is this: If you bid on it and you win, you buy it. eBay really means it.

3. **At this point, you have to sign in if you haven't already. If you're signed in, skip to Step 4.**

4. **If you agree to the terms, click Confirm Bid.**

   After you agree, the Bid Confirmation screen appears.

When you first start out on eBay, I suggest that you start with a *token bid* — a small bid that won't win you the auction but can help you keep tabs on the auction's progress. Personally, I keep an eye on the listing by adding it to my Watch list and letting my eBay Mobile app keep me apprised of the bidding action.

After you bid on an item, the item number and title appear on your My eBay page, listed under the Buy heading, as shown in Figure 6-8. (See Chapter 4 for more information on My eBay.) The Bidding list makes tracking your auction (or auctions, if you're bidding on multiple items) easy.

Figure 6-8:
Keep track of your bids on items on your My eBay page.

eBay considers a bid on an item to be a binding contract. You can save yourself a lot of heartache if you make a promise to *never bid on an item you don't intend to buy.* Don't make practice bids, assuming that because you're new to eBay, you can't win; if you do that, you'll probably win simply because you've left yourself open to Murphy's Law. Therefore, before you go to the bidding form, be sure that you're in this auction for the long haul — and make yourself another promise: *Figure out the maximum you're willing to spend.* (Read the section "The Agony (?) of Buyer's Remorse," later in this chapter, for doleful accounts of what can happen if you bid idly or get buyer's remorse.)

Bidding to the Max: Automatic Bidding

When you make a maximum bid on the bidding form, you actually make several small bids — again and again — until the bidding reaches where you told it to stop. For example, if the current bid is up to $19.99 and you put in a maximum of $45.02, your bid automatically increases incrementally so that you're ahead of the competition — at least until someone else's maximum bid exceeds yours. Basically, you bid by *proxy,* which means that your bid rises incrementally in response to other bidders' bids.

No one else knows for sure whether you're bidding by proxy, and no one knows your maximum bid. And the best part is that you can be out having a life of your own while the proxy bid happens automatically. Buyers and sellers have no control over the increments (appropriately called *bid increments*) that eBay sets. The bid increment is the amount of money by which a bid is raised, and eBay's system can work in mysterious ways.

The current maximum bid can jump up a nickel or a quarter or even a Washington, but there is a method to the madness, even though you may not think so. eBay uses a *bid-increment formula* (see Table 6-1) that uses the current high bid to determine how much to increase the bid increment. As you can see, the higher you bid, the larger the proxy (automatic) bidding amounts become. Here are a pair of examples:

- A 5-quart bottle of body lotion has a current high bid of $14.95. The bid increment is $0.50 — meaning that if you bid by proxy, your proxy will bid $15.45.

- A 5-ounce can of top-notch caviar has a high bid of $200. The bid increment is $2.50. If you choose to bid by proxy, your proxy will bid $202.50.

Table 6-1	eBay's Proxy Bid Increments
Current Bid	*Your Bid Increment*
$0.01–$0.99	$0.05
$1.00–$4.99	$0.25
$5.00–$24.99	$0.50
$25.00–$99.99	$1.00
$100.00–$249.99	$2.50
$250.00–$499.99	$5.00
$500.00–$999.99	$10.00
$1000.00–$2499.99	$25.00
$2500.00–$4999.99	$50.00
$5000.00 and up	$100.00

Table 6-2 shows you what kind of magic happens when you put the proxy system and a bid-increment formula together in the same cyber-room.

Table 6-2   Proxy Bidding and Bid Increments

Current Bid	Bid Increment	Minimum Bid	eBay Auctioneer	Bidders
$2.50	$0.25	$2.75	"Do I hear $2.75?"	Joe Bidder tells his proxy that his maximum bid is $8.00. He's the current high bidder at $2.75.
$2.75	$0.25	$3.00	"Do I hear $3?"	You tell your proxy your maximum bid is $25.00 and take a nice, relaxing bath while your proxy calls out your $3.00 bid, making you the current high bidder.
$3.00	$0.25	$3.25	"I hear $3.00 from proxy. Do I proxy hear $3.25?"	Joe Bidder's proxy bids $3.25, and while Joe Bidder is out walking his dog, he becomes the high bidder.

A heated bidding war ensues between Joe Bidder's proxy and your proxy while the two of you go on with your lives. The bid increment inches from $0.25 to $0.50 as the current high bid increases.

Current Bid	Bid Increment	Minimum Bid	eBay Auctioneer	Bidders
$7.50	$0.50	$8.00	"Do I hear $8.00?"	Joe Bidder's proxy calls out $8.00, his final offer.
$8.00	$0.50	$8.50	"The bid is at $8.00. Do I hear $8.50?"	Your proxy calls out $8.50 on your behalf, and having outbid your opponent, you win the auction.

Specialized Categories

After you get the hang of bidding on eBay, you may venture to the specialized auction areas. You can purchase a car or car parts and accessories from eBay Motors, or your own piece of land or a new home in the Real Estate category. eBay is always adding new specialty areas, so be sure to check the announcements as well as the home page.

Should you reach the big-time bidding, be aware that if you bid over $15,000 in an auction, you *must* register a credit card with eBay. All items in the special categories are searchable in eBay's search, so don't worry about missing your dream Corvette when you use the Search page.

eBay Motors

Visiting the automotive area of eBay is an auto enthusiast's dream. You can also find some great deals in used cars, and eBay offers creative ways to make buying vehicles of all shapes and sizes (as well as the largest array of parts you'll find anywhere on the planet) easy. Visit eBay Motors by clicking the Motors category link on the home page or by going to `http://www.ebay.com/motors`. Clicking the Vehicle Buyer Services link on the left will bring you to all sorts of ways to shop for a car with confidence.

- ✔ **Specialized search:** If you want to search for cars without coming up with hundreds of die-cast vehicles, eBay Motors has its own search available from the eBay Motors home page. Here you can input makes, models, and your ZIP code to see if there are any vehicles available in your area. There is a separate search where you can find parts or accessories for your existing car.

- ✔ **Vehicle shipping:** If you don't want to drive across the country to pick up your new vehicle, you can have it shipped through several eBay-recommended auto shippers. Check online for a free quote.

- ✔ **Inspections:** Many used-car buyers take advantage of eBay's independent inspection vendors. These companies offer a comprehensive inspection covering the mechanical condition and cosmetic appearance, and they supply a detailed inspection report. Once you've found the perfect vehicle for you, you can scroll below the bidding area and click the link labeled Order an Inspection.

✔ **Vehicle History Reports:** With the vehicle's VIN (Vehicle Identification Number), a seller can provide a free history report. If the seller has not offered this feature, click the Buy AutoCheck report link to order one on your own. A single report is $9.99, and a value pack of ten reports (for comparison shopping) is $14.99.

✔ **Financing:** Clicking the Get Low Monthly payments link, below the bidding area, will take you to the RoadLoans.com page to get an estimate. You can also apply for financing here for your purchase.

eBay Stores

The eBay Stores are a quick, easy, and convenient way to find items for sale that you can buy now. A large number of eBay sellers have opened eBay Stores for a monthly fee as an inexpensive way to display a large number of items for sale. They mostly carry fixed-price items and carry multiples of their items for sale.

When you're perusing the auctions on eBay, you'll see the store listings mixed in with the auctions. You can see the fixed-price listings by clicking one of the tabs at the top of a Search page or category listing, as shown in Figure 6-9.

See only auctions.

See only fixed-price sales.

Figure 6-9: Click the tab to see Auctions only or Buy It Now, fixed-price sales.

The Agony (?) of Buyer's Remorse

Maybe you're used to going into a shopping mall and purchasing something that you're not sure you like. What's the worst that could happen? You end up back at the mall, receipt in hand, returning the item. Not necessarily so on eBay. (Many of the top-rated sellers offer a 14-day return policy.) Even if you realize you already have a purple feather boa in your closet that's just like the one you bought yesterday on eBay, deciding that you don't want to go through with a transaction *is* a big deal. Not only can it earn you some nasty feedback, but it can also give you the reputation of a deadbeat.

It would be a shame to float around eBay with the equivalent of a scarlet *D* (for *deadbeat*) above your User ID. Okay, eBay sellers use a kinder term — *non-paying bidder* — but for many members, it boils down to the same thing. If you win an auction or buy an item and have to back out of your obligation — even through no fault of your own — you need some info that can keep you in good (well, okay, *better*) standing. Look no further; you've found it.

Retracting your bid

Remember, many states consider your bid a binding contract, just like any other contract. You can't retract your bid unless one of these three outstandingly unusual circumstances applies:

- ✔ If your bid is clearly a typographical error (you submitted a bid for $4,567 when you really meant $45.67), you may retract your bid. If this occurs, you should re-enter the correct bid amount immediately. You won't get any sympathy if you try to retract an $18.25 bid by saying you meant to bid $15.25, so review your bid before you send it.

- ✔ You have tried to contact the seller to answer questions on the item, and he or she doesn't reply in a timely fashion.

- ✔ If the seller substantially changes the description of an item after you place a bid (the description of the item changes from "can of tennis balls" to "a tennis ball," for example), you may retract your bid.

If you simply must retract a bid, try to do so long before the auction ends — and have a good reason for your retraction. eBay users are understanding, up to a point. If you have a good explanation, you should come out of the situation all right. So admit that you've made a mistake.

Buyer's remorse can pay off

Sometimes buyer's remorse does pay off. I know one eBay buyer who got a serious case of remorse after winning an auction. She decided to do the right thing and pay for the item even though she didn't want it. After receiving the item, she turned around and *sold* it on eBay for triple what she paid. If you really don't want the item, think like a seller — see whether you can turn a horrible mistake into a profitable venture. For more information on the benefits of selling, take a look at Chapter 9.

If you've made an error, you must retract your bid prior to the last 12 hours of the auction. At this point, a retraction removes all bids you have placed in the auction. Mistakes or not, when you retract a bid that was placed within the last 12 hours of the listing, only the most recent bid you made is retracted — your bids placed prior to the last 12 hours are still active.

Here's how to retract a bid while the auction's still going on:

1. **Go to** `http://offer.ebay.com/ws/eBayISAPI.dll?RetractBidShow.`

2. **Read the legalese and scroll down the page. Enter the item number of the auction you're retracting your bid from. Then open the drop-down menu and select one of the three legitimate reasons for retracting your bid.**

3. **Click the Retract Bid button.**

   You receive a confirmation of your bid retraction via e-mail. Keep a copy of it until the auction is completed.

If you made a mistake when making a Best Offer, go to the following: `http://offer.ebay.com/ws/eBayISAPI.dll?RetractBestOfferShow`

The seller may send you a message to ask for a more lengthy explanation of your retraction, especially if the item was a hot seller that received a lot of bids. Keep your replies courteous. After you retract one bid on an item, all your lower bids on that item are also retracted (unless the retraction is done within the last 12 hours), and your retraction goes into the bidding history — another good reason to have a really good reason for the retraction. The number of bids you've retracted also goes on your feedback-rating scorecard.

Avoiding deadbeat (unpaid item) status

Some bidders are more like kidders — they bid even though they have no intention of buying a thing. When honest eBay members spot these ne'er-do-wells, they often post the deadbeats' User IDs on Internet message boards. Some eBay members have created entire websites to warn others about dealing with the deadbeats . . . ahem . . . *non-paying bidders.* (Civilized but chilly, isn't it?)

Once a seller opens an unpaid item case (if you do not pay within two days), and you don't want to pay, you can be excused by appealing the case. You may also contact the seller explaining why. The following human mishaps are generally accepted by most sellers:

- ✔ A death in the family
- ✔ Computer failure
- ✔ A huge misunderstanding

If you have a good reason to call off your purchase, make sure that the seller knows about it. The seller is the only one who can excuse you from the sale.

If an unpaid item case is opened against you but you've paid for the item, eBay requires proof of payment. That would include a copy of the check (front and back) or money order, a copy of the payment confirmation from PayPal (or other online payment service), or an e-mail from the seller acknowledging receipt of payment. If the seller excused you from the auction, you need to forward the e-mail with all headers.

- ✔ Fax hard copies to eBay at 888-379-6251 (write Bidder Appeal on the fax cover page).
- ✔ Send the e-mail via an online form. Go to pages.ebay.com/help/buy/appeal-unpaid-item.html, click the link to the online unpaid item appeal form, and plead your case.

There's no guarantee that your appeal will be accepted. eBay will contact you after an investigation and let you know whether your appeal was successful.

eBay has a message for non-paying bidders: The policy is pretty strict. After the first complaint about a non-paying (deadbeat) bidder, eBay gives the buyer a warning. After the third offense, the violator may be suspended from eBay for good and becomes *NARU* (Not A Registered User). Nobody's tarred and feathered, but you probably won't see hide nor hair of that user again on eBay.

After the auction: Side deals or second chances?

If a bidder is outbid on an item that he or she really wants or if the auction's reserve price isn't met, the bidder may message the seller and see whether the seller is willing to make another deal. Maybe the seller has another similar item — or is willing to sell the item directly rather than run a whole new auction. You need to know that this could happen — but eBay doesn't sanction this outside activity.

If the seller has more than one of the item, or the original auction winner doesn't go through with the deal, the seller can make a Second Chance offer. This is a legal, eBay-sanctioned second chance for *underbidders* (unsuccessful bidders) who participated in the auction. Second Chance offers can also be made in reserve auctions if the reserve price wasn't met.

Any side deals other than Second Chance offers are unprotected. Here's an example: My friend Jack collects autographed final scripts from hit television sitcoms. So when the curtain fell on *Seinfeld,* he had to have a script. Not

surprisingly, he found one on eBay with a final price tag that was way out of his league. But he knew that by placing a bid, he made it likelier that someone else with a signed script to sell might see his name and try to make a deal. And he was right.

After the auction closed, he received a message from a guy who worked on the final show and had a script signed by all the actors. He offered it to Jack for $1,000 less than the final auction price on eBay. Tempted as he was to take the offer, Jack understood that eBay's rules and regulations wouldn't help him out if the deal turned sour. He was also aware that he wouldn't receive the benefit of feedback or any eBay Buyer Protection for the transaction.

If you even *think about* making a side deal, remember that not only does eBay *strictly* prohibit this activity, but eBay can also suspend you if you are reported for making a side deal. And if you're the victim of a side-deal scam, eBay's rules and regulations don't offer you any protection. My advice? Watch out!

Chapter 7

Winning eBay Strategies

. . . .

. . . .

*W*hen people think about eBay, they initially think all sales are auctions. This is not close to being true, of course, since many major brands have hung up their shingles on the site. Fixed-price sales have become the majority of eBay transactions. But, thank goodness, the folks at eBay still let us enjoy the fun of an auction. Bidders love them and sellers even more - especially when the item up for sale is worth more than the seller ever expects to get.

I travel the country and am often asked about eBay. I speak to so many people who find an auction on eBay, bid on it, and at the last minute — the last hour, or the last day — are outbid. Sad and dejected, they find losing an auction often cuts to the core and makes them feel like losers.

You're *not* a loser when you lose an auction on eBay. You just may not know the fine art of sneaky bidding (my way of saying *educated* bidding).

When the stakes are high and you really, really want the item, you have to resort to a higher form of strategy. Sports teams study their rivals, and political candidates scout out what the opposition is doing. Bidding in competition against other bidders is just as serious an enterprise. Follow the tips in this chapter and see if you can come up with a strong bidding strategy of your own. (Feel free to e-mail me with any brilliant bidding plans; I'm always open to new theories.)

Make an Offer!

If you come across a fixed-price listing and you're in the mood to negotiate, why not make an offer? Sellers on eBay can use the Best Offer option any time they list a fixed-price item. When the seller selects this option, you'll see the Make Offer button on a listing, which should indicate to you that you're dealing with a seller who's motivated to sell. This is a great way to get bargains. You make an offer on the item and the seller will either accept your offer or send you a counteroffer.

Making an offer to buy an item has a drawback: The seller has 48 hours to respond to you, and you may find the same item from another seller at a better price before then. By making an offer, you guarantee that you will buy the item at the price of your offer if the seller agrees to it. If that doesn't happen, you're off the hook and can find another of the item elsewhere.

To make an offer, click the Make Offer button (rather than the Buy It Now button); see Figure 7-1.

Click this button to make an offer.

Figure 7-1: Use the Make Offer option any time you're not in a rush and want to wangle a good deal.

When making an offer, you might think you want to put in a really, really low offer. But be sensible; if the item is new, the seller may have only a little wiggle room on the price. Also, putting in a ridiculously low offer (say $10 on a $25 item) may just annoy the seller and he or she may turn you down without giving you an opportunity to negotiate.

Find Out an Item's Bidding History

You can access the bidding history by clicking the Number of Bids link, which appears to the right of the current bid on the item page. The bidding history lists everyone who is bidding on the item. You can see how often and at what time bids are placed, but you can't see the bidder's real eBay username because (to protect the innocent) eBay changes User IDs to a gibberish of asterisks and numbers. Each bidder is assigned a faux bidder ID in the history.

Pay attention to the times at which bidders are placing their bids; you may find that, like many eBay users, the people bidding in this auction seem to be creatures of habit — making their bids about once a day and at a particular time of day. They may be logging on before work, during lunch, or after work. Whatever their schedules, you have great info at your disposal in the event that a bidding war breaks out: Just bid after your competition traditionally logs out, and you increase your odds of winning the auction.

You'll also notice when someone has placed a much higher proxy bid — as when a single bidder continually ups the bid and still doesn't have the highest, winning bid. Look at Figure 7-2 to see the bidding history on an auction where I didn't bust the winning bidder's proxy bid.

Figure 7-2: The bidding history tells you the date and time of day at which the bidders placed their bids, as well as the amount.

Bid history			
Bidders: 5 Bids: 5 Time left: **3 days 13 hours 47 mins** Duration: **7 days**			
You've been outbid. Bid again before it's too late!			

Only actual bids (not automatic bids generated up to a bidder's maximum) are shown. Automatic bids may be placed days or hours before a listing ends. Learn more about bidding

Show automatic bids

Bidder ⓘ	Bid Amount	Bid Time
j***e (539 ⭐)	US $8.27	**Aug-09-13 18:12:51 PDT**
u***c (669 ⭐)	US $7.77	Aug-07-13 23:11:41 PDT
marsha_c (8190 ⭐)	US $5.25	Aug-09-13 13:05:30 PDT
1***1 (1898 ⭐)	US $2.00	Aug-06-13 23:57:03 PDT
r***c (134 ⭐)	US $2.00	Aug-07-13 17:05:36 PDT
Starting Price	US $0.99	Aug-06-13 08:00:52 PDT

Item info

AUTHENTIC BRAND NEW IN BOX CARTIER GRIS SUNGLASSES

Current bid: **US $8.27**
Shipping: Free -- Standard Shipping
Item number: 281146679970

Enter your maximum bid.

Bid Again

(Enter US $8.77 or more)

Early in an auction, there may not be much of a bidding history for an item, but that doesn't mean you can't still check out the dates and times a bidder places bids. You can also tell that a bidder practices *sniping* (discussed later in this chapter) if his or her bid zips in during the last few minutes (or even seconds!) of the auction. You may have a fight on your hands if the bidder does practice sniping.

Get to Know the Other Bidders

It used to be an easy task to study up on your competition, but the brains at eBay got smart and made it all but impossible. That is, all *but* impossible to me! In this section I show you how I figured out the now-circuitous route you can use to research your competition.

The anonymized ID of the person the item would belong to if the auction ended right now is listed on the auction item page. You can tell whether the auction has bidders because the number of bidders appears on the listing page.

Take a look at this ID because you may see this bidder again later in this auction. By clicking the ID, you are presented with a page like the one shown in Figure 7-3, which shows just what that bidder has been up to — bidding-wise.

Figure 7-3:
Clicking an
ID in the
bid history
reveals a lot
about the
competi-
tion. Here
someone
is clearly
highly inter-
ested in
the fashion
category.
(A dealer,
perhaps?)

The tale of the 3-plus-negative seller

A friend of mine took a risk and bid on an old Winchester rifle (now a banned item — see Chapter 9 for a rundown of what you're allowed and not allowed to sell on eBay) without reading the seller's feedback. The seller had a (3) next to his User ID, which at a glance might say that the user is new to eBay. Good thing my friend lost the auction. It turned out that the seller had a whopping 20 negative feedback messages. He had 23 positives, mostly posted by suspicious-looking names. These days, a seller like this would be suspended by eBay . . . eventually. Repeat after me: *Always read the feedback comments!*

Strategies to Help You Outsmart the Competition

Your two cents *do* matter — at least on eBay. Here's why: Many eBay members tend to round off their bids to the nearest dollar figure. Some choose nice, familiar coin increments such as 25, 50, or 75 cents. But the most successful eBay bidders have found that adding 2 or 3 cents to a routine bid can mean the difference between winning and losing. So I recommend that you make your bids in oddish figures (such as $15.02 or $45.57) as an inexpensive way to edge out your competition. If you have a proxy bid in, say for $22.57, and a sniper jumps in at the last second and places a bid for $22.50 — you still win! The highest bid placed always wins. For the first time ever, your 2 cents (or in this case 7 cents) may actually pay off!

Pirates of the Caribbean . . . or Carribean?

Just before the original *Pirates of the Caribbean* movie premiered, Disneyland gave out exclusive movie posters to its visitors. My then-college-student daughter, savvy eBayer that she is, snagged several copies to sell on the site. She listed them (one at a time) when the movie opened and couldn't get more than the starting bid of $9.99 for each of them.

When we searched eBay for *pirates poster,* we found that the very same posters listed with a misspelled title, "Pirates of the Carribean," were selling for as high as $30 each. After selling out her initial stock, my daughter found another seller who had ten for sale — in one auction — with the proper spelling. She bought those as well (for $5 each) and sold them with misspelled titles on the site for between $15 and $27!

The moral of this story is always to search alternate spellings of your item; you might possibly eke out a gem without any competition.

That's just one of the many strategies to get you ahead of the rest of the bidding pack without paying more than you should. ***Note:*** The strategies in this section are for bidders who are tracking an item over the course of a week or so — so be sure that you have time to track the item and plan your next moves. Also, get a few auctions under your belt before you throw yourself into the middle of a bidding war.

Here's a list of dos and don'ts that can help you win your item. Of course, some of these tips *are* eBay endorsed, but I had to get you to notice what I have to say somehow:

- **Don't bid early and high.** Bidding early *and* high shows that you have a clear interest in the item. It also shows that you're a rookie, apt to make mistakes. If you bid early and high, you may give away just how much you want the item.

  Of course, a higher bid does mean more bucks for the seller and a healthy cut for the middleman. So it's no big mystery that many sellers recommend it. In fact, when you sell an item, you may want to encourage it too.

  If you must bid early and can't follow the auction action (you mean you have a life?), use software or an online sniping service like BidRobot. Then feel free to place your highest possible bid! You can find out more about that in Chapter 20.

- **Do wait and watch your auction.** If you're interested in an item and you have the time to watch it from beginning to end, I say that the best strategy is to wait. Click the Watch This Item link to move it to your My eBay page — and remember to check it. But if you don't have the time, go ahead — put in your maximum bid early and cross your fingers.

- **Don't freak out if you find yourself in a bidding war.** Don't keel over if, at the split second you're convinced that you're the high bidder with your $45.02, someone beats you out at $45.50.

  You can increase your maximum bid to $46.02, but if your bidding foe also has a maximum of $46.02, the tie goes to the person who put in the highest bid *first*. Bid as high as you're willing to go, but bid at the very end of the auction.

- **Do check the item's bidding history.** If you find yourself in a bidding war and want an item badly enough, check the bidding history and identify your fiercest competitor; then refer to the previous section, "Get to Know the Other Bidders," for a pre-auction briefing.

  To get a pretty exact picture of your opponent's bidding habits, make special note of the times of day when he or she has bid on other auctions. You can adjust your bidding times accordingly.

- **Do consider sniping**. Further in this chapter I discuss *sniping* - a term I coined in the early days of eBay to describe a technique for bidding at the last possible second of an auction.

✔ **Do remember that most deals go through without a problem.** The overwhelming majority of deals on eBay are closed with no trouble, which means that if the auction you're bidding in is typical and you come in second place, you've lost. Or maybe not . . .

If the winning bidder backs out of the auction or the seller has more than one of the item, the seller *could* (but isn't obligated to) come to another bidder and offer to sell the item at the second bidder's price through eBay's Second Chance option. (See Chapter 13 for more details on this feature.)

Time Is Money: Auction Strategy by the Clock

You can use different bidding strategies depending on how much time is left in an auction. By paying attention to the clock, you can find out about your competition, beat them out, and end up paying less for your item.

Most auctions on eBay run for a week; the auction item page always lists how much time is left. However, sellers can run auctions for as short as one day or as long as ten days. So synchronize your computer clock with eBay's master time and become the most precise eBay bidder around. Figure 7-4 shows eBay's Official Time page, which you can find at the very bottom of many eBay pages — or go directly to http://viv.ebay.com/ws/eBayISAPI.dll?EbayTime.

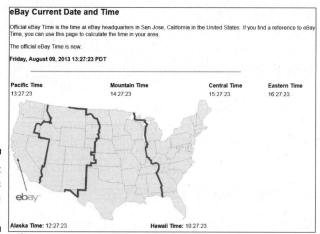

Figure 7-4: eBay's Official Time page.

To synchronize your clock, make sure that you're logged on to the Internet and can easily access the eBay website. Then follow these steps:

1. **Go into your computer's Control Panel and double-click the icon that represents your system's date and time functions.**

2. **On the eBay home page, scroll down to the Legal & More tab at the bottom of the page and click it.**

3. **In the Tools and Apps area, click the eBay Official Time link.**

4. **Check your computer's time against eBay's current time.**

5. **Click the minutes in your computer's clock and then click the Reload button (sometimes it's called Refresh) on your browser.**

   Clicking Reload ensures that you see the latest, correct time from eBay.

6. **Type the minutes displayed on the eBay Official Time page as soon as the newly reloaded page appears.**

7. **Repeat Steps 5 and 6 to synchronize your computer's seconds display with eBay's.**

This process takes a little practice, but it can mean the difference between winning and losing an auction.

You don't need to worry about the hour display unless you don't mind your system clock displaying Pacific time.

Most bidding on eBay goes on during East Coast work time and early evening hours, which gives you a leg up if you live out West. Night-owl bidders will find that after 10:00 p.m. Pacific time (about 1:00 a.m. Eastern time), lots of bargains are to be had. And believe it or not, lots of auctions end in the wee hours of the morning. Monday holidays are also great for bargains, as are Thanksgiving and the day after. While everyone is in the living room digesting and arguing about what to watch on TV (or getting up at 5:00 a.m. to buy the big discount deal at Walmart), fire up eBay and be thankful for the great bargains you can win.

For simplicity's sake, go over to my website and print my quick and easy eBay time-conversion chart. It's located at `www.coolebaytools.com/tools/usa-time-zones`.

Using a laid-back strategy

Sometimes the best strategy at the beginning of an auction is to do nothing at all. That's right; relax, take off your shoes, and loaf. Go ahead. You may want to make a *token bid* (the very lowest you are allowed) or mark the page to watch in your My eBay area. I generally take this attitude through the first six days of a week-long auction I want to bid on, and it works pretty well. Of course, I check in every day just to keep tabs on the items I'm watching on my My eBay page, and revise my strategy as time goes by.

The seller has the right to up his minimum bid — if his auction has received no bids — up to 12 hours before the auction ends. If the seller has set a ridiculously low minimum bid and then sees that the auction is getting no action, the seller may choose to up the minimum bid to protect his investment in the item that's up for sale. By placing the minimum token bid when you first see the auction, you can foil a Buy It Now sale from another bidder (because the Buy It Now feature is disabled after a bid has been placed unless there is a reserve on the listing) or prevent the seller from upping the minimum. If it's important enough, you can see whether the seller has done this in the past, by searching the seller's completed auctions (see "Get to Know the Other Bidders," previously in this chapter, to find out how to do this search). All pre-closing changes are available for public view; just click View All Revisions to see item specifics on the item page. See Figure 7-5 for a sample.

Item Revisions summary for item #220255908883

The seller has revised the following item information:

Date	Time	Revised Information
Jul-14-08	10:58:44 PDT	Description
Sep-16-08	15:31:01 PDT	Title Description
Sep-16-08	18:55:25 PDT	Description
Oct-13-08	17:56:03 PDT	Description
Oct-13-08	18:03:32 PDT	Description
Oct-27-08	11:50:51 PDT	Description
Oct-30-08	11:52:54 PDT	Description
Nov-25-08	16:34:20 PST	Description

Figure 7-5: This page shows the revisions made by the seller during this auction.

If you see an item that you *absolutely must* have, mark it to watch on your My eBay page (or make that token bid) and plan and revise your maximum bid as the auction goes on. I can't stress enough how important this is.

As you check back each day, take a look at the other bids and the high bidder. Is someone starting a bidding war? Look at the time that the competition is bidding and note patterns. Maybe at noon eastern time? During lunch? If you know what time your major competition is bidding, when the time is right, you can safely bid after he or she does (preferably when your foe is stuck in the dentist's chair while trying to use the eBay app, without a signal, to bid).

If you play the waiting game, you can decide if you really want to increase your bid or wait around for the item to show up again sometime. You may decide you really don't want this particular item after all. Or you may feel no rush because many sellers who offer multiple items put them up one at a time.

Using the beat-the-clock strategy

You should rev up your bidding strategy during the final 24 hours of an auction and decide, once and for all, whether you really *have* to have the item you've been eyeing. Maybe you put in a maximum bid of $45.02 earlier in the week. Now's the time to decide whether you're willing to go as high as $50.02. Maybe $56.03?

No one wants to spend the day in front of the computer (ask almost anyone who does). You can camp out by the refrigerator or at your desk or wherever you want to be. Just place a sticky note where you're likely to see it, reminding you of the exact time the auction ends. If you're not going to be near a computer when the auction closes, you can also use an automatic bidding site to bid for you; see Chapter 20 for details.

In the last half-hour

With a half-hour left before the auction becomes ancient history, head for the computer and dig in for the last battle of the bidding war. I recommend that you log on to eBay about five to ten minutes before the auction ends. The last thing you want to have happen is to get caught in Internet gridlock and not get access to the website. Go to the item you're watching and click the auction title.

With an hour to go, if your auction has a lot of action, eBay reloads the bidding action every second so you can get the most current info on what people are bidding.

Sniping to the finish: The final minutes

The rapid-fire, final flurry of bidding is called *sniping* — the fine art of waiting until the very last seconds of an eBay auction and then outbidding the current high bidder just in time. Of course, you have to expect that the current high bidder is probably sniping back.

With a hot item, open a second window on your browser (in Internet Explorer or Firefox, you do that by pressing the Ctrl key and the N key together); keep one open for bidding and the other open to watch eBay's constant reloading during the final few minutes. With the countdown at 60 seconds or less, make your final bid at the absolute highest amount you will pay for the item. The longer you can hold off — I'm talking down to around 15 seconds — the better. It all depends on the speed of your Internet connection (and how strong your stomach is), so practice on some small auctions so you know how much time to allow when you're bidding on your prize item. Keep watching the time tick to the end of the auction, as in Figure 7-6.

The story of the Snipe sisters

Cory and Bonnie are sisters and avid eBay buyers. Bonnie collects vases. She had her eye on a Fenton Dragonfly Ruby Verdena vase, but the auction closed while she was at work and didn't have access to a computer. Knowing that, her sister Cory decided to snipe for it. With 37 seconds to go, she inserted the high bid on behalf of her sister. Bang, she was high bidder at $63. But, with 17 seconds left, another bidder sniped back and raised the price to $73. It was, of course, Bonnie, who had found a way to get access to a computer from where she was. Bonnie got the vase, and they both had a good laugh.

Figure 7-6:
Watching the seconds count down.

If you want to be truly fancy, you can open a third window for bidding and have a backup high bid in case you catch another sniper swooping in on your item immediately after your first snipe. (I recently received an e-mail from one of my readers who used my somewhat paranoid method — which she learned from a previous edition of this book — and by using the second snipe, she won her item!) You can avoid the third-window routine if you've bid your highest bid with the first snipe. Then if you're outbid, you know that the item went for more than you were willing to pay. (I know; it's some consolation, but not much.)

Some eBay members consider the practice of sniping highly unseemly and uncivilized — it's like when dozens of parents used to mob the department store clerks to get to the handful of Beanie Babies that were just delivered. (Come to think of it, whatever happened to *those* collectibles?) Of course, sometimes a little uncivilized behavior can be a hoot.

I say that sniping is an addictive, fun part of life on eBay auctions. And it's a blast. So my recommendation is that you try sniping. You're likely to benefit from the results and enjoy your eBay experience even more — especially if you're an adrenaline junkie.

Here's a list of things to keep in mind when you get ready to place your last bid:

- Know how high you're willing to go. If you know you're facing a lot of competition, figure out your highest bid to the penny. You should have already researched the item and know its value at this point. Raise your bid only to the level where you're sure that you're getting a good return on your investment; don't go overboard. Certainly, if the item has some emotional value to you and you just have to have it, bid as high as you want (and can afford — but you knew that). But remember, you'll have to pay the piper later. You win it, you own it!

- Know the speed of your Internet connection.

- Remember, this is a game, and sometimes it's a game of chance, so don't lose heart if you lose the auction.

Although sellers love sniping because it drives up prices and bidders love it because it's fun, a sniper can ruin a week's careful work on an auction strategy. The most skillful snipers sneak in a bid so close to the end of the auction that you have no chance to counterbid, which means you lose. Losing too often, especially to the same sniper, can be a drag.

If your Internet connection is slower than most, and you want to do some sniping, make your final bid _2 minutes before the auction ends_ — and adjust the amount of the bid as high as you feel comfortable with so you can beat out the competition.

If you can make the highest bid with less than 20 seconds left, you most likely will win. With so many bids coming in the final seconds, your bid might be the last one that eBay records.

This stuff is supposed to be fun, so don't lose perspective. If you can't afford an item, don't get caught up in a bidding war. Otherwise the only person who wins is the seller. If you're losing sleep, barking at your cat, or biting your nails over an item, it's time to rethink what you're doing. Shopping on eBay is like being in a long line in a busy department store. If it's taking too much of your life or an item costs too much, be willing to walk away — or log off — and live to bid (or shop) another day.

Chapter 8

Winner! Winner! Chicken Dinner?

In This Chapter

▶ Getting yourself organized

▶ Having some straight talk with the seller

▶ Ironing out the details and sending your payment

▶ Dealing with an item that arrives "not as expected"

▶ Finishing the transaction with feedback

*P*erhaps there's no chicken dinner, but the thrill of the chase is over, and you've bought your first eBay item. Congratulations — now what do you do? You have to follow up on your victory and keep a sharp eye on what you're doing. In this chapter, you can get a handle on what's in store for you after you buy your item. I clue you in on what the seller is supposed to do to make the transaction go smoothly and show you how to grab hold of your responsibilities as a buyer. I give you info here about following proper post-sale etiquette, including the best way to get organized, communicate with the seller professionally, and send your payment without hazards. I also brief you on how to handle an imperfect transaction.

eBay Calling: You're a Winner

The Buy section of your My eBay page highlights the titles of items you've won or purchased and indicates the amount of your purchase price. If you think you may have won an auction and don't want to wait around for eBay to contact you, check out the Buy section for yourself and find out whether you're a winner. If you install eBay's mobile app on your smartphone, it will also notify you of any transactional information. In Chapter 18, I help you with the plusses and minuses of the mobile app.

Throughout an auction's bidding process, dollar amounts of items that you're winning appear in green on your My eBay Bids/Offers page. If you've been outbid, the bid amounts appear in red. After an auction ends, there's no marching band, no visit from a celebrity with a camera crew, no armful of roses, and no oversized check to duck behind. In fact, you're more likely to find out that you've won the auction from either an eBay notification or by visiting the Won section of your My eBay page. (An item you bought outright through Buy It Now shows up in your Purchase History.) eBay gets its End of Sale e-mails out pronto, but there may be a bit of lag time if you're not paying constant attention. For a look at the information in the winner's e-mail, see Figure 8-1.

Figure 8-1: Everything you need to know about your transaction is included in eBay's e-mail.

The notification on the Android mobile app takes you to a page shown in Figure 8-2. You will receive this as well as the e-mail notification.

Figure 8-2: The mobile app notification takes you to a page where you can pay for your auction win.

Getting Your Paperwork Together

Yeah, I know that PCs were supposed to create a paperless society, but cars were supposed to fly by the year 2000, too. Maybe it's just as well that some predictions don't come true (think of the way some people drive or steer shopping carts). Paper still has its uses, and when you're just starting out on eBay, printing copies of your purchase records can help you keep your transactions straight.

The item page shows the amount of your winning bid, the item's description, and other relevant information. The second you find out that you've won the item, click the Print link that appears to the right of the Description tab and print a copy of the item page for your files.

If you're the techie type, like me, you might just want to take a screen grab of the item's description.

Many people keep a separate folder on their computer to keep screen grabs of the item descriptions. Be sure to name the JPEGs with the item title so, if necessary, you can find the transaction later. To keep your eBay e-mails together, make a new folder in your e-mail program and drag all purchase-related e-mails there.

eBay displays listings for only 90 days in the Bidder search, so don't put off saving the details from that final item page for your records. If you save your End of Sale e-mails that you get from eBay, you can access the listing for up to 90 days if you use the link in the e-mail.

Many sellers have multiple listings going at the same time, so the more organized you are, the more likely you will receive the correct item (and quick feedback) from the seller. Here's a list of the items you should keep in your item purchases folder:

- ✔ A copy of your e-mail from eBay. *Don't* delete the e-mail! You may need to refer to the e-mail later, and there's no way to get another copy.

- ✔ Archive copies of any e-mail correspondence between you and the seller that details specific information about the item or circumstances of shipping arrangements.

- ✔ A copy of the final listing page.

Sellers can update their listings while they're in progress, so keep your eyes peeled for changes in the listing as you monitor it. If the seller makes major changes, you are within your rights to withdraw your bid. (Check out Chapter 6 for more on the bidding process.)

An order of fries with a menu on the side

In 1999, one seller auctioned an old menu from Howard Johnson's, estimating its era as the 1950s based on the cars pictured on the cover — and the prices (fried clams were $1.25). Also included was a separate menu card that listed fresh seafood and had a liquor menu (with Pieman logo) on the back — plus a list of locations in the New York City area. Except for a couple of staple holes at the top of the front cover (maybe evidence of daily specials past), the menu was in very good condition. The starting bid was $5; the item sold for $64. These menus are even harder to come by now but are selling in the $25 range. (I wonder how much they want for fried clams in New York City these days . . . .)

Getting in Contact

If you've won an item and intend to pay through PayPal, it's *de rigueur* for you to go to the item as soon as possible after you've won. If the item is an auction that you won while away from your computer, you will see a Pay Now link on the item page. Clicking that link takes you to a page where you can review your order and make payment.

You can also check the PayPal transaction page in your PayPal account where you will find the seller's e-mail address. A good thing to tuck away should the need arise. Know that any contact you have with the seller should be done through eBay's monitored messages; they become part of the transaction's record. Should a problem come up, the folks at eBay will be able to see the communications between you and the seller.

Sending the Payment Promptly and Securely

So how many times have you heard the saying "The payment is in the mail?" Yeah, I've heard it about a thousand times, too. If you're on the selling end of a transaction, hearing this line from the buyer but not getting the money is frustrating. If you're on the buying end, it's very bad form and may also lead to bad feedback for you.

Being the good buyer that you are (you're here finding out how to do the right thing, right?), you'll get your payment out pronto via PayPal. Do it immediately — why wait? (The sooner you pay, the sooner you get that charming Wizard of Oz Flying Monkey decanter you won!)

Most sellers expect to get paid within a couple of business days after the close of an auction. (Buy It Now items are paid immediately.) Although this timeline isn't mandatory, it makes good sense to let the seller know if there will be any delay in payment.

Send your payment promptly. If you have to delay payment for any reason (you have to go out of town or you are over your credit card limit), let the seller know as soon as possible. Most sellers understand if you send them a kind and honest e-mail. Let the seller know what's up, give him or her a date by which the money can be expected, and then meet that deadline. If the wait is unreasonably long, the seller may cancel the transaction. In that case, you can kiss your positive feedback goodbye.

The bottom line is that just about every eBay seller accepts PayPal as the main payment option. Let me help you feel more comfortable about why PayPal is the safest way to pay on eBay. eBay sees to it that PayPal is incredibly easy to use because PayPal is the official payment service on eBay. After an auction is over, a link you can use to pay appears. If you prefer, wait until you hear from the seller. You can make your payment in several ways:

- ✔ **Credit or Debit Card:** You can use your American Express, Discover, Visa, or MasterCard to make your payment through PayPal. The cost of the item is charged to your card, and your statement will reflect a PayPal payment with the seller's ID.

- ✔ **eCheck:** Sending money with an eCheck is easy. It debits your checking account just like a paper check. It does not clear immediately, and the seller probably won't ship until PayPal tells him or her that the eCheck has cleared your bank.

✔ **PayPal's Bill Me Later:** If you'd like to open up a credit line with PayPal you can (as long as you qualify). By clicking the Bill Me Later option, you can open up a credit account in a minute or so.

✔ **Instant Transfer:** An instant transfer is just like an eCheck, except that it clears immediately and the money is directly posted to the seller's account. It is only available to users in the United States who have linked a U.S. bank account and a debit or credit card to their PayPal account. When you send an instant transfer, your credit or debit card will be a backup (should the payment from your bank be denied).

PayPal is my favorite payment service when shopping at other websites as well. PayPal also has a buyer protection program, which covers your purchases in the case of possible fraud (if your item arrives not as described). Read more about that in Chapter 16.

When the auction is over, you can pay in a few ways. Click the Pay Now button on the e-mail you receive from eBay to check out and confirm your transaction details. If you don't pay immediately from the item page or the eBay e-mail, click the Pay link on the drop-down menu to the left of your item on your My eBay Purchase History area. After you click, just follow these steps:

1. **If this is your first encounter with PayPal, register.**

2. **Check to be sure your shipping address is correct.**

3. **See that the appropriate transaction appears and decide how to pay.**

If you're new to PayPal, they take you step by step through the process of filling out a payment form to identify the auction you're paying for, as well as your shipping information. Then you're all done. Your credit card information is held safely with PayPal, and the payment is deposited into the seller's PayPal account. The seller receives notice of your payment and notifies you about how quickly he or she will ship your item.

By paying with PayPal, you can instantly pay for an eBay item without hassle. Your credit card information is kept private, and your payment is deposited into the seller's PayPal account.

You can always view your Checkout status or track the package by going to your My eBay: Purchase History. Click the drop-down menu in the Action column for the item in question.

So, What's Your Number?

If something comes up between buying and receiving an item you've purchased, or an e-mail you've sent gets no response, then you need to get more contact information. Remember back when you registered and eBay asked for a phone number? eBay keeps such information for times like this.

To get an eBay member's phone number, click the Advanced Search link next to the Search box and then click the Members: Find the Contact Information link on the left side of the screen. You need to enter the seller's User ID and the number of the item that you're trading with the other member; then click the Submit button.

eBay automatically generates an e-mail to both you and the other user.

eBay's e-mail includes the seller's User ID, name, e-mail address, company, city, state, and country of residence, as well as the seller's phone number and date of initial registration. eBay sends this same information about you to the user you want to get in touch with.

Often, sellers jump to attention when they receive this e-mail from eBay and swiftly get the ball rolling to complete the transaction.

eBay doesn't tolerate any abuses of its contact system. Make sure that you use this resource only to communicate with another user about a specific transaction. To use contact information to complete a deal outside eBay is an infringement of the rules. If you abuse the contact system, eBay can investigate you and eject you from the site.

Fixed-price sales: Buy It Now or Add to Cart?

When you are shopping and buying eBay Fixed Price listings, you'll notice a Buy It Now button — as well as an Add to Cart button (both shown in the figure).

They represent two different procedures:

- **Buy It Now:** This button takes you to a review page, where you confirm that your item is one you want and your mailing address is correct. Then you just click Pay Now and the item is yours.

- **Add to Cart:** Clicking this button allows you to hold that particular item in your cart, so you can continue shopping around the site and find other items to buy. As you find them, just click Add to cart. When you've accumulated your full bounty, you can pay for all the items with just a click.

Keep in mind that any items in your cart are not yours until you pay for them. So if a seller only has one of the item left in stock, another buyer can swoop in and purchase it while you are dillydallying.

Checking Out

When you buy something in a store, you need to check out to pay. eBay isn't much different. eBay's Checkout is a convenient way to pay for your completed auctions and Buy It Now sales with a credit card or eCheck through PayPal.

Checkout is integrated directly onto the item page so that you can win and pay for an item in less than a minute. You may also be forwarded to a link to the seller's Checkout page if the seller uses a third-party Checkout system. When an auction is over, the item page will have Checkout information, as shown in Figure 8-3.

Figure 8-3:
Click the
Pay Now
button to
pay for
the item
immediately
through
PayPal.

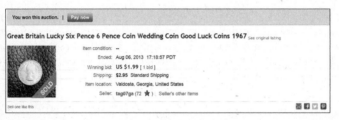

When you click the Pay Now button, you're taken through the Checkout process. You pay for the item, and the seller is notified. You also get an e-mail confirming your payment, along with the seller's e-mail address.

If you don't have a balance in your PayPal account (from selling items), PayPal defaults to taking the payment from your registered bank account. If you prefer to pay with a credit card, you must find the link as I did in Figure 8-4 to change your payment method.

Select payment method here.

Figure 8-4:
Use the
elusive
drop-down
menu to
select your
preferred
payment
method.

If you're dealing with a Buy It Now or fixed-price listing, the page won't change much after you've purchased the item. After you commit to buy and confirm to eBay that you want to make a purchase, you're taken immediately to a page with a Confirm and Pay button.

Communicating with the Seller

Top-notch sellers know that communication is the absolute key to a successful transaction, and they do everything they can to set a positive tone for the entire process with speedy and courteous e-mails (or, at the very least, polite invoices when needed).

After the transaction is over and it's time to leave feedback, communication is one of the points on which you're asked to rate the seller. Top-rated eBay sellers depend on high (5-star) ratings to maintain their reputation on the site. Things to consider when judging a seller's communication include (a) how accurate the seller's description was of the item and (b) how quickly you receive confirmation of your purchase.

Contact you may receive from a professional eBay seller might include the following information:

- ✔ The link for paying with PayPal or a secure website for credit card processing
- ✔ A review of the shipping options, if applicable
- ✔ Contact information
- ✔ The date the item will be shipped and when you should expect delivery
- ✔ The tracking number so you can follow your item's progress through the mail

You should pay immediately upon receipt of the invoice. If you have a question before paying, contact the seller immediately — he or she will be expecting your payment.

If you see significant differences between the e-mail you receive from the seller after the sale and what's on the item page, address those differences immediately with the seller before you proceed with the transaction. For more on clarifying payment options during the buying process, see Chapter 6.

Keeping in Touch: Dealing with an AWOL Seller

The eBay community, like local towns and cities, is not without its problems. With the millions of transactions that go on every week, transactional difficulties do pop up now and then.

You may be faced with an AWOL seller — the kind of person who pesters you for payment and then disappears. Just as you're expected to hustle and get your payment off to the seller, the seller has an obligation to notify you after receiving your payment to let you know that the item has been shipped. If you sent the payment but you haven't heard a peep in a while, *don't* jump the gun and assume the person is trying to cheat you, but *do* follow up.

Follow this step-by-step approach if you've already paid for the item but haven't heard from the seller:

- ✔ **The gentle-nudge approach:** In your My eBay Purchase History area, click the arrow below more actions on your transaction. Click Contact Seller; ask whether your item has been shipped, and would they be so kind as to send you the tracking number. You'll find that the old saying, "You can attract a lot more bees with honey than with vinegar," works great on eBay.

- ✔ **Civil-but-firm approach:** Send a message through eBay again. Be civil but firm, and request the information. Meanwhile, tap into some of eBay's resources. See the section "So, What's Your Number?" earlier in this chapter, to find out how to get an eBay user's phone number. After you have this information, you can send a follow-up e-mail or make a call.

- ✔ **Take-action time:** If you still haven't heard from the seller within a week, go to your My eBay Purchase History area, and in the drop-down menu next to the item in question, choose Resolve a Problem. You can then open a case for an Item Not Received (or for one stating that the item is Not as Described). Know that eBay will investigate the case — and if everything pans out, you will receive a refund. Turn to Chapter 16 to find out more about filing complaints and using other tools to avoid problems.

You Get the Item . . . Uh-Oh What's This?

The vast majority of eBay transactions go without a hitch. You buy, you send your payment, you get the item, you check it out, you're happy. If that's the case — a happy result for your transaction — skip this section and go leave some positive feedback for the seller!

On the other hand, if you're not happy with the item you receive, the seller may have some 'splaining to do. Message or call the seller immediately and politely ask for an explanation if the item isn't as described. Some indications of a foul-up are pretty obvious:

- ✔ The item's color, shape, or size doesn't match the description.

- ✔ The item is scratched, broken, or dented in ways that don't match the description (the description said the doll was new, but the box is tattered and the doll has seen more than its share of action).

- ✔ You purchased a set of candlesticks and received a vase instead.

A snag in the transaction is annoying, but don't get steamed right away. Contact the seller and see whether you can work things out. Keep the conversation civilized. The majority of sellers want a clean track record and good feedback, so they'll respond to your concerns and make things right. Assume the best about the seller's honesty, unless you have a real reason to suspect foul play. Remember, you take some risks whenever you buy something that you can't touch. If the item has a slight problem that you can live with, leave it alone and don't go to the trouble of leaving negative feedback about an otherwise-pleasant, honest eBay seller.

Of course, while I can give you advice on what you *deserve* from a seller, you're the one who has to live with the item. If you and the seller can't reach a compromise and you really think you deserve a refund, ask for one.

If the item arrives at your home pretty well pulverized, call the seller to alert him or her about the problem. Give the seller all the details needed to make an insurance claim (if the insurance was purchased by the seller).

With any luck, you and the seller can work things out. If not, file a claim with eBay's Buyer Protection to get your money back. Check out Chapter 12 for more tips on how to deal with shipping catastrophes. And jump over to Chapter 16 to find out how to file your eBay Buyer Protection claim.

Filing to Get a Refund

If your item never arrives or (as described in the previous section) isn't what you expected based on the description, you can get a refund on tangible goods through PayPal. (This comes under the PayPal Buyer Protection plan.) To do so, follow these steps:

1. **Go to your My eBay Purchase History, and in the drop-down menu next to the item in question, choose Resolve a Problem.**

2. **Verify that this is the item in question.**

3. **Click Resolve a Problem.**

4. **Answer the questions on the resulting page and you'll get a link to report your case.**

    You will have an opportunity to negotiate with the seller. If the case can't be resolved, and eBay agrees that you're right, you'll receive a refund.

Don't Forget to Leave Feedback

Good sellers should be rewarded, and potential buyers should be informed of good transactions. That's why no eBay transaction is complete until the buyer fills out the feedback form. Before leaving any feedback, though, always remember that sometimes no one's really at fault if some transactions get fouled up; communication meltdowns can happen to anyone. (For more info on leaving feedback, see Chapter 4.) Here are some scenarios that give you an idea on what kind of feedback to leave for a seller:

- ✔ **Positive:** If the transaction could have been a nightmare, but the seller really tried to make it right and meet you halfway, that's an easy call — give the seller the benefit of the doubt and leave positive feedback.

- ✔ **Positive:** Whenever possible, reward someone who seems honest or tried to fix a bad situation. For example, if the seller worked at a snail's pace but you eventually got your item and you're thrilled with it, you may want to leave positive feedback with a caveat. Something like "Item as described, good seller, but very slow to deliver" sends the right feedback message.

- ✔ **Neutral:** If the seller worked at a snail's pace and did adequate packaging and the item was kinda-sorta what you thought, you may want to leave neutral feedback; the transaction wasn't bad enough for negative feedback but doesn't deserve praise, either. Here's an example of what you might say: "Really slow to deliver, didn't say item condition was good not excellent, but did deliver." Wishy-washy is okay as a response to so-so; at least the next buyer will know to ask very specific questions.

- ✔ **Negative:** If the seller never shipped your item or the item seriously didn't match the description when it arrived, *and* you had to file a claim, you need to leave negative feedback. Make sure that both conditions apply. Never write negative feedback in the heat of the moment — and never make it personal. Keep it mellow and just state the facts. Do expect a response but don't get into a name-calling war. Life's interesting enough without taking on extra hassles.

The Accidental Deadbeat might be an intriguing title for a movie someday, but being a deadbeat isn't much fun in real life. See Chapter 6 for details on buyer's remorse and retracting a bid *before* the end of an auction.

Properly Giving the Seller's Detailed Star Rating (DSRs)

In addition to a feedback comment and rating (positive, negative, or neutral), buyers should leave detailed seller ratings, too. The DSR part of the feedback system asks you to rate sellers by filling in 1 to 5 stars. A 5-star rating doesn't cost you anything as the buyer, and if the sellers you buy from are Top Rated Sellers, feedback can affect a discount they receive on their eBay fees. Table 8-1 outlines what the stars mean to me when I leave a rating.

Table 8-1	What the DSR Stars Mean	
Rating Question	*# of Stars = Meaning*	*In the Real World*
How accurate was the item's description?	1 = Very inaccurate 2 = Inaccurate 3 = Neither inaccurate nor accurate 4 = Accurate 5 = Very accurate	In my world, the item was either described right or wrong — to me, there is no in-between. So when I rate a seller, either the item is as advertised (5) or it isn't (1).
How satisfied were you with the seller's communication?	1 = Very unsatisfied 2 = Unsatisfied 3 = Neither unsatisfied nor satisfied 4 = Satisfied 5 = Very satisfied	As a buyer, I lean more with being very satisfied that I got enough communication from the seller, or not. If I get one e-mail, I'm usually satisfied and give a 5. But if I haven't heard from a seller until the item reaches my door and there's a problem, I'm definitely rating in the 2-star range.
How quickly did the seller ship the item?	1 = Very slowly 2 = Slowly 3 = Neither slowly nor quickly 4 = Quickly 5 = Very quickly	When you're a buyer, it's only fair to check the postmark on the package you receive. If the seller ships the next day or the next day after — you really should click 5 (Very quickly), no matter how long the postal service took to get it there.

(continued)

Table 8-1 *(continued)*

Rating Question	# of Stars = Meaning	In the Real World
How reasonable were the shipping and handling charges?	1 = Very unreasonable 2 = Unreasonable 3 = Neither unreasonable nor reasonable 4 = Reasonable 5 = Very reasonable	When I purchase an item, I know what the shipping cost will be. The only surprise here is when you get an item in a small envelope and you paid $9 for shipping — or if you paid for Priority Mail and it comes in another class of service. This is, to me, pretty black-and-white. The shipping and handling charges are either reasonable or unreasonable.

Here are some other items to keep in mind when you're deciding on what Detailed Star Rating to leave for a seller:

- ✔ **Shipping takes time:** You have to realize that Ground shipping can take up to ten days. This isn't the seller's fault. So before leaving this rating, make sure to check the postmark or the date on the shipping label.

- ✔ **Shipping costs money:** Sellers have to add a little to cover the costs of tape, boxes, and packing materials. As a buyer, you have to keep that in mind. If you're unfamiliar with postage rates, you should also know that a package costs a lot more to ship across the country than to ship to the next state. So do a little homework and evaluate shipping costs *before* you buy. If the shipping is too high, go to another seller.

You may notice when leaving feedback that some start categories are grayed out (you can't click them). This is because the seller fulfilled requirements such as posting a tracking number quickly, or the package was delivered within the stated time.

If your seller is a Top Rated Seller, you should also know that your star ratings affect the fees he or she pays to eBay. Being a good seller (with high DSRs) can save as much as 20 percent on final value fees, so your rating is a very serious matter.

Part III
Making Money the eBay Way

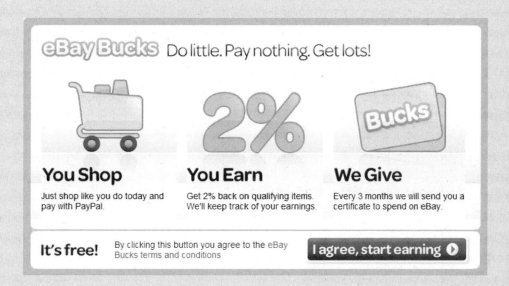

Visit www.dummies.com/extras/ebay for deeper information about your eBay listings.

In this part...

- ✔ Selling and shipping your items on eBay
- ✔ Conducting auctions
- ✔ Keeping track of money you make and taxes you pay
- ✔ Dressing up auctions with pictures and basic HTML

Chapter 9

Selling in Your Bunny Slippers for Fun and Profit

*F*inding items to sell can be as easy as opening your closet (garage? kitchen drawer?) or as challenging as acquiring antiques overseas (I even took the leap and imported items from Taiwan to sell on eBay). Either way, establishing yourself as a successful eBay seller isn't as difficult as it seems when you know the ropes. In this chapter, you find out how to look for items under your own roof, figure out what they're worth, and turn them into ready cash. But before you pick your house clean (I know eBay can be habit-forming, but please keep a *few* things for yourself!), read up on the eBay rules of the road — such as how to sell, when to sell, and what *not* to sell. If you're interested in finding out how to set up your auction page, get acquainted with Chapter 10; if you want to read up on advanced selling strategies, the appendix is where to find them.

Why Should You Sell Stuff on eBay?

Whether you need to clear out 35 years of odd and wacky knickknacks cluttering your closets or you seriously want to earn extra money, the benefits of selling on eBay are as diverse as the people doing the selling. The biggest plus to selling on eBay is wheeling and dealing from your home in pajamas and bunny slippers (every day is Casual Friday in my office — see Figure 9-1). But no matter where you conduct your business or how you dress, many more important big-time rewards exist for selling on eBay.

Figure 9-1:
My bunny slippers at work, listing items on eBay (I even sold a few pairs).

Most people starting a business have to worry about rounding up investment capital (startup money they may lose), building inventory (buying stuff to sell), and finding a selling location such as a booth at a swap meet or even a small store. Today, even a little mom-and-pop startup operation requires a major investment. eBay helped to level the playing field a bit; everybody can get an equal chance to start a small business with just a little money. Anyone who wants to take a stab at doing business can get started with just enough money to purchase initial items.

Get a few transactions under your belt. Sell your old collection of postcards, ashtrays, or souvenir spoons. See how you like the responsibilities of marketing, collecting money, shipping, and customer service. Grow a bit more, and you'll find yourself spotting trends, acquiring inventory, and marketing your items for maximum profit. In no time, you'll be making items disappear faster than magician David Copperfield (though you may have a little trouble with the Statue of Liberty — how'd he *do* that, anyway?). If you think you're ready to make eBay a full or part-time business, take a look at the appendix. If you still want to go long on eBay, please take a look at my book, *Starting an eBay Business For Dummies* (or, for gung-ho entrepreneurs, my *eBay Business All-in-One For Dummies*) for a complete reference to your online business. They give you just what you need to ramp up from hobbyist to big-time e-commerce tycoon making a few hundred (or even several thousand) dollars a month!

A fun way to get your feet wet on eBay is to buy some small items. When I say small, I mean it. Some of the least expensive items you can buy on eBay are recipes. Type **recipe** in the search box and sort the results by Lowest Prices First. You'll find recipes that range from a penny up. You don't have to pay a shipping charge, either. The sellers are required to send you a copy in the mail, but they often also e-mail the recipe direct to you after you pay. You can also begin selling your very own secret recipes. This is a great way to become familiar with how eBay works, and you'll be gaining experience with feedback — as well as building yours!

Life lessons learned on eBay

If you have children, they will benefit if you get them involved with your eBay transactions. They'll get real-life lessons they can't learn in school. Give them a feel for meeting deadlines and fulfilling promises. Get them writing e-mails (if they aren't already) and when you sell, help to pack the items. eBay is a great place to learn basic economics and how to handle money. When I first started on eBay, I taught my preteen daughter about geography by using eBay. Every time I completed a transaction, she used a search engine to look up the city in which the buyer (or seller) lived — and then marked the city by placing a pin on a huge map of the United States. She graduated from college, having majored in business and marketing, and has a good job today. (Thank you, eBay!)

Get creative and make eBay a profitable learning experience, too. Remember, however, that eBay doesn't let anyone under the age of 18 register, buy, or sell — so make sure that you're in charge of handling all transactions. Your kids can help out, but they need to be under your supervision at all times.

Finding Stuff to Sell

Finding merchandise to sell on eBay is as easy as checking your garage and as tough as climbing up to the attic. Just about anything you bought and stashed away (because you didn't want it, forgot about it, or it didn't fit) is fair game. Think about all those unwanted birthday and holiday presents (hey, it was the thought that counted — and the givers may have forgotten about them, too). Now you have a place you can try to unload them for cash. They could even make someone else happy.

In your closet, find what's just hanging around:

- ✔ Clothing that no longer fits or is out of fashion. (Do you really want to keep it if you wouldn't be caught dead in it or you know it will never fit?) Don't forget the pair of shoes you wore once and put away.

   You may not get top dollar for used items, but selling them will give you experience, build your feedback, and fill your pocket with a few well-earned dollars.

- ✔ Any item with a brand-name label that's in new or almost-new condition.

- ✔ Gifts. Have you received many well-meaning gifts that you've never used? You stashed them in the closet, right? One man's trash is another man's (or woman's) treasure.

- ✔ Kids' clothes. (They outgrow things fast. Use profits from the old items to buy new clothes they can grow into. Now, that's going green.)

Have the articles of clothing in the best condition possible before you put them up for sale. For example, shoes can be cleaned and buffed till they're like new. According to eBay's policies, clothing *must* be cleaned before shipping.

And consider what's parked in your basement, garage, or attic:

- **Old radios, stereo and video equipment, and 8-track systems:** Watch these items fly out of your house — especially the 8-track players (believe it or not, people love 'em).

- **Books you finished reading long ago and don't want to read again:** Some books with early copyright dates or first editions by famous authors earn big money on eBay.

- **Leftovers from an abandoned hobby:** Who knew that building miniature dollhouses was so much work?

- **Unwanted gifts:** Have a decade's worth of birthday, graduation, or holiday gifts collecting dust? Put them up on eBay and hope Grandma or Grandpa doesn't bid on them because they think *somebody* needs another mustache comb!

Saleable stuff may even be lounging around in your living room or bedroom:

- **Home décor you want to change:** Lamps, chairs, and rugs (especially if they're antiques) sell quickly. If you think an item is very valuable but you're not sure, get it appraised first.

- **Exercise equipment:** If you're like most people, you bought this stuff with every intention of getting in shape, but now all that's building up is dust. Get some exercise boxing up all that equipment after you've sold it on eBay — remember the USPS will pick up for free.

- **Vinyl records:** Have a few boxes of vintage vinyl? If you're not buying a turntable any time soon, put them up for sale! (Think records are dead? You may be surprised.)

- **Autographs:** All types of autographs — from sports figures, celebrities, and world leaders — are popular on eBay. A word of caution, though: A lot of fakes are on the market, so make sure that what you're selling (or buying) is the real thing. If you're planning on selling autographs on eBay, be sure to review the special rules that apply to these items. Here's where to find them:

  http://pages.ebay.com/help/policies/autographs.html

Know When to Sell

Warning . . . warning . . . I'm about to hit you with some of my clichés: *Timing is everything. Sell what you know and know when to sell. Buy low and sell high. Fast quarters are better than slow dollars.*

Okay, granted, clichés may be painful to hear over and over, but they do contain nuggets of good information. (Perhaps they're repeated for a reason?)

Experienced eBay sellers know that when planning a sale, timing is almost everything. Fur coats don't sell well in July, and as a seller of collectibles you don't want to be caught with 200 Nintendo WiiU games during a run on Xbox. (Hold on to them; vintage games do sell well.) *Star Wars* action figures are traditionally good sellers unless a new sci-fi title is all the rage.

Some items — such as good antiques, rugs, baseball cards, and sports cars — are timeless. But timing still counts. Don't put your rare, antique paper cutter up for auction if someone else is selling one at the same time. I guarantee that will cut into your profits.

Timing is hardly an exact science. Rather, timing is a little bit of common sense, a dash of marketing, and a fair amount of information gathering. Do a little research among your friends. What are they interested in? Would they buy your item? Use eBay itself as a research tool. Search Sold listings to see whether anyone's making money on the same type of item. If people are crazed for some fad item and you have a bunch of those, *yesterday* was the time to sell. (In other words, if you want your money out of 'em, get crackin' and get packin'.)

If the eBay market is already flooded with dozens of an item and no one is making money on them, you can afford to wait before you plan your listing.

Know Thy Stuff

At least that's what Socrates would have said if he'd been an eBay seller. Haven't had to do a homework assignment in a while? Time to dust off those time-trusted skills. Before selling your merchandise, do some digging to find out as much as you can about it.

Snapping up profits

Way back in 1980, when Pac-Man ruled, my friend Ric decided to try his hand at photography. Hoping to be the next Ansel Adams — or to at least snap something in focus — he bought a Kowa 66, one of those cameras you hold in front of your belt buckle while you look down into the viewfinder. Soon after he bought the camera, Ric's focus shifted. The camera sat in its box, instructions and all, for over 15 years until he threw a garage sale.

Ric and his wife didn't know much about his Kowa, but they knew that it was worth something. When he got an offer of $80 for it at the garage sale, his wife whispered "eBay!" in his ear, and he turned down the offer.

Ric and his wife posted the camera on eBay with the little information they had about its size and color, and the couple was flooded with questions and information about the camera from knowledgeable bidders. One bidder said that the silver-toned lens made it more valuable. Another gave them the camera's history.

Ric and his wife added each new bit of information to their description and watched as the bids increased with their every addition — until that unused camera went for more than $400 in a flurry of last-minute sniping in 1999. These days, when Ric posts an item for sale, he always asks for additional information and adds it to the listing page.

What difference does a year make? You'll find that the values of all items on eBay trend up and down. In 2000, this camera sold on eBay for over $600; in late 2001, it sold for $455. In the winter of 2003, interest in it was waning; it sold in the $375 to $400 range. In 2009, one sold for $390, in 2011, $440. Believe it or not, in these days of digital cameras, one *just* closed on eBay for $401. Not bad, considering "everyone is saying" film cameras are dead merchandise.

Getting the goods on your goods

Here are some ideas to help you flesh out your knowledge of what you have to sell:

- **Hit the books.** Study historic guides and collector magazines; perhaps even check your local library (yes, they still exist) for books about the item. Even out of print books will give you valuable information.

  Even though collectors still use published price guides when they put a value on an item, so much fast-moving e-commerce is on the Internet that printed price guides often lag behind the markets they cover. Take their prices with a grain of salt.

- **Go surfin'.** Conduct a web search and look for info on the item on other e-commerce sites. If you find a print magazine that has some good information, check to see whether the magazine is available on the web by typing the title of the magazine into your browser's search window. (For detailed information on using search engines to conduct a more thorough online search, check out Chapter 5.)

- ✔ **When the shopping gets tough, go mobile.** If you're out and about searching tag sales or resale shops, use eBay's handy smartphone app and see whether (and for how much) the item is selling on eBay. (Find more on eBay's handy apps in Chapter 18.)

  When you understand the demand for your product (whether it's a collectible or a commodity) and how much you can realistically ask for it, you're on the right track to a successful auction.

- ✔ **Call in the pros.** Need a quick way to find the value of an item you want to sell? Call a dealer or a collector and say you have one to sell. A merchant who smells a good deal will make an offer, and then ask them what it would sell for in their store.

- ✔ **Bing to the rescue.** Run a search of your keywords on Bing.com. You can run a search on Google, but Bing provides more Internet-wide results. When I ran a search on Google, the entire first page consisted of eBay results.

For information on how items are graded and valued by professional collectors, jump to Chapter 5, where I discuss grading your items.

Be certain that you know what you have — not only what it is and what it's for, but also *whether it's genuine.* Make sure that it's the real McCoy. You are responsible for your item's authenticity; counterfeits and knock-offs are not welcome on eBay. In addition, manufacturers' legal beagles are on the hunt for counterfeit and stolen goods circulating on eBay — and they *will* tip off law enforcement.

Spy versus spy: Comparison selling

Back in the old days, successful retailers like Gimbel and Macy spied on each other to figure out ways to get a leg up on the competition. Today, in the bustling world of e-commerce, the spying continues, and dipping into the intrigue of surveilling the competition is as easy as clicking your mouse.

Say that you're the biggest *Dukes of Hazzard* fan ever and you collect *Dukes of Hazzard* stuff, such as DVDs of the show, movie memorabilia, General Lee models, and lunch boxes. Well, good news: That piece of tin that once held a lunchtime PB&J may very well fetch a nice sum. To find out for sure, you can do some research on eBay. To find out the current market price for a *Dukes of Hazzard* lunch box, you can conduct a sold listings search (as described in Chapter 5) and find out exactly how many *Dukes of Hazzard* lunch boxes have been sold in the past few weeks. You can also find out their high selling prices and how many bids the lunch boxes received by the time the auctions were over. And repeating a completed search in a week or two is not a bad idea — you can get at least a month's worth of data to price your item. Figure 9-2 shows the results of a Sold items search sorted by the highest prices first.

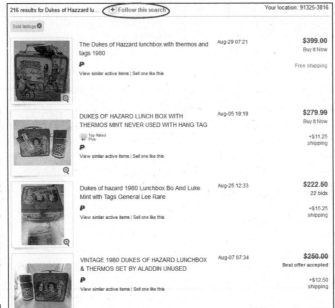

Figure 9-2:
Use the
sold listings
search to
find out
what an item
is currently
selling for.
Excuse me
while I look
for an old
lunch box.

You can easily save your searches for pricing research on eBay. Just click the star next to Save Search link at the top to add a search to your favorite searches. Then it's on your My eBay Lists page, and you can repeat the search with a click of your mouse.

Look at the pictures on item pages for each item that your sold listings search turns up. That way, you can confirm that the items (lunchboxes, for example) are identical to the one you want to sell. And when you do your research, factor in your item's condition. Read the individual item descriptions. If your item is in better condition, expect (and ask for) more money for it; if your item is in worse condition, expect (and ask for) less. Also, note the categories the items are listed under; they may give you a clue about where eBay members are looking for items just like yours.

If you want to be extremely thorough in your comparison selling, go to a search engine to see whether the results of your eBay search mesh with what's going on elsewhere. If you find that no items like yours are for sale anywhere else online, and are pretty sure that people are looking for what you have, you may just find yourself in Fat City.

Don't forget to factor in the history of an item when you assess its value. Getting an idea of what people are watching, listening to, and collecting can help you assess trends and figure out what's hot. For more about using trend-spotting skills to sniff out potential profits, take a look at the appendix.

Know What You Can (and Can't) Sell

The majority of items sold on eBay are aboveboard. But sometimes eBay finds out about listings that are either illegal (in the eyes of the state or federal government) or prohibited by eBay's rules and regulations. In either case, eBay steps in, calls a foul, and makes the item invalid.

eBay doesn't have rules and regulations just for the fun of it. eBay wants to keep you educated so you won't unwittingly bid on, buy — or sell — an item that has been misrepresented. eBay also wants you to know what's okay and what's prohibited so that if you run across an item that looks fishy, you'll help out your fellow eBay members by reporting it. And eBay wants you to know that getting your listing shut down is the least of your worries: You can be suspended if you knowingly list prohibited items. And I won't even talk about criminal prosecution.

You need to know about these three categories:

- ✔ **Prohibited** lists the items that may *not* be sold on eBay under any circumstances.
- ✔ **Restricted** lists the items that may be sold under certain conditions.
- ✔ **Potentially Infringing** lists the types of items that may be in violation of copyrights, trademarks, or other rights.

You may not even offer to *give away for free* a prohibited or an infringing item, nor can you give away a questionable item that eBay disallows; giving it away doesn't relieve you of potential liability.

The items that you absolutely *cannot* sell on eBay can fit into *all three* categories. Those items can be legally ambiguous at best — not to mention potentially risky and all kinds of sticky. To find a detailed description of which items are prohibited on the eBay website, follow these steps:

1. **Click the Policies link, which is on the bottom of all eBay pages.**

   You arrive at the friendly eBay Rules & Policies page.

2. **Scroll to the Prohibited and Restricted items link and click.**

   You are presented with the lists and links that help you decipher whether selling your item falls within eBay's policy boundaries.

   Or, if you're reading this in an e-book or you don't mind typing, you can go directly to `http://pages.ebay.com/help/policies/overview.html`.

Sometimes an item is okay to own but not to sell. Other times the item is prohibited from being *sold and possessed.* To complicate matters even more, some items may be legal in one part of the United States but not in others. Or an item may be illegal in the United States but legal in other countries.

Because eBay's base of operations is in California, United States law is enforced — even if both the buyer and seller are from other countries. Cuban cigars, for example, are legal to buy and sell in Canada, but even if the buyer *and* the seller are from Canada, eBay says *"No permiso"* and shuts down sales of Havanas fast. Figure 9-3 shows an auction that was shut down soon after I found it.

Figure 9-3:
In 1999, I found this auction for a Cuban cigar before eBay found it (and removed it).

Prohibited items

Even though possessing (and selling) many of the items in the following list is legal in the United States and elsewhere, you are absolutely, positively *prohibited* from buying and selling the following on eBay:

- ✔ **Firearms of all types:** This also means firearm accessories — including antique, collectible, sport, or hunting guns; air guns; BB guns; silencers; converters; kits for creating guns; gunpowder; high-capacity ammunition magazines (receptacles designed to feed ten rounds or more into a gun, not the publications about ammo); and armor-piercing bullets. You can't even sell a gun that *doesn't* work.

  You *can* buy and sell single bullets, shells, and even antique bombs and musket balls — as long as they have nothing explosive in them.

- ✔ **Firearms and military weapons:** No way can you sell any type of firearm that is designed to propel a metal (or similar) projectile, regardless of whether it works. (If we're talking paintball, archery, or spud pistols — that's another story.) Military weapons? Items included in that category are bazookas, grenades, and mortars.

- ✓ **Police and other law-enforcement badges and IDs:** Stop in the name of the law if you're thinking about buying or selling any of these items, including actual United States federal badges or reproduction badges. In fact, selling just about any U.S. government badge (even the Forest Service) can get you in hot water.

  You also can't own or sell those agencies' identification cards or credential cases or those really cool jackets they use in raids. Selling a copy or reproduction of any of these items is prohibited, too, because these items are copyrighted (see the section on infringing items in this chapter).

  If you find a badge that's legal to sell and own, you need to provide a letter of authorization from the agency. The same letter of authorization is required for fake badges, such as reproductions or movie props.

- ✓ **Replicas of official government identification documents or licenses:** Birth certificates, drivers' licenses, and passports fall into this category.

- ✓ **Current vehicle license plates or plates that claim to resemble current ones:** Note that expired license plates (at least three years old) are considered collectible — as long as they are no longer valid for use on a vehicle and you mention the plate's age in the listing.

- ✓ **Lockpicking devices:** These items can be sold only to authorized recipients. Federal law prohibits the mailing of such devices.

- ✓ **Human parts and remains:** Hey, we all have two kidneys, but if you get the urge to sell one to pay your bills, eBay is not the place to sell it. You can't sell your sperm, eggs, blood, or anything else you manage to extricate from your body. What's more, you can't even *give* away any of these items as a free bonus with one of your auctions.

- ✓ **Drugs or drug paraphernalia:** Narcotics, steroids, or other controlled substances may not be listed, as well as gamma hydroxybutyrate (GHB). Drug paraphernalia includes a swath of items that are primarily intended or designed for using a controlled substance, including vaporizers, bongs, and water pipes.

- ✓ **Anything that requires a prescription from a doctor, a dentist, or an optometrist to dispense:** Listen, just because it's legal to use doesn't mean that it doesn't require special permission to get. For example, even though penicillin is legal to buy in the United States, only a doctor can prescribe it — which is why, when you get sick, you have to stand in that *loooong* line at the pharmacy sneezing on all the other sick people. And if you're looking for Viagra auctions on eBay, don't even *go* there.

- ✓ **Stocks, bonds, or negotiable securities:** Nope, you can't sell stock in your new pie-baking company or an investment in property you may own. And if you're thinking of offering credit to someone, you can't do that either. (Note that collectible items are permitted.)

✔ **Bulk e-mail lists:** No bulk e-mail or mailing lists that contain personal identifying information. You may not even sell tools or software designed to send unsolicited commercial e-mail or promote social "likes" or "followers."

✔ **Pets and wildlife, including animal parts from endangered species:** If you've had it with Buster, your pet ferret, don't look to eBay for help in finding him a new home. And you can't sell your stuffed spotted owls or rhino-horn love potions, either. If you're in the animal business — _any_ animal business — eBay is not the place for you.

✔ **Child pornography:** Note that this material is strictly prohibited on eBay, but you can sell other forms of erotica. (See the section later in this chapter about questionable items.)

✔ **Forged items:** Autographs from celebrities and sports figures are big business — and a big opportunity for forgers. Selling a forgery is a criminal act. The state of New York is taking the lead on this issue, investigating at least two dozen suspected forgery cases linked with online auctions.

If you're in the market for an autograph, don't even consider bidding on one unless it comes with a _Certificate of Authenticity_ (COA). eBay requires that sellers give buyers the right to a full refund if any doubt about authenticity crops ups. Figure 9-4 shows an item that comes with a COA from an auction on eBay. Find out more about authentication services in Chapter 16.

✔ **Items that infringe on someone else's copyright or trademark:** Take a look at the very next section for details on infringing items.

✔ **Stolen items:** Need I say more? (Seems obvious, but you'd be surprised.) If what you're thinking about selling came to you by way of a five-finger discount or fell off a truck, don't sell it on eBay.

Figure 9-4:
When bidding on an item with a COA, be sure that the seller is reputable (check the feedback).

The item you are bidding on is a 3x5 Card , Autographed by the late James Stewart ....

The card is white and in mint condition... Signed bold and clear , in black felt tip pen ...

This Autograph is 100% Genuine , and I will provide my COA that Guarantees it for life...

Ignorance is no excuse. If you list an item that's in any way prohibited on eBay, eBay will end your auction. If you have any questions, always check eBay's Trust & Safety department at `http://pages.ebay.com/help/policies/items-ov.html`.

Infringing items

In school, if you copied someone's work, you were busted for plagiarism. Even if you've been out of school for a while, you can still get busted for copying someone else's work. Profiting from a copy of someone else's legally owned *intellectual property* is an *infringement* violation. Infringement, also known as *piracy,* is the encroachment on another person's legal ownership rights on an item, a trademark, or a copyright. eBay prohibits the selling of infringing items at its site.

All the legal mumbo jumbo, translated to English, comes down to this: Profiting from someone else's idea, original work, or patented invention without legal permission is very bad and can get you in hot water.

Here's a checklist of no-no items commonly found at the center of infringement violations:

- Music that's been recorded from an original compact disc, cassette tape, or record.

- Movies that have been recorded from an original DVD, laser disc, or commercial VHS tape.

- e-books you purchased for your own use and do not have the rights to resell or distribute.

- Television shows that have been recorded off the air, off cable, or from a satellite service.

  Selling a used *original* CD, tape, commercial VHS movie cassette, DVD, or CD-ROM is perfectly legal. Some television shows have sold episodes on tape; you can sell those originals as well. But if you're tempted to sell a personal copy that you made of an original, you are committing an infringing violation.

- Software and computer games that have been copied from CD-ROMs or disks (and that includes hard drives — anybody's).

- Counterfeit items (also called *knock-offs*), such as clothes and jewelry, that have been produced, copied, or imitated without the permission of the manufacturer. (Bart Simpson knock-off T-shirts abounded in the early '90s.)

Hot property busted

In 1961, a young jockey named John Sellers won his first Kentucky Derby on a horse named Carry Back. He was so emotional about the victory that he was crying as he crossed the finish line. Seventeen years later, someone broke into his California home and stole his priceless trophy. But today, more than two decades after it was stolen, it's back in his possession — thanks to an observant eBay member. The prized trophy was put up for auction in 1999 by a seller who had bought it legitimately. An eBay member who knew the history of the trophy saw that it was for sale and alerted the seller. The seller stopped the auction immediately, contacted the former jockey, and personally returned the trophy to him. Now that's a great finish!

If you pick up a brand-name item dirt cheap from a discount store, you can check to see whether it's counterfeit by taking a look at the label or comparing it on the web with like items. If something isn't quite right, the item may be a knock-off.

Trademark and copyright protection don't just cover software, music, and movies. Clothing, toys, sunglasses, and books are among the items covered by law.

Intellectual property owners actively defend their rights and, along with help from average eBay users, continually tip off eBay to fraudulent and infringing auctions. Rights owners can use eBay's Verified Rights Owner (VeRO) Program, as well as law-enforcement agencies. (See "Intellectual Property Violations," later in this chapter, for info about the VeRO program.)

Restricted items: Know the laws

Because some items are prohibited in one place and not another, eBay lists a few items that you can trade but that are restricted and regulated. As a member of eBay, you're responsible for knowing the restrictions in your area — as well as those on the eBay website.

Certain items are illegal in one geographic area and not another. This list mentions a few of the major questionable items:

✔ **Event tickets:** Laws regarding the resale of event tickets vary from state to state, even city to city. Some laws prohibit reselling the ticket for a price higher than the amount printed on the face of the ticket. Some states limit the amount you can add to the ticket's face value. Be sure to double-check your state website for laws covering ticket sales. A website keeps a pretty up-to-date listing of the laws. You can find it on Seat Geek at

```
http://seatgeek.com/blog/ticket-industry/
ticket-resale-laws#lawsbystate
```

Be certain that you're following the appropriate laws for your area.

✔ **Wine and alcohol:** Selling wine and alcohol on eBay — and anywhere else, for that matter — is tricky business. For starters, you have no business in this business unless you're at least 21 years old. eBay does not permit sales of any alcohol products unless they are sold without their contents for their "collectible" containers. You may sell wine for consumption if you have a license to sell and ship wine and are pre-approved by eBay.

For the latest news and all the clickable links you need to keep your wine-shipping business on the good side of the law, visit www. wineinstitute.org/initiatives/stateshippinglaws or check with the Alcoholic Beverage Control (ABC) agency of your state. The Wine Institute page also gives the latest info on the status of shipping wine in the United States.

✔ **Erotica:** Some forms of erotica are allowed on eBay, some in Adult-only and others in the Health & Beauty➪Health Care➪ Sexual Wellness category. To see what eBay allows and what it prohibits, type `http:// pages.ebay.com/help/policies/adult-only.html` into your browser.

Forbidden items

The folks on eBay didn't just fall off the turnip truck. eBay staffers have seen just about every scam to get around paying fees or following policy guidelines. Chances are good that if you try one of these scams, you'll get caught. Then eBay cancels the listing. Do it once, and shame on you (don't count on getting the listing fee credited back to you). Do it a lot, and you're no longer welcome on eBay.

The following items are definitely forbidden:

✔ **Raffles and prizes:** You need to *sell something* in your auction; you can't offer a chance to win a prize either by chance or a giveaway. You can offer to give away a bonus product with a sold item.

✔ **Advertisements:** An eBay auction is not the place to make a sales pitch (other than attractive copy describing your item, that is) for an item for sale elsewhere. Some eBay bad guys list an auction name and then use the auction to send bidders to some other auction or website. The Real Estate category and eBay Motors are exceptions. You can run an ad there to sell property.

✔ **Bait-and-switch tactics:** These are a variation on the ugly old sales technique of pretending to sell what you're not really selling. Some eBay users who are selling an unfamiliar brand of item try to snag bidders by putting a more familiar brand in the title. For instance, writing *Designer Chanel purse — not really, but a lot like it!* is a fake-out. eBay calls it *keyword spamming.* I call it lousy.

✔ **Choice listings:** You cannot offer your bidder a choice of significantly different items. But you can offer variations of the same item. For example, if you're selling a particular T-shirt, list small, medium, and large sizes.

✔ **Mixing apples with oranges:** This gambit tries to attract more bidders to view an item by putting it in a high-traffic category where it doesn't belong. Forget it. eBay may move it for you if necessary, but keeping that rutabaga recipe book *away* from the list of automotive repair manuals is more considerate.

✔ **Duplicate listings:** You may not list more than one fixed price listing of an identical item at the same time. If you are running an auction, you may have more than one listing for identical items. Auctions for identical items listed by the same seller will be filtered by eBay and only one duplicate listing without bids will appear at a time.

Reporting a Problem Listing

You probably don't think that eBay can monitor millions of items for sale on a daily basis. You're right; it can't. eBay relies on eBay members like you to let it know when you suspect a shady listing is afoot. If you ever smell something fishy, for goodness' sake, report it to eBay. Sometimes eBay takes a few days to cancel a listing, but rest assured that eBay invests time to protect its users from fraudulent listings and violations of policy.

If you see something that just doesn't look right, you should report the listing using an online form by clicking the Report Item link, which is on the right, on the same line as the Description tab on every eBay item page or go directly to this page:

```
http://ocs.ebay.com/ws/eBayISAPI.dll?ReportItemMember
```

Intellectual Property Violations

If you own intellectual property that you think is being infringed upon by an item for sale on the eBay site, you should take advantage of the eBay *Verified Rights Owner* (VeRO) Program. Owners of trademarked or copyrighted items and logos, as well as other forms of intellectual property, can become members of this program for free.

You can find out more about the VeRO Program by going to `http://pages.ebay.com/help/tp/vero-rights-owner.html`. Read the information, and if you qualify, click to download the form, fill it out, and fax it to eBay. Then you're on your way to protecting your intellectual property from being auctioned to the highest bidder. Remember, only *you* can stop the infringement madness. If eBay agrees with you that your intellectual property is being infringed upon, it invalidates the sale and informs the seller by e-mail that the auction "is not authorized." The high bidders in an auction are also notified and warned that there was an issue with the listing.

I am a member of the VeRO Program. Should someone think it's a good idea to digitize and sell counterfeit copies of my books, I file my VeRO notice, and the listing is removed within hours.

eBay understands that sometimes people don't know that they're selling infringing items, but it draws a hard line on repeat offenders. eBay not only shuts down the offenders' listings but can also suspend repeat offenders. Also, eBay cooperates with the proper authorities on behalf of its VeRO Program members.

If eBay deems your listing or transaction to be invalid because the item doesn't meet eBay's policies and guidelines, you can find out why by checking the page at `http://pages.ebay.com/help/sell/questions/listing-ended.html`. If you still feel that you're in the right, find the Contact Us link. Click there to plead your case.

eBay Fees? What eBay Fees? Oops . . .

The "Cliché Police" are going to raid me sooner or later, but here's one I'm poking a few holes in this time around: *You gotta spend it to make it.* This old-time business chestnut means that you need to invest a fair amount of money before you can turn a profit. Although the principle still holds true in the real world (at least most of the time), on eBay you don't have to spend much to start your business. This is one reason why eBay has become one of the most successful e-commerce companies on the Internet and a darling of Wall Street. eBay keeps fees low and volume high.

For the beginning seller (without an eBay Store), eBay charges the following types of fees for listing on the site:

- ✔ **Auction Insertion Fees:** Up to 50 auction listings are free per month. After that, it can range from $0.10 to $2.

- ✔ **Fixed-price listing fees:** For an item selling at $0.99 or more, you pay a flat $0.50.

- ✔ **Real estate listing fees:** These vary because you have the choice of listing your property as an ad rather than an auction. Because eBay real estate auctions are *nonbinding* (due to legalities), you may be better off running an ad. eBay charges different prices for different types of real estate:

  - *Timeshares, manufactured homes, and land*

    Auctions: 1-, 3-, 5-, 7-, or 10-day listing ($35); 30-day listing ($50)

    Ad format: 30-day listing ($150); 90-day listing ($300)

  - *Residential, commercial, and other real estate*

    Auctions: 1-, 3-, 5-, 7-, or 10-day listing ($100); 30-day listing ($150)

    Ad format: 30-day listing ($150), 90-day listing ($300)

- ✔ **Automotive fees:** The first six listings are free per calendar year, with subsequent listings $50; motorcycles are only $20.

- ✔ **Additional reserve-price auction fees:** $2; auctions with reserves over $200 are 1 percent of the reserve with a maximum of $50.

- ✔ **Final Value Fees:** A percentage of the sales price (read further on).

- ✔ **Optional fees:** Vary.

Insertion Fees are negligible

Every item (after your first 50 listings a month) listed on eBay is charged an *Insertion Fee*. If you are listing more than 50 items a month, you might consider opening an eBay Store (as long as you are *selling* the majority of the items you list).

The Insertion (or listing) Fee kicks in after those initial 50 items and is based on whether you are listing fixed-price items or auctions. Later in this chapter, I explain how an auction reserve price affects what you have to pay.

Take a look at Table 9-1 for eBay's Insertion Fee structure.

Table 9-1	Basic Insertion Fees
Number of listings	*Insertion Fee*
First 50 listings per month (whether auction or fixed price)	Free
Additional listings over 50 (per month)	$0.05 for fixed-price Books, DVDs & Movies, Music, and Video Games listings $0.30 for auction and fixed-price listings in all other categories

If you're running a reserve-price auction (explained in detail in Chapter 10), eBay bases its Insertion Fee on the reserve price, not the starting bid. eBay also charges a fee to run a reserve-price auction.

Here's a snapshot of how a reserve price affects your auction Insertion Fee. If you set a starting bid of $0.99 for a gold Rolex watch (say what?) but your reserve price is $5,000 (that's more like it), you're charged a $50 Insertion Fee based on the $5,000 reserve price (reserve fee is 1 percent of the reserve price). (See Table 9-2, later in this chapter, for the reserve auction fees.)

So what does the Insertion Fee buy you on eBay?

- ✔ A really snazzy-looking display page for your item that millions of eBay members can see, admire, and breathlessly respond to. (Well, we can only hope.)

- ✔ The use of eBay services, such as the Trust & Safety program, which protects your selling experience. (Chapter 16 tells you how to use Trust & Safety during and after your sale.)

Final Value Fees

If you follow the movie business, you hear about some big A-list stars who take a relatively small fee for making a film but negotiate a big percentage of the gross profits. This is known as a *back-end deal* — in effect, a commission based on how much the movie brings in. eBay does the same thing, taking a small

Insertion Fee when you list your item and then a commission on the back end when you sell your item. This commission is called the *Final Value Fee* (FVF) and is based on the total amount of the sale (the selling price of the item, shipping, and any other fees a seller may charge, excluding any sales tax).

eBay doesn't charge a Final Value Fee on a listing in the Real Estate/Timeshares category as they do in other categories; instead, they charge a flat *notice fee* of $35 rather than an FVF for Timeshares, Land and Manufactured Homes. There's no fee for Residential, Commercial and Other. But in the Automotive category, you pay a flat transaction services fee of $60 for passenger vehicles if your auction ends with a final bid amount under $2,000. If your item's final bid is over $2,000, you'll pay a $125 fee.

In real life, when you pay sales commissions on a big purchase such as a house, you usually pay a fixed percentage. It is the same on eBay. A listing's Final Value Fee (whether auction or fixed price) is 10 percent. This is taken from the total amount of the sale, including the final price of the item, shipping charges, and any other amounts you may charge the buyer. Sales tax is not included.

Final Value Fees are different (and lower) for eBay Store owners. Chapter 11 will explain that and more.

Here's a sample Final Value Fee calculation for a successful auction:

- ✔ You sell an item for $95 with a shipping cost of $5.
- ✔ Your Final Value Fee on the total amount is 10 percent of $100 ($10.00).

If you try to work out your own Final Value Fees, you may get an extreme headache — and come up with fractional cents. Know that eBay rounds up fees of $0.005 and more and drops fees below $0.005. These roundings are done on a per-transaction basis, and generally even out over time.

Optional fees

You don't have to pay a license fee and destination charge, but setting up your auction can be like buying a car. eBay has a nice array of options to jazz up your listings. I explain how all these bells, whistles, and white sidewalls dress up your auction in Chapter 10.

As a hint of things to come, Table 9-2 lists the eBay listing options and what they'll cost you.

Table 9-2	eBay Optional-Feature Fees	
Option	*Fee (Auction or Fixed Price, 3, 5, 7, 10 Days)*	*Fixed-Price Fee (per 30 Days)*
Value Pack (Gallery Plus, Subtitle, and Listing Designer)	$0.65	$2.00
Boldface title	$2.00	$4.00
Gallery Plus	$0.35	$1.00
List in two categories	Double-listing and upgrade fees	Double-listing and upgrade fees
10-day auction	$0.40	n/a
Listing Designer	$0.10	$0.30
Subtitle	$0.50	$1.50
International site visibility	Auctions on a tiered scale based on starting price from $0.10 to $0.40	All fixed-price listings $0.50
Auction BIN (Buy It Now) fee	Free	

The auction Buy It Now feature is free. See Chapter 10 for more on how to use this valuable selling tool.

Keep current on your profits

When you've finished all the legwork needed to make some money, do some brain work to keep track of your results. The best place to keep watch on your eBay sales is on your My eBay page, a great place to stay organized while you're conducting all your eBay business. (I describe all the functions of the page in Chapter 4.) When it comes to calculating your bottom line, it's best to get used to using a program like QuickBooks.

Before you list, calculate your fees. eBay has a very basic fee calculator at `http://www.fees.ebay.com/feeweb/feecalculator`. If you'd rather be able to calculate every last penny (and discount), there's a couple super, free, more-detailed eBay calculators at `http://salecalc.com/` and `http://www.rememberingrolbe.com/ebay.htm`.

Here's a checklist of what to watch out for after the sale ends:

- ✔ **Keep an eye on how much you're spending to place items up for sale on eBay.** You don't want any nasty surprises, and you don't want to find out that you spent more money to set up your listing than you received selling your item.

- ✔ **If you decide to turn your eBay selling into a business, keep track of your expenses for your taxes.** I explain Uncle Sam's tax position on eBay next. Stay tuned.

- ✔ **Make sure that you get refunds and credits when they're due.**

- ✔ **Double-check your figures to make certain eBay hasn't made mistakes.** If you have any questions about the accounting, let eBay know.

Uncle Sam Wants You — to Pay Your Taxes

What would a chapter about money be without a discussion of taxes? As Ben Franklin knew (and we've all found out since), you can't escape death and taxes. (Hey, it's not a cliché; it's accepted wisdom.) Whether in cyberspace or face-to-face life, never forget that Uncle Sam is always your business partner.

Beginning in 2011, the IRS will receive a 1099-K form reflecting the total transaction amounts for sellers with over 200 transactions or who have sold over $20,000 on eBay. You will have to include this income on your annual income tax filing, so filing your taxes may become a bit more complex.

You will have to file a schedule 1040-C, "Profit or Loss From Business." Here you will have to post your income (and expenses) for your eBay business.

Be sure to keep track of all your eBay business expenses to offset your profits. If you live outside the United States, check the tax laws in that country so you don't end up with a headache down the road.

As with offline transactions, knowledge is power. The more you know about buying and selling on eBay before you actually start doing it, the more savvy the impression you make — and the more satisfying your experience.

For more details on taxes and bookkeeping, check out my book, *eBay Business All-in-One For Dummies.*

Two wild rumors about federal taxes

I've heard some rumors about not having to pay taxes on eBay profits. If you hear any variation on this theme, smile politely and don't believe a word of it. I discuss two of the more popular (and seriously mistaken) tax notions running around the eBay community these days.

The U.S. government uses two laws on the books to go after eBay outlaws. One is the Federal Trade Commission (FTC) Act, which prohibits deceptive or misleading transactions in commerce. The other is the Mail or Telephone Order Merchandise Rule, which requires sellers to ship merchandise in a timely manner or offer to refund a consumer's money. The FTC is in charge of pursuing these violations. If you have a question about federal laws, you can find a lot of information online. For example, I found these three websites that keep fairly current lists of U.S. law and federal codes:

www.law.cornell.edu/uscode

www.ftc.gov

www.fourmilab.ch/ustax/ustax.html

Rumor #1: e-commerce isn't taxed

One story claims that "there will be no taxes on e-commerce sales (sales conducted online) for three years." No one ever seems to know when those three years start or end.

Something new is on the horizon: the *Marketplace Fairness Act of 2013* regarding Internet sales tax. Although this may sound like the states will be charging state sales tax on all e-commerce purchases, the reality isn't that simple. The bill would require all online sellers with total sales over $1,000,000 to pay sales tax in each state in which they have transactions. When you get to a million dollars in sales, many states have joined a streamlined tax act that allows businesses to pay such tax on one form. Someday I hope I have to worry about this issue.

Rumor #2: Profits from garage sales are tax exempt

"eBay is like a garage sale, and you don't have to pay taxes on garage sales." (Uh-huh. And the calories in ice cream don't count if you eat it out of the carton. Who comes up with this stuff anyway?)

This notion is just an urban (or shall I say *suburban*) legend — somebody's wishful thinking that's become folklore. If you make money on a garage sale, you have to declare it as income — just like anything else you make money on. Most people never make any money on garage sales because they usually sell things for far less than they bought them for. However, the opposite is often true of an eBay transaction.

Even if you lose money, you may have to prove it to the government, especially if you're running a small business. You most definitely should have a heart-to-heart talk with your accountant or tax professional as to how to file your taxes. If something might look bad in an audit if you *don't* declare it, consider that a big hint.

To get the reliable word, I checked with the IRS's e-commerce office. The good folks there told me that even if you make as little as a buck on any eBay sale after all your expenses (the cost of the item, eBay fees, shipping charges), you still have to declare it as income on your federal tax return.

If you have questions about eBay sales and your taxes, check with your personal accountant, call the IRS Help Line at 800-829-1040, or visit the IRS website at www.irs.gov. And be friendly. (Just in case.)

State sales tax

If your state has sales tax, a *sales tax number* is required before you *officially* sell something. If sales tax applies, you may have to collect the appropriate sales tax for every sale that falls within the state that your business is in. A 1992 U.S. Supreme Court decision said that states can only require sellers that have a physical presence in the same state as the consumer to collect so-called use taxes, but all that may have changed.

To find the regulations for your state, visit one of the following sites, which supply links to every state's tax board. The tax board should have the answers to your questions.

www.taxsites.com/State-Links.html

www.aicpa.org/ADVOCACY/STATE/STATECONTACTINFO/Pages/
StateContactInformation.aspx

State income taxes

Yes, it's true. Not only is Uncle Sam in Washington, D.C., looking for his slice of your eBay profits, but your state government may also be hankering to join the feast.

If you have a good accountant, give that esteemed individual a call. If you don't have one, find a tax professional in your area. Tax professionals actually do more than just process your income tax returns once a year; they can help you avoid major pitfalls even before April 15.

Here's how to find out what your responsibilities are in your home state:

✔ You may need to collect and pay state sales taxes, but only if you sell to someone in your state.

✔ You can get tax information online at this website:

www.taxadmin.org/fta/rate/tax_stru.html

The site has links to tax information for all 50 states.

✔ You can also call your state tax office and let the good folks there explain the requirements. The state tax office should be listed in the government section of your state government website.

Chapter 10

Make It Sell: Completing the Cyber Paperwork

*I*t's time to make some money. Are you ready? Yes? (Call it an inspired guess.) You're on the threshold of adding your items to the hundreds of thousands that go up for sale on eBay every day (and perhaps also shedding from your home some of the valuable things you haven't touched in years). Some listings are so hot that the sellers quadruple their investments. Other items, unfortunately, are so stone cold that they may not even register a single bid.

In this chapter, I explain the facets of the Sell Your Item pages — the page you fill out to get your auction going (or item selling) on eBay. You get some advice that can increase your odds of making money, and you find out the best way to position your item so buyers can see it and bid on it. I also show you how to modify, relist, or end your listing when you need to.

A caveat here: To keep the marketplace vibrant, eBay's programmers are constantly working to improve the site, and improvement means change. The form you use to list an item for sale (as I describe in this chapter) can change from time to time, but the basic decisions you need to make will not. The selling philosophy laid out in this chapter should help you ride the waves of change on eBay — whatever they may be.

Getting Ready to List Your Item

After you decide what you want to sell, find out as much as you can about it and conduct a little market research. Then you should have a good idea of the item's popularity and market value. To get this info, check out Chapter 9.

Before you list your item, make sure that you have these bases covered:

✔ **The specific category under which you want the item listed:** Ask your friends or family where they'd look for such an item — and remember the categories you saw most frequently when you conducted your market research with the eBay search function. (Further on, I show you how eBay will help you here as well.)

To find out which category will pay off best for your item, run a search and then check sold listings. See how many of this type of item are selling now (and whether people are actually buying those items). Scroll down to the left of the page and click the sold listings box. This tells you which items sold recently on eBay and the price for which they sold. Then sort your results by *Price: Highest First* and look over the sales to see in which categories the most successful items are listed. (For more information on eBay's search, visit Chapter 5.)

✔ **What you want to say in your item description:** Jot down your ideas. Take a good look at your item and make a list of keywords that describe it. *Keywords* are single descriptive words that can include the following (this is hardly a complete list):

- Brand name
- Complete model name (research helps here)
- Size of the item (citing measurements if appropriate)
- Age or date of manufacture
- Condition
- Rarity
- Color
- Size
- Material

I know all about writer's block. If you're daunted by the listing page, struggle through it anyway. This way you've finished the hard work before you even begin.

✔ **Whether you want to attach a picture (or pictures) to your description via a Uniform Resource Locator (URL):** Pictures help sell items and it's important to have at least one. You can upload photos from your computer, or store them on a website and use the URL to bring them into your item's description for extra punch. (This information won't be on the test, but if you want to know more about using pictures in your listings, see Chapter 14.)

✔ **The price at which you think you can sell the item:** Be as realistic as you can. (That's where your market research comes in.)

Examining the Sell Your Item Page

Begin by clicking the word *Sell* in the navigation bar at the top of the eBay page. Once clicked, you will need to sign in and then the Sell Your Item form appears. Filling out this virtual paperwork requires a few minutes of clicking, typing, and answering all kinds of questions. The good news is that when you're finished, your listing is up and running and (I hope) starting to earn you money.

Before you begin, you have to be a registered eBay user. If you still need to register, go to Chapter 2 and fill out the preliminary online paperwork. If you've registered but haven't provided eBay with your financial information (credit card or checking account), you'll be asked for this information to set up your seller account before you proceed. Fill in the data on the secure form. Then you're ready to roll.

Just like the dizzying menu in a Chinese restaurant, you have lots of choices for selling an item on eBay — three, in fact. Three ways may not seem to be very dizzying, unless you're trying to decide psychically which format is the best for you. Here's what you need to know about each type:

✔ **Auction:** This is the tried-and-true traditional sale format on eBay. This is what the newbies look for, and you can combine this with a Buy It Now for those who want the item immediately. Often, if you're selling a collectible item, letting it go to auction may net you a much higher profit — just remember to do your research *before* listing.

✔ **Fixed-price:** As with shopping at the corner store or any e-commerce shopping site, a fixed-price sale is easy for the buyer to comprehend and complete. The only problem is that some potential buyers may lean toward an auction because of the perception that they *may* get a better deal. This includes items you sell in your eBay Store.

A variation on a fixed-price listing is to add the Make an Offer option. This enables buyers to assume that they can get a great deal — but you have the opportunity to accept the offer or make a counteroffer. Cultural leanings toward bargaining may mean some buyers prefer this method. You may not. It can be fun and is just another way to spur sales for a slow-selling product.

✔ **Classified ad:** If you don't want to put your property or other valuable item up for auction and you'd like to correspond with the prospective buyer, this is the option for you. Although this option originated with eBay real estate sales, the ad format is available in many categories. The cost of your ad is $9.95 for a 30-day listing. If you're interested in finding out which types of items you can sell with a classified ad, check out this URL:

`http://pages.ebay.com/help/sell/adformatfees.html`

Say, for example, that you want to list a good old-fashioned eBay auction. You want to sell your item for a fixed price but are willing to take a chance on an auction.

To find eBay's Sell Your Item form from the eBay home page, you can use either of these methods:

✔ Click the Sell link on the navigation links at the top of the page. eBay allows you to select your category and download the Sell Your Item page in seconds.

✔ Start your listing from your My eBay page. Just click the Sell Similar link (on the Sell page) next to one of your existing items. Using the form that appears, you can change the item data.

When listing your item, here's some of the info you're asked to fill out (each of these items is discussed in detail later in this chapter):

✔ **Category:** The category where you've decided to list your item (required).

✔ **Title:** The name of your item (required).

✔ **Description:** What you want to tell eBay buyers about your item (required).

✔ **eBay Picture Services or image web address:** Upload your images that you want to appear at the top of your listing. You are allowed 12 for free (the first picture becomes your Gallery photo which appears in searches). If you are selling a very rare item, consider adding more to your description (there's no extra charge for this). (Chapter 14 has more information on using images in your listings.)

✔ **Item location:** The region, city, and country from which the item will be shipped (required).

✔ **Quantity:** The number of items you're putting up for sale in this listing. In an auction it is always one (required).

✔ **Starting price:** The starting price (sometimes called a *minimum bid*) you set (required in an auction).

✔ **Selling price:** If this is a fixed-price listing, you have to post the selling price of the item.

✔ **Duration:** The number of days you want the auction or fixed-price listing to run (required).

✔ **Reserve price:** The hidden target price you set for an auction. This is the price that must be met before this item can be sold (optional).

eBay charges you a fee for the reserve-price feature. See Chapter 9 for the pricing of eBay's optional features.

✔ **Private auction:** You can keep the identity of all bidders secret with this option (optional). This type of auction is used only in special circumstances.

✔ **Buy It Now:** You can sell your item directly to the first buyer who meets this price (optional).

✔ **List item in two categories:** If you want to double your exposure, you can list your item in two categories. Note that double exposure equals double listing fees (optional).

✔ **Free counter:** If you want to avail yourself of a free counter that keeps track of how many prospective buyers view your item, indicate so here (optional).

✔ **Ship-to locations:** Here's where you can indicate where you're willing to ship an item. If you don't want the hassle of shipping out of the United States, check that option only. You can individually select different countries as well (optional).

You may want to consider whether you *really* want to be in the international shipping business. Buyers pick up the tab, but you have to deal with customs forms and post-office paperwork. (You can make that easier by printing your customs forms along with your postage from your computer — see Chapter 12). Keep in mind that if you don't ship internationally, you're blocking a bunch of possible high bidders. Depending on what you're selling, shipping internationally may or may not be worth the investment in extra time.

✔ **Shipping and handling charges:** eBay requires you to show your shipping charge in the listing. Buyers are more likely to bid or buy right then and there if they feel your shipping costs are reasonable or free. Consider that when you list a flat shipping charge (or even free shipping) on your listing, eBay will take that into account when deciding how your item shows up in search results. For larger items, see information on eBay's handy shipping calculator, later in this chapter, in the section "Setting shipping terms."

✔ **Payment instructions:** Here's the place you put any after-sale information. You are required to accept PayPal or at least one electronic payment or Internet merchant credit card option for your items. (These are the safest options anyway.) If you want to offer the option to pay with a different electronic payment service, mention that as well. This information appears at the top of your listing when the sale is completed, under the Shipping and Payment tabs of the listing while it's active, and in the End of Listing e-mail (optional).

✔ **PayPal and immediate payment:** Fill in this area if you want to require the high bidder to pay through PayPal immediately when using Buy It Now. Add the Immediate Payment option if you want the winner to pay with a click of the mouse (optional).

✔ **Return policy:** You are required to state whether you are willing to accept returns. You can give the customer as few as three days to return the item (that cuts down on spurious returns). It's okay if you don't accept returns, but you must post that information in your listing.

Filling In the Required Blanks

Yes, the Sell Your Item form looks daunting, but filling out its many sections doesn't take as long as you may think. Some of the questions you're asked aren't things you even have to think about; just click an answer and off you go. Other questions ask you to type information. Don't sweat a thing; all the answers you need are right here. In this section I describe all the required info; later in this chapter, I talk about optional stuff. After you click your category, you land on the official Sell Your item page.

eBay has two different types of listing pages. One is "advanced" and the other is "basic." If you do not see all the options mentioned in the chapter, eBay may make some unintended decisions about how you wish to list your item for sale. To be able to fully customize your listing, click the Switch to Advanced Tool link in the upper-right corner of the page to get the full-featured Sell Your Item form.

Selecting a category

Many eBay sellers will tell you that selecting the exact category isn't crucial to achieving the highest price for your item — and they're right. The bulk of buyers (who know what they're looking for) just input search keywords into eBay's search box and look for their items. Others may select a category and peruse the items for sale to see whether a particular one strikes their fancy (just like going to the mall but without the parking hassles).

On the first page of the Sell Your Item form, you select the main category for your item. Type the UPC or the ISBN number from the code of a new product. If there is no visible barcode, type at least three keywords that best describe your item in the box provided and click Search. Figure 10-1 shows you how the results come up after you type your words, making it easy to select a main category.

Figure 10-1:
Let eBay
do some of
the work
in finding
the proper
category for
your item.

Here's where your creativity can come into play. Who says that a box of Blue Dog (the famous doggie icon painted by Cajun artist George Rodrigue) note cards belongs in *Everything Else* (where most greeting cards are listed)? If you look around, you may find a better category, such as *Art*. The Find Categories tool appears the second you open the Sell Your Item page. Just click the associated link to browse for categories. Check to see whether anyone else is selling the item (and in which category) — or just let this tool help you pick a good category.

You can also browse the categories by clicking (surprise!) the Browse Categories tab on this page. This will help you select your main category, and the thousands of subcategories. eBay offers you this wealth of choices in a handy point-and-click way. If you're unfamiliar with the types of items you can actually *find* in those categories, you may want to pore over Chapter 3 before you choose a category to describe *your* item. Figure 10-2 shows you how to narrow the subcategory listings manually on the Sell Your Item page.

Figure 10-2:
Narrowing
your subcat-
egories.

To select a category, here's the drill:

1. **Click one of the main categories.**

   In the next box, you see a list of subcategories.

2. **Select the most appropriate subcategory.**

3. **Continue selecting subcategories until you have narrowed your item listing as much as possible.**

   You know you've come to the last subcategory when you don't see any more right-pointing arrows in the Categories.

Most bidders scan for specific items in subcategories. For example, if you're selling a Bakelite fruit pin, don't just list it under Jewelry; keep narrowing your choices. In this case, you can put it in a costume-jewelry category that is especially for Bakelite. (I guarantee that the real Bakelite jewelry collectors out there know where to look to find the jewelry they love.) To narrow the category of your item, just keep clicking until you hit the end of the line.

Some subcategories aren't for everyone

If you've chosen to list an item, bid on an item, or even just browse in the Everything Else: Adult Only category, you need to follow separate, specific guidelines because that category contains graphic nudity or sexual content that may offend some community members. You must

✔ Be at least 18 years of age (but you already know that all eBay customers must be 18 or older in the first place).

✔ Have a valid credit card.

✔ Complete a waiver stating that you're voluntarily choosing to access adults-only materials. For more on how to do this (and a handy primer on privacy issues), see Chapter 15.

If you have adult or erotic items that you'd like to sell in a private auction, check out the later section, "I want to be alone: The private auction."

Creating the perfect item title

After you figure out what category you want to list in, eBay wants to get down to the nitty-gritty — what the heck to call that thing you're trying to sell.

Think of your item title as a great newspaper headline. The most valuable real estate on eBay is the 80-character title of your item. *The majority of buyers do title searches, and that's where your item must come up to be sold!* Give the most essential information right away in the form of keywords to grab the eye of the reader who's just browsing. Be clear and informative enough to get noticed by eBay's search engine. Figure 10-3 shows examples of good titles. Note how one of these titles contains a subtitle.

Figure 10-3:
These keyword-filled titles are effective because they're clear and concise.

> NEW Tito's Handmade Vodka Metal Tin Sign Sealed in Plastic 12' x 8" Austin Texas
>
> SHARK TANK Mission Belt Co VADER Adjustable Ratchet Dress Leather Black Belt
>
> New Balance Minimus 1010 Men's EXTRA WIDE 2E (EE) Barefoot Trail Running Shoes
>
> TRADER JOES Natural Lavender Oil Sea Salt Scrub LARGE 20 oz Exfoliating Joe's
>
> Limited 1998 STAR TREK the EXPERIENCE Las Vegas Hilton Hotel Room Card Key
>
> PRO CLOUD DOME Digital Phototography Light Diffuser Kit & 7" EXTENSION Photo Box

Here are some ideas to help you write your item title:

- ✔ Use the most common name for the item.
- ✔ If the item is rare, vintage, or hard to find, mention that.
- ✔ State the item's condition and whether it's new or old.
- ✔ Include the item's special qualities, such as its style, model, or edition.
- ✔ Avoid fancy punctuation or unusual characters, such as $, multiple hyphens, and L@@K, because they just clutter up the title — and buyers don't search for them.

When you get into advanced selling mode, you should take a look at one of my other books, coauthored by Patti Louise Ruby, *eBay Listings That Sell For Dummies*. It covers eBay photography and HTML in depth.

Ordinarily, I don't throw out French phrases just for the fun of it. But where making a profit is an issue, I definitely have to agree with the French that choosing or not choosing *le mot juste* can mean the difference between having potential bidders merely see your auction and having an all-out bidding war on your hands. Read on for tips about picking *the best words* to let your listing shine.

Look for a phrase that pays

Here's a crash course in eBay lingo that can help bring you up to speed on attracting buyers to your item. The following words are used frequently in eBay listings, and they can do wonders to jump-start your title:

- ✔ Mint
- ✔ One of a kind (or OOAK — see the abbreviation list in Table 10-1)
- ✔ Vintage
- ✔ Collectible
- ✔ Rare
- ✔ Unique
- ✔ Primitive
- ✔ Well-loved

There's a whole science (called *grading*) to figuring out the value of a collectible. You're ahead of the game if you have a pretty good idea of what most eBay members mean. Do your homework before you assign a grade to your item. If you need more information on what these grades actually mean, Chapter 5 provides a translation.

eBay lingo at a glance

Common grading terms and the phrases in the preceding section aren't the only marketing standards you have at your eBay disposal. As eBay has grown, so has the lingo that members use as shortcuts to describe their merchandise.

Table 10-1 gives you a handy list of common abbreviations and phrases used to describe items. (***Hint:*** *Mint* means "may as well be brand new," not "cool chocolate treat attached.")

Table 10- 1	A Quick List of eBay Abbreviations	
eBay Code	**What It Abbreviates**	**What It Means**
MIB	Mint in Box	The item is in the original box, in great shape, and just the way you'd expect to find it in a store.
MOC	Mint on Card	The item is mounted on its original display card, attached with the original fastenings, in store-new condition.
NRFB	Never Removed from Box	Just what it says, as in "bought but never opened."
COA	Certificate of Authenticity	Documentation that vouches for the genuineness of an item, such as an autograph or painting.
OEM	Original Equipment Manufacture	You're selling the item and all the equipment that originally came with it, but you don't have the original box, owner's manual, or instructions.
OOAK	One of a Kind	You are selling the only one in existence!
NR	No Reserve Price	A reserve price is the price you can set when you begin your auction. If bids don't meet the reserve, you don't have to sell. Many buyers don't like reserve prices because they don't think that they can get a bargain. (For tips on how to allay these fears and get those bids in reserve-price auctions, see "Writing your description," later in this chapter.) If you're not listing a reserve for your item, let bidders know.
HTF, OOP	Hard to Find, Out of Print	Out of print, only a few ever made, or people grabbed up all there were. (HTF doesn't mean you spent a week looking for it in the attic.)

Often, you can rely on eBay slang to get your point across, but make sure that you mean it and that you're using it accurately. Don't label something MIB (Mint in Box) when it looks like it's been Mashed in Box by a meat grinder. You can find more useful online abbreviations on my website, www.coolebaytools.com/tools/online-acronyms-and-ebay-abbreviations.

Don't let your title ruin your salability

Imagine going to a supermarket and asking someone to show you where the stringy stuff that you boil is rather than asking where the spaghetti is. You might end up with mung bean sprouts — delicious to some but hardly what you had in mind. That's why you should check and recheck your spelling. Savvy buyers use eBay search to find merchandise; if the name of your item is spelled wrong, the search engine may (or may not) be able to find it. Poor spelling and incomprehensible grammar also reflect badly on you. If you're in competition with another seller, the buyer is likelier to trust the seller *hoo nose gud speling*.

If you've finished writing your item title and you have spaces left over, ***please*** fight the urge to dress it up with lots of asterisks and exclamation points!!!!!!!!!!! (See how annoying that is?) No matter how gung-ho you are about your item, the eBay search engine may overlook your item if the title is encrusted with meaningless **** and !!!! symbols. If bidders do see your title, they may become annoyed by the virtual shrillness and ignore it anyway!!!!!!!! (It's even more annoying the second time around.)

Another distracting habit is overdoing capital letters. To buyers, seeing everything in caps is LIKE SEEING A CRAZED SALESMAN SCREAMING AT THEM TO BUY NOW! Using all caps is considered *shouting,* which is rude and tough on the eyes. Use capitalization SPARINGLY, and only to finesse a particular point to attract the buyer's eye.

Giving the title punch with a subtitle

A handy feature on eBay are subtitles. eBay allows you to buy an additional 55 characters, which will appear under your item title on a search results page. The fee for this extra promotion is $0.50 for 7 days and $1.50 for a 30-day listing, and in many circumstances, it's definitely worth your while. Any text that you input will really make your item stand out when many sellers have the same item up for sale. But (you knew there would be a *but* didn't you?) these additional 55 characters won't come up as part of a title search. In other words, if the subtitle includes essential information ("NR MIMB," for example) that isn't in the main title, people searching for the terms *NR MIMB* won't find your listing. So if you have all those words in your description, the words will be found either way with a title and description search. If you choose this option, choose attention-getting info that isn't absolutely needed for the title itself.

Writing your description

After you hook potential bidders with your title, reel 'em in with a fabulous description. Don't think Hemingway here; think infomercial (the classier and more fact-filled the better). Figure 10-4 shows a concise description with a sales pitch. You can write a description that sells as well — all you have to do is click in the box and start typing.

Figure 10-4:
A good description can mean the difference between success and failure.

Brand New - PUMA Men's Tarun Leather Cell Running Shoes - Model 181035-26 - Black With Lime and Silver Accents - Medium Width - Leather Upper. The original shoebox is not included.

With a perforated leather upper, tons of cushioning, and a grippy rubber outsole, the Tarun doesn't mess around. But its versatility is what really sets it apart: designed to support you during a workout, these kicks also look unmistakably awesome with jeans.

Features:

- Leather upper with perforated details for breathability
- Lace closure for a snug fit
- Cushioned construction with a cell cushioning unit in the heel for added comfort and shock absorption
- Midfoot TPU shank for stability
- Grippy rubber outsole
- PUMA Formstrip at medial and lateral sides
- PUMA Logo at tongue
- Trio of PUMA Cat Logos and CELL callout at heel
- PVC Free

Here's a list of suggestions for writing an item description:

✔ **Accentuate the positive.** Give the buyer a reason to buy your item and be enthusiastic when you list all the reasons everyone should bid on it. Unlike the title, here you can use as much space as you want. Even if you use a photo, be precise in your description — its size, color, kind of fabric, design, and so on. Refer to "Creating the perfect item title," earlier in this chapter, as well as Table 10-1, for ideas on what to emphasize and how to word your description.

✔ **Include the negative.** Don't hide the truth of your item's condition. Trying to conceal flaws costs you in the long run; you get tagged with bad feedback. If the item has a scratch, a nick, a dent, a crack, a ding, a tear, a rip, missing pieces, replacement parts, faded color, dirty smudges, or a bad smell (especially if cleaning might damage the item), mention it in the description. If your item has been overhauled, rebuilt, repainted, or hot-rodded, say so. You don't want the buyer to send back your merchandise because you weren't truthful about imperfections or modifications and report you to eBay because it arrived "not as described."

✔ **Be precise about all the logistical details of the post-sale transaction.** If you are going to charge for shipping, figure out the cost and add that to your description. You may not charge extra for shipping insurance.

✔ **While you're at it, promote yourself too.** As you accumulate positive feedback, tell potential bidders about your terrific track record. You can even take it a step further by inviting prospective bidders to your eBay user page. Chapter 17 gives you some tips on how to make your auction seen by a wider audience.

✔ **Wish your potential bidders well.** Communication is the key to a good transaction, and you can set the tone for your listing and post-sale exchanges by including some simple phrases that show your friendly side. Always end your description by wishing bidders good luck, inviting potential bidders to ask questions, and offering the option of providing additional photos of the item if you have them are always a nice touch.

When you type your description, you have the option of jazzing things up with a bit of HTML coding, or you can use eBay's HTML text editor, as shown in Figure 10-5. If you know how to use a word processor, you'll have no trouble touching up your text with this tool. Table 10-2 shows you a few additional codes if you'd like to manually insert the code in the HTML view.

Figure 10-5: The HTML text editor shows you the description area with HTML-coded text and additional free photo inserted.

Table 10-2	A Short List of HTML Codes	
HTML Code	**How to Use It**	**What It Does**
`<b></b>`	`<b>cool collect-ible</b>`	**cool collectible** (bold type)
`<i></i>`	`<i>cool collect-ible</i>`	*cool collectible* (italic type)
`<b><i></i></b>`	`<b><i>cool collectible</b></i>`	***cool collectible*** (bold and italic type)
`<font color=red></font>`	`<font color=red>cool collectible</font>`	Selected text appears in red. (This book is in black and white so you can't see it.)
`<font size=+1></font>`	`<font size=+3>cool</font> collectible`	**cool** collectible (font size normal +1 through 4, increases size x times)
` `	`cool collectible`	cool collectible (inserts line break)
`<p>`	`cool<p>collectible`	cool collectible (inserts paragraph space)
`<hr>`	`cool collectible<hr>cheap`	cool collectible _____ cheap (inserts horizontal rule)
`<h1><h1>`	`<h1>cool collect-ible</h1>`	**cool collectible** (converts text to headline size)

You can go back and forth from the HTML text editor to regular input and add additional codes here and there by clicking from the Standard form to the HTML entry form tabs. I often prepare my listings ahead of time and save them in my eBay folder as plain HTML files — that way they're always retrievable for use (I just copy and paste) — no matter what program or form I'm using to list. See Chapter 20 for more on software to help you with your auctions.

To insert additional photos in your description, use the following code. (Just insert the URL of your hosted picture, along with the photo file name). My example in Figure 10-5 uses the following code:

```
<img scr="http://www.collierad.com/catbed.jpg">
```

Occasionally, sellers offer an item as a *presale,* or an item that the seller doesn't yet have in stock but expects to. If you're offering this kind of item, make sure that you spell out all the details in the description. eBay policy states that you must ship a presell item within 30 days of the auction's end, so be sure that you will have the item within that time span. Don't forget to include the actual shipping date. I have found that putting an item up for sale without having it in hand is a practice fraught with risk. The item you're expecting may not arrive in time or may arrive damaged. I've heard of one too many sellers who have had to go out and purchase an item at retail for a buyer to preserve their feedback when caught in this situation.

Listing the number of items for sale

Unless you're planning on holding a Multiple Item listing, the number of items is always 1, which means that you're holding a traditional auction or listing a single item up for sale. If you need to change the quantity number from 1, just type the number in the box.

A matching set of cuff links is considered one item, as is the complete 37-volume set of *The Smith Family Ancestry and Genealogical History since 1270.* If you have more than one of the same item (two sets of cuff links), I suggest that you sell them one at a time. You are much more likely to get higher final bids for your items when you sell them individually. Never try to sell items that belong in a set as separate items.

Sellers can't have more than one identical fixed-price listing up at a time. You may have duplicate auctions, but only one of the duplicate auctions without bids will appear on eBay at a time.

Setting a starting price — how low can you go?

What do a baseball autographed by JFK, a used walkie-talkie, and a Jaguar sports car all have in common? They all started with a $0.99 starting price. eBay requires you to set a *starting price,* also called a minimum bid — the lowest bid allowed in an auction. You may be surprised to see stuff worth tens of thousands of dollars starting at just a buck. These sellers haven't lost their minds. Neither are they worried that someone could be tooling down the highway in a $100,000 sports car they bought for the price of a burger.

Setting an incredibly low minimum (just type it in the box *without* the dollar sign but *with* the decimal point) is a subtle strategy that gives you more bang for your buck. You can use a low starting price to attract more bidders who will, in turn, drive up the price to the item's real value — especially if, after doing your research, you know that the item is a hot seller.

If you're worried about the outcome of the final bid, you can protect your item by using a *reserve price* (the price the bidding needs to reach before the item can be sold). Then you won't have to sell your item for a bargain-basement price; your reserve price protects your investment. The best advice is to set a reserve price that is the lowest amount you'll take for your item and *then* set a minimum bid that is ridiculously low. Use a reserve only when absolutely necessary because some bidders pass up reserve auctions. (For more info about setting a reserve price, see the section "Your secret safety net — reserve price," later in this chapter.)

The more bids you get, the more people who will want to bid on your item because they perceive the item as desirable. A hot item with lots of bids draws even more bidders the way a magnet attracts paper clips.

Before you set any starting price, do your homework and make some savvy marketing decisions. If your auction isn't going as you hoped, you *could* end up selling Grandma Ethel's Ming vase for a dollar. Think about your strategy. See "Midcourse Corrections: Fixing Current Listings," later in this chapter on how you can make changes in your listing if you've made some egregious error.

When entering a starting price, type only the numbers and a decimal point. Don't use dollar signs ($) or cents signs (¢).

Buy It Now for auctions

eBay's Buy It Now (*BIN* in eBay-speak) is available for auctions. This feature allows buyers who want to purchase an item *now* to do so. Have you ever wanted an item really badly and didn't want to wait until the end of an auction? If the seller offers Buy It Now, you can purchase that item immediately. If you're the seller, you can entice your bidders to pay just a tad more to have the satisfaction of walking away with the item free and clear. Just specify the amount the item can sell for in the Buy It Now price area — the amount can be whatever you want. If you choose to take advantage of selling a hot item during the holiday rush, for example, you can make the BIN price as high as you think it can go. If you just want the item to move, make your BIN price the average price you see the item go for on eBay.

When your item receives a bid, the BIN option disappears, and the item goes through the normal auction process. If you have a reserve price on your item, the BIN feature doesn't disappear until a bidder meets your reserve price through the normal bidding process. To list an item with Buy It Now, the Buy It Now price needs to be at least 30 percent higher than the auction's opening bid, and you need to list the item for at least $0.99.

Setting your auction time

How long do you want to run your auction? eBay gives you a choice — 1, 3, 5, 7, or 10 days. Just click the number you want in the box. If you choose a 10-day auction, you add $0.40 to your listing fee.

My auction-length strategy depends on the time of year and the item I'm selling, and I generally have great success. If you have an item that you think will sell pretty well, run a 7-day auction (be sure that it will cover a full weekend) so bidders have time to check it out before they decide to bid. However, if you know that you have a red-hot item that's going to fly off the shelves — such as a rare toy or a hard-to-get video game — choose a 3-day auction. Eager bidders tend to bid higher and more often to beat out their competition if the item is hot and going fast. Three days is long enough to give trendy items exposure and ring up bids.

No matter how many days you choose to run your auction, it ends at exactly the same time of day as it starts. A 7-day auction that starts on Thursday at 9:03:02 a.m. ends the following Thursday at 9:03:02 a.m.

Although I know the gang at eBay is a pretty laid-back group, they do run on military time. That means they use a 24-hour clock set to Pacific time. So 3:30 in the afternoon is 15:30, and one minute after midnight is 00:01. Questions about time conversions? Look at the table on my website in the Tools area, which has a printable conversion chart of eBay times (`www.coolebaytools.com/tools/usa-time-zones/tools.html`). There's also one with international time conversions.

With auctions running 24 hours a day, 7 days a week, you should know when the most bidders are around to take a gander at your wares. Here are some times to think about:

✔ **Saturday/Sunday:** Always run an auction over a weekend. People log on and off eBay all day.

Don't start or end your auction on a Saturday or Sunday — *unless* your completed auction research indicates that you should. Certain types of bidders love sitting at their computers waiting for auctions to end on the weekends, but many bidders are busy having lives, and their schedules are unpredictable. Although a few eager bidders may log on and place a maximum bid on your auction, you can bet that they won't be sitting at a computer making a last-minute flurry of competitive bids if they have something better to do on a Saturday or Sunday.

✔ **Holiday weekends:** If a holiday weekend is coming up around the time you're setting up your auction, run your auction through the weekend and end it a day after the "holiday" Monday. This gives prospective bidders a chance to catch up with the items they perused over the weekend and to plan their bidding strategies.

Don't end an auction on the last day of a three-day holiday; try the day after. People in the mood to shop are generally at department stores collecting bargains. If eBay members aren't shopping, they're out enjoying an extra day off.

✔ **Time of day:** The best times of day to start and end your auction are during eBay's peak hours of operation, which are 5:00 p.m. to 9:00 p.m. Pacific time, right after work on the West Coast. Perform your completed auction research, however, to be sure that this strategy applies to your item. Your timing depends on the item you're listing and whether 5:00 p.m. to 9:00 p.m. Pacific time is the middle of the night where you live.

Unless you're an insomniac or a vampire and want to sell to werewolves, don't let your auctions close in the middle of the night. Not enough bidders are around to cause any last-minute bidding that would bump up the price.

Your secret safety net — reserve price

Here's a little secret: The reason sellers list big-ticket items like Ferraris, grand pianos, and high-tech computer equipment with a starting bid of $1 is because they're protected from losing money with a *reserve price*. The reserve price is the lowest price that must be met before the item can be sold. It's not required by eBay but can protect you. eBay charges an additional fee for this feature that varies, depending on how high your reserve is.

For example, say you list a hardback book — a first edition of John Steinbeck's *The Grapes of Wrath*. You set the starting price at $1, and you set a reserve price at $80. That means that people can start bidding at $1, and if at the end of the auction the bidding hasn't reached the $80 reserve, you don't have to sell the book.

As with everything in life, using a reserve price for your auctions has an upside and a downside. Many choosy bidders and bargain hunters blast past reserve-price auctions because they see a reserve price as a sign that proclaims "No bargains here!" Many bidders figure that they can get a better deal on the same item with an auction that proudly declares *NR* (for *no reserve*) in its description. As an enticement to those bidders, you see lots of NR mentions in auction titles.

If you need to set a reserve on your item, help the bidder out. Many bidders shy away from an auction that has a reserve, but if they're really interested, they will read the item description. To dispel their fears that the item is way too expensive or out of their price range, add a line in your description that states the amount of your reserve price. "I have put a reserve of $75 on this item to protect my investment; the highest bid over $75 will win the item." A phrase such as this takes away the vagueness of the reserve auction and allows you to place a reserve with a low opening bid. (You want to reel ' em in, remember?)

On lower-priced items, I suggest that you set a higher starting price and set no reserve. Otherwise, if you're not sure about the market, set a low minimum bid but set a high reserve to protect yourself.

If bids don't reach a set reserve price, some sellers e-mail the highest bidder and offer the item at what the seller thinks is a fair price. Sending a Second Chance offer through the eBay system makes much more sense. Two caveats if you try to circumvent eBay fees and contact the bidders:

- *Side deals that circumvent eBay fees are strictly prohibited.* eBay can suspend the seller *and* the buyer if a side deal is reported to Trust & Safety.

- eBay won't protect buyers or sellers if a side deal goes bad.

I want to be alone: The private auction

In a private auction, bidders' User IDs are kept under wraps. Sellers typically use this option to protect the identities of bidders during auctions for high-priced big-ticket items (say, that restored World War II fighter). Wealthy eBay users may not want the world to know that they have the resources to buy expensive items. Private auctions are also held for items from the Adult/Erotica category. (Gee, what a shock.)

A private auction might have helped John Stamos

The famous sign that was pictured in almost every Disneyland promotion (for the first 40 or so years of Disneyland's existence) was put up for sale on eBay in 2000. Legend has it that the sign was purchased by actor John Stamos for a high bid of $30,700. Unfortunately for John, the Disney auction did not use the private auction feature (and in those days eBay did not mask bidder IDs). After news of the winner's name hit the tabloids, the entire world knew John's eBay User ID! He had to change his ID in a hurry to end the throngs of lovey-dovey e-mail headed to his computer!

Put me in the Gallery

The Gallery is a legacy term that refers to the first picture you post to accompany your listing. It causes a postage-stamp-size version of your image to appear next to your listing in the category or search. Many buyers enjoy browsing the Gallery view, and it's open to all categories. (I explain how to post your pictures in Chapter 14.)

Filling out the item location

eBay wants to list the area and country where you live. The idea behind telling the bidder where you live is to give him or her a heads-up on what kind of shipping charges to expect. They'll fill in your ZIP code from your registration. If you live in a big area — say, suburban Los Angeles (who, me?), which sprawls for miles — you may want to think about narrowing your region a little. You may find a bidder who lives close to you, and that convenient fact could swing your auction. If you do a face-to-face transaction, doing it in a public place is a good idea. (I picked up an eBay purchase at Starbucks recently.)

Listing Designer

How many times have you seen an item on eBay laid out on the page all pretty with a decorative border around the description? If that sort of thing appeals to you, eBay's Listing Designer will supply you with accents and borders for almost any type of item for $0.10. Selecting your design is as easy as clicking the menu (see Figure 10-6). You can designate where you'd like to place your image on the page relative to the description (left, right, top, or bottom).

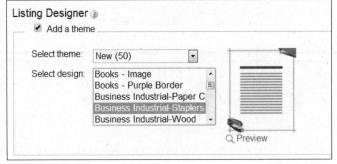

Figure 10-6: Selecting a graphic in Listing Designer is as simple as clicking your mouse.

Will the pretty borders increase the amount of bids your auction will get? It's doubtful. A clean item description with a few good clear pictures of your item is really all you need.

There's a special combination deal called the Value Pack. For $0.65, you can place a subtitle on your listing, add a Gallery Plus picture (a larger version of your picture in search results), and doll things up with Listing Designer. All those features would normally cost $0.95, so you can net some savings if you run several listings a week.

Listing the payment methods you'll accept

Yeah, sure, eBay is loads of fun, but the bottom line to selling is the phrase "Show me the money!" eBay allows the following payment options: PayPal, credit or debit card processed through an Internet merchant account, ProPay, or Skrill. You make the call on what you're willing to take as money from the buyer of your item.

In some cases, you may still accept checks and money orders in certain categories. Because these categories can change per eBay's policy, I suggest you check `http://pages.ebay.com/help/policies/accepted-payments-policy.html` to see if your category is listed.

eBay's rules say that you must clearly state the payment methods you accept and can't make generalized statements or ask buyers to contact you for additional payment methods.

Some sellers who use credit card services try attaching an additional fee (to cover their credit card processing fees) to the final payment. However, that's against the law in California, home of eBay — and therefore against eBay's rules. So forget about it. eBay can end your listing if it catches you.

Setting shipping terms

Ahoy, matey! Hoist the bid! Okay, not quite. Before you run it up the mast, select your shipping options. Here are your choices:

- ✔ **Ship to the United States only:** This option is selected by default; it means that you ship only domestically.

- ✔ **Will ship worldwide:** The world is your oyster. But make sure that you can afford the time for the extra processing of customs forms.

- ✔ **Will ship to United States and the following:** If you're comfortable shipping to certain countries but not to others, make your selections here; they show up on your item page.

When you indicate that you will ship internationally, your item shows up on the eBay International sites, which is a fantastic way to attract new buyers! (Although, you can pay up to $0.50 extra for U.S. seller's listings to appear on the International sites.) eBay has lots of good international users, so you may want to consider selling your items around the world. If you do, be sure to clearly state in the description all extra shipping costs — and that the buyer is responsible for any customs charges. (See Chapter 12 for more information on how to ship to customers abroad.)

The buyer pays for shipping (unless you choose to offer free shipping), and this is the point at which you must decide how much to charge. You also have to calculate how much this item will cost you to ship. If it's a small item (weighing under a pound or so), you may decide to charge a flat rate to all buyers. To charge a flat rate, click the Flat Shipping Rates tab and fill in the shipping amount. Before you fill in the amount, be sure to include your costs for packing (see Chapter 12 for more info on how much to add for this task) and how much the insurance charges will be.

TIP

If your item weighs 2 pounds or more, you may want to use eBay's versatile shipping calculator. Because UPS and the U.S. Postal Service now charge variable rates for packages of the same weight, based on distance, using the calculator simplifies things for your customers (and you). Be sure that you weigh the item and know how much your handling charge will be. The calculator allows you to input a handling amount and adds it to the overall shipping total but does not break out the amount separately for the customer. The calculator also conveniently calculates the proper insurance amount for the item. Figure 10-7 shows how simple the form is.

Figure 10-7: The correct shipping amount is posted automatically on the buyer's view of your listing, based on his or her registered ZIP code.

Shipping Calculator								
Package Description Package (or thick envelope) (0 lbs. 6 oz.) Change				**Seller's ZIP Code** 90210 Change				
				Packaging and Handling Fee $0.00 Change				
Compare services and costs To calculate Domestic or International rates for various shipping services, select a destination or enter a ZIP code below and click Show Rates.								
Domestic Rates Sample Rates ▾ ZIP Code: Show Rates				**International Rates** Worldwide Sample Rates ▾ Show Rates				
UNITED STATES POSTAL SERVICE				ups				
To add services to your listing (up to three), use the checkboxes below and click Offer Services. Offer Services Close								
					UPS prices based on UPS Retail Rates			
	Chicago	New York City	Los Angeles			Chicago	New York City	Los Angeles
☐ US Postal Service First Class Mail® Estimated delivery 2-5 days	$2.02	$2.02	$2.02	☐ UPS Ground Guaranteed in 1-6 days*		$10.19	$10.37	$9.00
☐ US Postal Service Parcel Post® Estimated delivery 2-9 days	$4.55	$4.55	$4.02	☐ UPS 3 Day Select℠ Guaranteed in 1-3 days*		$16.16	$16.56	$9.75
☐ US Postal Service Priority Mail®	$4.95	$4.95	$4.95	☐ UPS 2nd Day Air® Guaranteed in 1-2 days*		$21.06	$21.36	$14.80

The calculator automatically appears on the item page so that prospective buyers can type in their ZIP codes and immediately know how much shipping will be to their locations. Check out Chapter 12 for more information on shipping options.

Checking Your Work and Starting the Listing

After you fill in all the blanks on the Sell Your Item form, you come to the Preview Your Listing page. Scroll down the page and confirm that all the information appears as you intended. If you think you're ready to join the world of e-commerce, follow these steps:

1. **Under the heading titled How Your Listing Will Appear in Search Results, click the Preview Your Listing link, as shown in Figure 10-8.**

   A pop-up page opens, showing you exactly how your listing will appear on eBay. Here's where you can catch mistakes before your item is listed. The bottom of the sell page shows you a condensed version of all your information and tallies how much eBay is charging you in fees and options to run this listing.

Figure 10-8:
The Preview Your Listing link is the last place you can double-check for errors before the listing begins.

You also may find the preview page helpful as a last-minute chance to get your bearings. You can go back to any of the areas that need correcting by clicking the Edit Listings links on the Preview Your Listing page. Make category changes or any other changes and additions, and then head for the Verification page again.

2. **Check for mistakes.**

   Nitpick for common, careless errors; you won't be sorry. I've seen eBay members make goofs such as the wrong category listing, misspelling and grammatical errors, and missing information about shipping, handling, insurance, and payment methods.

3. **When you're sure that everything's accurate and you're happy with your item listing, click the Submit button.**

   A Confirmation page pops up. At that precise moment, your listing begins, even though a few hours may pass before it appears in eBay's search and listings updates. If you want to see your listing right away and check for bids, your Confirmation page provides a link for that purpose. Click the link, and you're there. You can also keep track of your items by using the My eBay page. (To find out how, see Chapter 4.)

All item pages come with this friendly warning: *Seller assumes all responsibility for listing this item. You should contact the seller to resolve any questions before bidding.* Some eBay veterans just gloss over this warning after they've been wheeling and dealing for a while, but it's an important rule to remember. See Chapter 9 for details on the rules sellers must follow and Chapter 12 for tips on your role in closing the deal and receiving good feedback.

For the first 24 hours after your sale is underway, eBay stamps the item page with a funky sunrise icon next to the listing. This is just a little reminder for buyers to come take a look at the latest items up for sale.

Midcourse Corrections: Fixing Current Listings

Don't worry if you make a mistake filling out the Sell Your Item page but don't notice it until after the auction is up and running. Pencils have erasers, and eBay allows revisions. You can make changes at two stages of the game: before the first bid is placed and after the bidding war is underway. The following sections explain what you can and can't correct — and when you have to accept the little imperfections of your item page.

Making changes before bidding begins

Here's what you can change about your auction before bids have been placed (and when there are more than 12 hours to go):

- The title or description of your auction
- The item category
- The item's starting price
- The item's Buy It Now price
- The reserve price (you can add, change, or remove it)
- The duration of your listing
- The URL of the picture you're including with your auction
- A private listing designation (you can add or remove it)
- Accepted payment methods, Checkout information, item location, and shipping terms

When you revise a listing, eBay puts a little notation on your auction page that reads: `Description(revised)`. (Think of it as automatic common courtesy.)

To revise a fixed-price listing or any auction before bids have been received, follow these steps:

1. **Go to your My eBay page and find the item you want to revise. Click the Revise link from the drop-down menu on the right side of the item.**

   If the item hasn't received any bids, a message appears on your screen to indicate that you may update the item.

2. **You arrive at the Revise Item page, which looks like the Sell an Item form.**

3. **Make changes to the item information and then click the Save and Continue button at the bottom of the page when you're finished.**

   A summary of your newly revised page appears on your screen.

4. **If you're happy with your revisions, click Save Changes.**

   You're taken to your newly revised item page, where you see a disclaimer from eBay that says you've revised the listing before the first bid. If you instead want to make further revisions, click the Back button of your browser and redo the Edit Your Listing page.

Making changes after bidding begins

If your listing is up and running and already receiving bids, you can still make some slight modifications to it. Newly added information is clearly separated from the original text and pictures. In addition, eBay puts a time stamp on the additional info in case questions from early bidders crop up later.

After your item receives bids, eBay allows you to add to your item's description. If you feel that you were at a loss for words in writing your item's description, if you discover new information (that vase you thought was a reproduction is actually the real thing!), or if a lot of potential bidders are asking the same questions, go ahead and make all the additions you want. But whatever you put there the first time around stays in the description as well.

Don't let an oversight grow into a failure to communicate — and don't ignore iffy communication until the auction is over. Correct any inaccuracies in your auction information now to avoid problems later.

Always check your messages to see whether bidders have questions about your item. If a bidder wants to know about flaws, be truthful and courteous when responding. As you get more familiar with eBay (and with writing descriptions), the number of buyer questions will decrease. If you enjoy good customer service in your day-to-day shopping, here's your chance to give some back.

Chapter 11

Shopping or Selling with an eBay Store

. . . .

. . . .

*T*here are plenty of times that you don't want to participate in an auction. Sometimes you want to buy your item *now*. The easiest place to go for this type of transaction is to purchase an item from a fixed-price listing where you find ready-to-buy items. Visiting a seller's eBay Store can save you money because buying multiple items from one seller allows several items to be shipped in a single box. Even if the items have to be shipped separately, many sellers will discount shipping costs on multiple purchases.

Regular eBay sellers run these stores, which are easily accessed by clicking the blue-door icon in the seller info box on any listing page, as shown in Figure 11-1. Not every seller has an eBay Store, but when you see an item you want to buy, and the seller has a store, you can check there to find more goodies.

The requirements for opening an eBay Store are basic. However, I highly recommend that you transact business (sell) on the site for quite a while before you open an eBay Store because you need a solid understanding of how eBay works and how to handle all types of transactions. These are eBay's requirements:

✔ You must be registered as an eBay seller, with a credit card on file.

✔ You must have a Verified Premier PayPal account.

Figure 11-1:
A quick
click on the
Stores blue-
door icon
takes you to
the seller's
store.

PRO CLOUD DOME Digital Phototography Light Diffuser Kit & 7" EXTENSION Photo Box

Item condition: **New**

Time left: 28d 00h (Sep 26, 2013 12:54:05 PDT)

Quantity: 1   6 available

Price: US $162.99   Buy It Now

Add to cart

Best Offer: Make Offer

Seller information
marsha_c (8206)
100% Positive feedback

Save this seller
See other items
Visit store: Marsha Collier's F...

Top
Rated
Plus

To get to the eBay Stores main information area, visit the eBay home page and click the Stores link in the Legal & More section at the bottom of the page. Alternatively, you can type `http://stores.ebay.com` in the address box of your web browser.

Selling from Your Own Virtual Storefront

After you've shopped the eBay Stores, you may be thinking that this is a good place to open your own store. There's great news on that end because eBay Stores have the most reasonable rent on the Internet. At an eBay Store, you are not constrained by the auction format of a 1-to-10-day maximum. You can list your fixed-price items in your eBay Store on a "good till cancelled" basis.

I don't like to pull punches with my readers, so let me give you a bit of advice. Opening an eBay Store without a large stock of items, or many items that you stock in multiples, makes no sense. Opening an eBay Store is really for experienced sellers — those who make a business on the eBay site selling merchandise they bought for the purpose of reselling. Retailers who come to the eBay site to expand their business can be successful with the stores, but certainly it helps to know the e-commerce ropes already. To catch up on all you need to know, you can always read my *eBay Business All-In-One For Dummies,* 3rd Edition.

Too many readers who are new to eBay e-mail me after reading this book and tell me that they opened a store and have had no sales. You must list a bunch of items on eBay in the auction format (or at a fixed price) to draw people to your store — simple as that.

Paying the landlord

When paid annually, the rent for a Basic eBay Store is as low as $15.95 per month, Premium stores $49.95, and Anchor stores (just like your local department store) pay $179.95 a month. The benefits of each level of store are based on your sales revenue: The more you sell, the better the deal you get on insertion fees. There are also other benefits to owning a store: cost-per-click advertising, sales management tools, vacation holds, Markdown Manager, and lots of promotional benefits for your merchandise.

The reasonable pricing behind eBay Stores is a remarkable bargain. For as little as $15.95 a month, you have the opportunity to sell your merchandise to over 140 million registered users!

Stores get a prescribed number for free listings (auction or fixed-price) per month:

✔ Basic Store 150 listings

✔ Premium Store 500

✔ Anchor store 2,500

After stores have exhausted their free listings, they are charged a nominal fee. See Table 11-1 for the fees.

Table 11-1	eBay Store Listing Fees after Using Free Quota		
Type of Store	**Auctions**	**Category Books, DVDs & Movies, Music, and Video Games**	**Other Categories**
Basic	25¢	5¢	20¢
Premium	15¢	5¢	10¢
Anchor	10¢	5¢	5¢

Listing fees and monthly rent can be just the tip of the iceberg if you choose to get fancy by using all kinds of options. My recommendation? Don't spend too much on them until you're fully entrenched in an eBay business — by that time, you'll have the experience to know what to add and when. Stick with the basics.

The *Final Value Fees* are based on the total amount paid by the customer, including shipping. Check them out in Table 11-2.

Table 11-2	Store Final Value Fees
Categories	*Final Value Fee (Maximum $250)*
Computers, Tablets & Networking Video Game Consoles	4%
Coins & Paper Money, Stamps	6%
Select Consumer Electronics Cameras & Photo	6%
Musical Instruments & Gear	7%
Motors Parts & Accessories	8%
Clothing, Shoes & Accessories	9%
Collectibles	9%
Home & Garden	9%
Camera & Photo Accessories	9%
Cell Phone Accessories	9%
All Other Categories	9%

When pricing your items for sale — or even deciding whether to have an eBay Store, use a calculator like the one at www.ebcalc.com to work out the numbers. There is also a "Fee Illustrator" on eBay at http://pages.ebay.com/sellerinformation/news/FeeIllustrator.html.

Running an auction is easy too

When you have an eBay Store, you'll have a bunch of fixed-price listings, but no doubt you'll want to run an auction from time to time. Your auctions are included in your free monthly listing quota; once you exceed that number you have to pay an Insertion Fee. On the good side, your Final Value Fees are lower than if you do not have a store.

Opening your eBay Store

Because this book is your introduction to eBay, I just give you some ideas about opening an eBay Store. In my more advanced book, *Starting an eBay Business For Dummies*, I take you step by step through the basics of opening your store.

Once open, your store will have its own personalized URL, which you can link to in your e-mails or from your Facebook business page (or other social media sites). The web address for my store is `http://stores.ebay.com/Marsha-Colliers-Fabulous-Finds`

Naming your eBay Store is your first challenge. Choose a name that describes the types of items your store will carry or one that includes your User ID. Don't choose a name that is so esoteric or overly creative that it doesn't give possible shoppers a clue as to what you carry. A creative store name and logo are pictured in Figure 11-2.

Figure 11-2:
The eBay Store page for ShopIt Fashion.

As you can see from the ShopIt Fashion Store page, each store can have its own categories. You get to make them up yourself so your customers can find items within your store in an organized manner. You can define up to 300 custom categories up to three levels deep. Each category can have a maximum of 29 characters for each name in your store.

Your eBay Store home page has links for your Store Information: Store Policies and About the Seller page. The About the Store page is the same as your About Me page (which I discuss in Chapter 14). You can also create up to 15 other custom pages.

Spend some serious time on eBay before you open an eBay Store. Study some of the successful stores. You need to have enough know-how to make your store a success!

Chapter 12

Closing the Deal and Shipping It Out

*T*he sale is made and you have a buyer, who has paid via PayPal and the money is in your account. Sounds perfect, doesn't it? It is if you watch your step, keep on top of things, and communicate like a professional.

In this chapter, I help you figure out how to stay organized by showing you what documents you need to keep and for how long. I also include tips and etiquette on communicating with the buyer so that you're most likely to come out with positive feedback. In addition, you find out how to pack your item, assess costs, and make sure that the item reaches the buyer when you said it would (oh, yeah . . . and in one piece).

Bookkeeping and Staying Organized

Although I don't recommend lining your nest with every scrap from every sale you run, you can safely keep some documents without mutating into a giant pack rat. Until you become an eBay expert and are comfortable with other ways to electronically store your information (if you are, be sure to keep files with the following information), you might like to print and file these essentials:

✔ **The listing page as it appeared before the item closed:** This page gives you a record of the item name and number and a lot of other useful information. The page also includes the auction item description (and any revisions you made to it), which is handy if the buyer argues that an item's disintegrating before his eyes and you honestly described it as just "well-loved."

Use the Print feature on the item page located just above the description on the right. You will get all the details, including the seller's description and images.

You can also look it up in your Purchase History on your My eBay page. Figure 12-1 shows how you can access your purchases as far back as three years. However, if you use the custom link that appears in your End of Listing (or Order Confirmation in the case of a buyer) e-mail (see the next bullet), you can access the listing online for up to 90 days. Print the page *before* you forget about it, file it where you know you can find it, and *then* forget about it.

Figure 12-1:
eBay
Purchase
History
holds three
years of
your pur-
chases.

✔ **The Order Confirmation or Listing End e-mail you receive from eBay that notifies you that the sale is over:** If you lose this e-mail, you can't get it back because eBay doesn't keep it. Sellers can find your ended listings, whether sold or unsold, for 90 days via their My eBay pages.

I set up a separate folder in my Microsoft Outlook e-mail program (you can set up a label in Gmail as well) for my sold item e-mails. When one comes in, I read it and then drag it over to its special folder. That way, I can always check this folder for the information I need.

✔ **Messages between you and the buyer:** In the virtual world, e-mail is as close to having a face-to-face conversation as most people get. Your e-mail correspondence is a living record of all the things you discuss with the buyer to complete the transaction. When you use eBay messages, the record is archived online for you (or eBay) to inspect should there be an issue.

✔ **PayPal payment notices:** You get a notice from PayPal when the buyer pays for the item. The notice has the listing information and the buyer's shipping information. (When that e-mail arrives, the clock begins to tick on sending the item.)

✔ **Any insurance forms:** Until the item has arrived and you're sure that the customer is satisfied, be sure to keep those shipping and insurance receipts.

✔ **Refund requests you make:** If you make a request to eBay for a refund from a sale that doesn't go through, keep revisiting it until you can view the credit on your statement.

✔ **Tracking numbers:** PayPal and eBay want to have a tracking number for every item you ship, and you should upload them as you print the labels. When you print your shipping labels on eBay, they are automatically inserted into the transaction record. If the customer claims it never arrived, the tracking number can prove that it did. I explain more about tracking and electronic options later in this chapter.

✔ **Receipts for items that you buy for the sole purpose of selling on eBay:** This comes in handy as documentation at tax time.

Someday, the Internal Revenue Service (or the government agency that collects taxes in your area) may knock on your door. Scary, but true. Like hurricanes and asteroid strikes, audits happen. Any accountant worth his or her salt will tell you that the best way to handle the possibility of an audit is to be prepared for the worst — even if every eBay transaction you conduct runs smooth as silk and you've kept your nose sparkling clean. See Chapter 9 for more tax information.

If you accept online payments by PayPal (PayPal Premier or Business members only), you can download your transaction history for use in QuickBooks, Quicken, or Excel. Additionally, these programs are excellent sources for your documentation.

Tales from the former Type A

Confession time: When I first started buying and selling online back in 1996, I used to keep all my paperwork — listings, e-mails, the works. Now I keep the e-mails and receipts sent to me until I know a transaction is complete. Then they go wafting off to the Recycle Bin. That said, I do keep my PayPal downloads eternally.

These days, I stay on top of my eBay finances with eBay's Selling Manager Pro, a feature that helps me keep track of who has paid me and who hasn't. Programs like these can also help you figure out your expenses, profit, and other financial calculations, almost painlessly. (See Chapter 20 for more information on programs and apps.)

When you're starting your career as a casual seller, once a month conduct a By Seller search on yourself so that you can print all the information on the bid histories of your most recent auctions. Do this independently of any auction applications you use. Having the listings neatly printed easily helps you see what sold for how much and when. Chapter 5 gives you the lowdown on how to perform this search.

When it comes to printouts or electronic archives of e-mails and documents generated during transactions, you can dump them as soon as the item arrives at the destination and you get your positive feedback. If you get negative feedback, hang on to your documentation a little longer (say, until you're sure that the issues it raises are resolved and everyone's satisfied). If selling on eBay becomes a fairly regular source of income, save all receipts for items you purchased to sell; for tax purposes, that's inventory.

If you sell specialized items, you can keep track of trends — and who your frequent buyers are — by saving your paperwork and connecting with them through social media. This prudent habit becomes an excellent marketing strategy when you discover that a segment of eBay users faithfully visits and purchases your items. A *community* of buyers. Imagine that.

Talking to Buyers: The ABCs of Good Communication

You've heard it countless times — talk is cheap. Compared to what? Granted, empty promises are a dime a dozen, but honest-to-goodness talk, comprehensive descriptions, and efficient messages are worth their weight in gold and good feedback — especially on eBay. Sometimes *not* talking is costly.

A smooth exchange of money and merchandise starts with you (the seller) and your attitude toward the transaction. Your listing description and then your first contact — soon after the sale is made — set the transaction in motion and the tone for that transaction. If all goes well, *no more than* a day should elapse between getting paid and sending the item.

I suggest contacting the buyer and sending an invoice even *before* you get eBay's e-mail. Here's how:

1. **Start at your My eBay Summary, Sold: Selling.**

   Locate your newly sold item. *Hint:* It should be at the top of the listings.

2. **Click the down arrow at the right end of the listing's line and select Send Invoice.**

   You are presented with a page that summarizes the transaction with a "working version" of the invoice.

3. **Examine the invoice displayed on this page. Make any changes if necessary.**

   If the buyer has purchased more than one item from you and hasn't used the shopping cart, click the link to combine purchases.

4. **Double-check that the shipping amount is correct (be sure alternatives are offered if you have some). When you're satisfied, click the Send Invoice button.**

   If you select the Copy Me check box on this invoice, you'll receive a copy of the invoice. The buyer's copy has a link in the invoice, enabling the buyer to pay directly to PayPal (if you accept PayPal for payment).

Signing in first puts a temporary *cookie* (a computer file that makes it easier to get around a website) in your computer so you don't have to go through this process again. Be sure to select the Stay Signed In check box when you sign in to eBay; your password is saved even if you cut off your Internet connection. Your login is saved until you click the Sign Out link. For more yummy info on cookies, see Chapter 15.

Another way to contact your buyers, should you have an additional message for them, is to go to your My eBay page, scroll down to the Items I've Sold area, find the transaction, and click the drop-down menu in the Actions column. From there, click the Contact Buyer link.

Thank you — I mean it

What do all the successful big-name department stores have in common? Yes, great prices, good merchandise, and nice displays. But with all things being equal, customer service always wins hands down. One department store in the United States, Nordstrom, has such a great reputation that the store happily took back a set of snow tires because a customer wasn't happy with them. No big deal, maybe — until you notice that Nordstrom doesn't even *sell* snow tires! (A word to the wise: They did that exactly once.)

A friend of mine who owns restaurants calls this level of customer satisfaction the Wow! factor. If customers (no matter what they're buying) say, "Wow!" during or after the transaction — admiringly or happily — you've satisfied the customer. A good rule to go by: *Give people the same level of service you expect when you're on the buying end.* The best eBay sellers are regular eBay buyers.

The best way to start satisfying the buyer is with an introductory e-mail — the buyer's e-mail can be found in the PayPal record. Congratulate the person on buying the item — making him or her feel good about the purchase — by saying thanks. A comprehensive e-mail provides these important details:

✔ Item name.

✔ Winning bid (or purchase) amount.

✔ Cost of shipping. (I give pointers on determining shipping costs later in this chapter.)

✔ Payment options.

✔ The shipping timetable.

You should also include a few vital details in the first e-mail:

✔ If you're using an online payment service such as PayPal, be sure to give buyers instructions on how they can pay for the item online.

✔ Include your "customer service" phone number and social media contacts (such as Twitter or Facebook).

✔ Suggest that if all goes well, you'll be looking forward to receiving their feedback. (See Chapter 4 for more on feedback.)

Most customers pay immediately upon purchase. Others, as in the case of an auction win, may need a little prodding to complete Checkout. Just click the Send Invoice link, verify all the information, and click Send Invoice. Figure 12-2 shows what the invoice e-mail looks like.

Figure 12-2: An eBay invoice, as sent to a buyer.

Note that there is an e-mail reference ID at the bottom of all eBay correspondence (It looks something like *Email reference id: [#d1f086e14987c9452d8c-16c86e2295a452#].*) This reference number, or one like it, appears on all official eBay e-mails. eBay uses them as a reference number to prove authenticity should you have to call them with an issue on your transaction.

Let's keep e-mailing

If you have a good transaction going (and the majority of them are good), the buyer will reply to your e-mail or pay the invoice within a business day. If your buyer has questions regarding anything about your item, you'll get those inquiries now. Most of the time, the only e-mail I ever get back is something like, "Thanks. I'll send the PayPal payment when I get paid on Thursday." Hey, that's all I ask.

If any last-minute details need to be worked out, usually the buyer asks to set up a time to call or request further instructions about the transaction. Respond to this communication as soon as possible. If you can't deal with it at the moment, let the buyer know that you're working on it and will shoot those answers back ASAP. ***Never* let an e-mail or eBay message go unanswered.**

For sample e-mail letters and deeper information, get your hands on a copy of my book on more advanced eBay selling, *Starting an eBay Business For Dummies*.

Shipping without Going Postal

Shipping can be the most time-consuming (and most dreaded) task for many eBay sellers. Even if the selling portion of your transaction goes flawlessly, the item has to get to the buyer in one piece. If it doesn't, the deal could be ruined — and so could your reputation.

This section briefs you on shipping etiquette, gives you details about the three most popular shipping options (the U.S. Postal Service, UPS, and FedEx Ground), and offers tips on how to make sure that your package is ready to ride.

The best way to avoid shipping problems is to do your homework beforehand, determine which method is likely to work best, and spell out in your item description exactly how you intend to ship the item. It's beneficial to give buyers an option should they want overnight or Priority shipping. Here's how I handle the process:

1. **Before listing an item, get a single package ready to ship.**

   You don't have to seal the package right away, but you should have it ready to seal because the two critical factors in shipping are weight and time. The more a package weighs and the faster it has to be delivered, the higher the costs. (I cover packing materials and tips later in this section.) The time to think about packing and shipping is *before* you put the item up for sale — that way, last-minute surprises are less likely to arise while your buyer waits impatiently for the item!

2. **Know your carrier options.**

   In the United States, the three main shipping options for most eBay transactions are the U.S. Postal Service, UPS, and FedEx. See the section "Shopping for a shipper" (try saying *that* five times fast) for how you can get rate options from each service, painlessly and online. Compare costs and services.

3. **Before quoting the shipping fees in the listing, make sure that you gather all appropriate costs.**

   Offering Free Shipping is very common on eBay, because it gives you an advantage in eBay searches. When you do, build the shipping cost into the price you ask for the item. When you budget your costs, you may want to add in a nominal handling fee (up to $1 isn't out of line) to cover your packing materials, labels, and time. These costs can add up quickly as you start making multiple transactions. You should also include any insurance costs and signature-confirmation costs, should they be necessary for the item. See the sidebar "Insuring your peace of mind (and your shipment)" for more information.

   Some shoddy eBay sellers inflate shipping and handling charges to make added profit. *Shame, shame, shame on them.* Purposely overcharging is tacky, ugly, and immature. (It's also a violation of eBay policy on circumventing fees — and will penalize your listings in Best Match search.) Often the buyer also figures it out after one look at the postage on the box — and that can easily net you a negative feedback.

   If you don't offer Free Shipping, post a flat shipping amount (or use the eBay online shipping calculator — see Chapter 10 for more on how to use this tool). This way, buyers can include this cost when they consider their bidding strategies. Figure out what the packed item will weigh and then give a good estimate; the online calculators can help.

   If the item is heavy and you need to use a shipping service that charges by weight and distance, be sure to say in your listing description that you're just giving an estimate and that the final cost will be determined after the listing is over. Optionally, you indicate that the buyer should use the eBay shipping calculator. You give the weight of the package when you put together your listing; eBay will calculate shipping costs for the buyer, based on your ZIP code and the buyer's.

   Occasionally, shipping calculations can be off-target, and you may not know that until after you take the buyer's money. If the mistake is in your favor and is a biggie, notify the buyer and offer a refund. But if shipping ends up costing you a bit more, take your lumps and pay it yourself. Consider it part of the cost of doing business. Spreading goodwill never hurts your reputation for future sales.

4. Send a thank-you note.

In every package you ship, you should include a thank-you note that promotes you as a seller and your business. The one I send in every shipment thanks the customer, mentions that I look forward to doing business with the buyer again, and provides a link to my website. I set up these notes to print four on an 8 ½" x 11" sheet of paper and print them on my color laser printer. (Don't forget to put in a plug for positive feedback.)

5. Send the package.

When should you ship the package? Common courtesy says it should go out as soon as the buyer has paid for the item and shipping charges. If the buyer has followed through with his or her side of the bargain, you should do the same. Ship that package no more than a day after payment. If you can't, contact the buyer immediately and explain the reason for the delay.

More often than not, you do get an e-mail back from the buyer to let you know that the item arrived safely. If you don't (and you haven't received any feedback), check the tracking number to see when the item was delivered. If it has, you can ask (through eBay messages) whether the buyer is satisfied with the purchase. It jogs the buyer's memory and demonstrates your professionalism as a seller.

Shopping for a shipper

If only you could transport your item the way they did on *Star Trek* — "Beam up that antique lamp, Scotty!" Alas, it's not so. Priority Mail via the U.S. Postal Service (USPS) is pretty much the eBay standard if you're shipping within the United States. Many American sellers also rely on the USPS to ship internationally. FedEx and UPS are global alternatives that work well, too.

Many sellers think that they are unequivocally covered by purchasing insurance. Not true — you are still responsible for making sure that the item arrives at the buyer's door. Federal mail-order laws state that when an item is paid for, it must be delivered to the buyer within 30 days unless there has been an agreement between the buyer and the seller for other arrangements. If it gets lost in the mail, you'll have to replace the item or refund the buyer's money.

Whether you're at the post office, UPS, FedEx, or your doctor's office, be ready, willing, and able to wait in line. There's definitely a "rush hour" at my neighborhood post office — everybody's in a rush, so everything moves at a glacial pace. Avoid both the noontime and post-work crunches (easier on the nerves). A good time to ship is around 10:30 a.m., when everyone is still in a good mood. If I have to go in the afternoon, I go about 2:00 p.m., when the clerks are back from their lunch breaks and friendly faces (mine, too — I always smile!) can take the edge off those brusque lunchtime encounters. If you can ship from home, why not save yourself the time and stress by requesting a free carrier pickup from the post office website? Here's the link:

```
https://tools.usps.com/go/ScheduleAPickupAction!input.
action
```

Be sure to visit my website, `www.coolebaytools.com`, for introductory offers for much of the software and services that I mention in this book.

U.S. Postal Service

The U.S. Postal Service (USPS) is the butt of many unfair jokes and cheap shots, but when it comes right down to it, I think USPS is still the most efficient and inexpensive way to ship items — eBay or otherwise. It also supplies free boxes and labels for Priority and Express Mail packages. Here are some ways eBay members get their items from here to there via USPS:

Insuring your peace of mind (and your shipment)

Sure, "damaged in the mail" is an excuse we've all heard hundreds of times, but despite everyone's best efforts, sometimes things do get damaged or misplaced during shipment. The universe can be a dangerous place; that's what insurance is for. I usually get insurance on expensive items, one-of-a-kind items, or very fragile items. On eBay, the expense for that insurance falls on the seller.

The major shippers all offer insurance that's fairly reasonably priced, so check out their rates on their websites. But don't forget to read the details. For example, many collectibles and gift items on eBay are sold MIMB (Mint in Mint Box). True, the condition of the original box often has a bearing on the final value of the item inside, but the U.S. Postal Service insures only what is *in* the box. So, if you sold a Malibu Barbie MIMB, USPS insures only the doll and not the collectible value of the doll in the original box. Pack carefully so that your buyer gets what's been paid for. Be mindful that shippers won't make good on insurance claims if they suspect you of causing the damage by doing a lousy job of packing.

Alternatively, when you're selling on eBay in earnest, you can purchase your own parcel-protection policy from a private insurer such as U-PIC. When you use this type of insurance, combined with preprinted electronic postage, you no longer have to stand in line at the post office to have your insured package logged in by the clerk at the counter.

Some sellers have their own form of *self-insurance*. Realize that I use the term "self-insurance" as a descriptive phrase only. You may not charge your buyer for insurance on eBay. Here's what I offer my buyers at no cost to them:

- ✔ On lower-priced items, I am willing to refund the buyer's money if the item is lost or damaged, per eBay policy.

- ✔ On some items I sell, I have a *risk reserve*. That means I have more than one of the item I sold. If the item is lost or destroyed, I can send the backup item as a replacement.

✔ **Priority Mail:** As I mentioned earlier, this is the *de facto* standard method of shipping for eBay users. I love the free boxes, and I like the rates. The promised delivery time is two to three days, although I've experienced rare delays of up to a week during peak holiday periods.

Cost? As of this writing (rates are always subject to change), Priority Mail costs as little as $5.05 for a 1-pound package within your local zone when you print your postage electronically. The fees go up and are calculated according to weight and distance unless you're using Flat-Rate boxes.

A $5.60 Flat-Rate Priority envelope is also available. You can ship as much stuff as you want — as long as you can fit it into the supplied 9½ x 12½ envelope. (You'll be surprised how much you can jam into those envelopes.) You can reinforce the envelope with clear packing tape.

Using flat-rate Priority Mail boxes (which come in a multitude of sizes), you can send heavy items at reduced rates. Order the boxes directly from the USPS. Table 12-1 shows you some of the wide selection!

To order your boxes, labels, forms, and just about anything else that you'll need to ship Priority Mail, go to the Postal Store (see Figure 12-3) at `http://bit.ly/GetMailing`. Orders can take up to a month to arrive, so be sure to order before you need more boxes.

To keep up on any changes in USPS service — it's rumored that Saturday mail service (although not package service) may be discontinued— be sure to visit `http://about.usps.com/news/` every once and a while.

To save money, print your postage electronically. You can do this through a service such as Endicia.com, stamps.com, eBay, or PayPal.

Table 12-1	Free Priority Mail Packaging
Size (in Inches)	*Description*
7 $\frac{9}{16}$" x 5$\frac{7}{16}$" x $\frac{5}{8}$"	DVD Box
9¼" x 6¼" x 2"	Large Video Box (#1096L)
7 $\frac{9}{16}$" x "5 $\frac{7}{16}$" x 1$\frac{3}{8}$"	Electronic Media
5 $\frac{3}{8}$" x 8 $\frac{5}{8}$" 1$\frac{5}{8}$"	Small Flat Rate
11½" x 13$\frac{1}{8}$" x 2$\frac{3}{8}$"	Medium (#1097)
11$\frac{7}{8}$" x 3$\frac{3}{8}$" x 13$\frac{5}{8}$"	Flat-Rate Medium (FBR2)
12$\frac{3}{8}$" x 15¼" x 3"	Large (#1095)
12$\frac{1}{8}$" x 13$\frac{3}{8}$" x 2¾"	Medium (#1092)
10" x 7" x 4¾"	Regional Rate A1
10$\frac{15}{16}$" x 2$\frac{3}{8}$" x 12$\frac{13}{16}$"	Regional Rate A2

(continued)

Table 12-1 (continued)

Size (in Inches)	Description
12" x 10¼" x 5"	Regional Rate B1
14⅜" x 2⅞" x 15⅞"	Regional Rate B2
14¾" x 11¾" x 11½"	Regional Rate C
6" x 38"	Large Triangle Tube
6" x 25"	Small Triangle Tube
7" x 7" x 6"	Small Square (BOX4)
12" x 12" x 8"	Medium Square (BOX7)
11 x 8½" x 5½"	Medium Flat-Rate (FBR1)
23¹¹⁄₁₆" x 11¾" x 3"	Large Board Game Flat-Rate
12" x 12" x 5½"	Large Flat-Rate Box
7.5" x 5.125" x 14.375"	Priority Mail Shoe Box
11.625" x 15.125"	Tyvek Envelope
9½" x 12½"	Padded Flat-Rate Envelope
6" x 10"	Cardboard Envelope
12½" x 9½"	Flat-Rate Cardboard Envelope
5" x 10"	Cardboard Window Envelope

Figure 12-3: USPS Flat-Rate Priority boxes ready and waiting for you!

✔ **Express Mail:** If the item needs to be delivered the next day, use Express Mail. The Postal Service promises delivery no later than noon the following afternoon (even on weekends or holidays). And you get free boxes.

Cost? Express Mail runs $14.10 for packages 8 ounces and under. Express Mail also has a Flat-Rate envelope, which is the same size as the Priority Flat-Rate envelope and ships for $19.95. (When you print your postage electronically, you save about 5 percent — with the aforementioned items at $13.09 and Flat-Rate at $18.11).

The Postal Service offers a free special pickup for Priority Mail and Express Mail, no matter how many separate packages are included. If you have several packages, carrier pickup is an excellent option.

Get to know your mail carrier and have your parcels ready and stacked up for him or her for the regular stop at your home. The mail carrier will be happy to take your packages back to the post office at no additional charge. (A bottle of icy-cold water for your letter carrier on hot days will go a long way to smooth your relationship!)

✔ **First-Class Mail:** If your item weighs 13 ounces or less, you can use First-Class Mail. First-Class Mail is considerably cheaper than Priority. I try to ship as much as I can via First-Class mail so I can have the edge on other sellers by offering lower shipping prices.

✔ **Media Mail:** This is a popular option among those who sell books on eBay. It's the new name for two older products, Book Rate and Special Standard Mail. Media Mail rates start at $2.53 for the first pound and increase by $0.45 for each additional pound. It's cheap and convenient, but your item can take up to two weeks to arrive.

✔ **Other options:** The Postal Service offers all sorts of add-ons. I always get a tracking number, because PayPal requires it as proof of the shipment. You can add it to Priority Mail, as well as with other mailing services such as First Class or Standard Post (previously known as Parcel Post). The cost is a mere $0.70 — and free on electronic purchases. It buys you the knowledge of when and where your item was delivered. Not only that, but if a buyer reports to PayPal that he or she wants a refund because an item was never received, the scan on the tracking number prevents you from getting a chargeback.

For items over $250 in value, you need a signature confirmation — as well as shipping tracking information — to cover your shipment under eBay's Seller Protection.

You can check on whether the package was delivered (or whether an attempt was made to deliver it) by typing the number online at `www.usps.com/shipping/trackandconfirm.htm`. You can also click the link to the tracking number in My eBay or PayPal after you've copied the number into the sales record.

Tracking numbers come in handy if you try to collect insurance for an item that was never delivered or if the buyer says the item was never delivered. It gives you proof from the Postal Service (or other shipper) that the item was sent. (I explain insuring shipments earlier in this chapter.) If your package gets lost in the mail for a few weeks, this number won't always reveal the location of your package until it's delivered.

The USPS website (www.usps.com) gives you an overview of the U.S. Postal Service rates so that you can see all your options. It sure beats standing in that endless line! For a complete explanation of domestic rates, check out www.usps.com/ship/service-chart.htm.

Even better, USPS has a page that can help you determine exactly what your item costs to mail (after you've packaged it and weighed it, of course). Start at the Rate Calculator page at http://postcalc.usps.gov/ and follow the instructions.

UPS

The folks in the brown UPS trucks love eBay. The options they offer vary, with everything from Overnight service to Ground service. UPS also takes many of the odd-shaped large boxes, such as those for computer equipment, that the U.S. Postal Service won't.

UPS makes pickups, but you have to know the exact weight of your package so that you can pay when the UPS driver shows up. UPS charges for this service unless you have a daily shipper account and ship a minimum number of packages with UPS per week.

The rates for the same UPS shipment can vary based on whether you have a business account with UPS, whether the package goes to or is picked up at a residence, and whether you use the right kind of form. If you're going to use UPS regularly, be sure to set up an account directly with UPS.

Although UPS offers "discounts" to eBay PowerSellers and Top Rated Sellers, don't be fooled. If you ship mostly a few small packages a week, you'd have to ship truckloads on a daily basis to compete with USPS rates.

You can find the UPS home page at www.ups.com. For rates, click the Shipping tab and then click Estimate Cost on the left side of the page, which gives you prices based on ZIP codes and package weights. (Note the ominous "estimate" rates.)

The UPS.com Quick Cost Calculator prices are based on what UPS charges its regular and high-volume users. When you get to the counter, the price may be higher than what you find on the web.

Sí, oui, ja, yes! Shipping internationally

Money's good no matter what country it comes from. I don't know why, but lots of folks seem to be afraid to ship internationally. Of course, sending an item that far away may be a burden if you're selling a car or a street-sweeper (they don't fit in boxes too well), but I've found that sending a package across the Atlantic can be just as easy as shipping across state lines. The only downside: my shipper of choice, the U.S. Postal Service, does not insure packages going to certain countries (check with your post office to find out which ones; they seem to change with the headlines), so I use private shipping insurance with U-PIC.

Here are a couple of other strategies for shipping internationally:

✔ You need to tell what's inside the package. Be truthful when declaring value on customs forms. Use descriptions that customs agents can figure out without knowing eBay shorthand terms. For example, instead of declaring the contents as "MIB Barbie," call it a "small child's doll." Some countries require buyers to pay special duties and taxes, depending on the item and the value. But that's the buyer's headache.

✔ Filling out customs forms is not a headache when you print your own labels via electronic postage. The vendors mentioned in this chapter generate these forms for you.

✔ Often foreign buyers request that you mark the package as a gift, or indicate a lower-than-actual valuation on the item. It's not a good practice to do this — because it's illegal, and eBay says you should report them for asking you to commit customs fraud.

If you do sell internationally, to protect your reputation from negative feedback, you must let your buyers know that this practice is illegal and your policy is not to do it. Here is sample text that I use on my items that are popular with international buyers:

NOTE to International Buyers: Import duties, taxes, and charges are not included in the item price or shipping cost. These charges are the buyer's responsibility. Please check with your country's customs office to determine what these additional costs will be prior to bidding or buying. Thank you for your business!

If an international buyer leaves you negative or neutral feedback for not falsifying customs documents, and eBay sees text in your listing that clearly states your no-falsification policy, they may expunge the feedback. I suggest you follow these rules to be sure the customer gets the message.

- Free standing or apart from other text in the item description

- In a font size no smaller than the majority of the other text in the item description

- Prominently displayed in the upper half of the item description

✔ Wherever you send your package (especially if it's going to a country where English is not the native language), write legibly. (Imagine, as an English speaker, getting a package from Russia and having to decipher a label written in the Cyrillic alphabet. *'Nuff said.*)

My favorite link on the UPS site is the transit map that shows the United States and how long it takes to reach any place in the country (based on the originating ZIP code). If you're thinking of shipping that compact refrigerator to Maine, you can check out this fun and informative page at

```
http://www.ups.com/maps?loc=en_PR
```

FedEx

I use FedEx Express Air all the time for rush business, but Express seems rather expensive for my eBay shipping. However, if the buyer wants it fast and is willing to pay, I'll send it by FedEx overnight, you bet.

FedEx Ground service has competitive prices and carries all the best features of FedEx. I use FedEx Ground for items that are heavy (say, pro-style barbells) or extremely large (such as a 1920s steamer trunk), because FedEx ships anything up to 150 pounds in a single box — 80 more pounds than the U.S. Postal Service takes. FedEx also delivers on Saturdays — which UPS won't. It also charges to pick up items from shippers whose shipping incurs less than $60 in weekly package charges.

I also like the FedEx boxes. These boxes are small *and* tough. But if you're thinking of reusing these boxes to ship with another service, forget it: The FedEx logo is plastered all over every inch of the freebies, and the company may get seriously peeved about it. You can't use those fancy boxes for its Ground service.

The FedEx Ground Home Delivery service is a major competitor for UPS. The rates are competitive, and FedEx offers a money-back guarantee (if it misses the delivery window) for residential ground delivery. For residential delivery, FedEx charges an additional $2.80 per package. A 2-pound package going from Los Angeles to a residence in New York City takes four days and costs $9.71 plus a $0.63 fuel surcharge for a total of $10.34, including the Home Delivery fee. FedEx includes online package tracking and insurance up to $100 in this price. You have to be a business to avail yourself of home delivery — but plenty of home businesses exist.

The same 2-pound U.S. Postal Service Priority Mail package with $100 insurance and a delivery confirmation costs you $12.33. (But remember, you know how to get free tracking, and insurance can cost much less with private package insurance!) Granted, the package will arrive within two to three days, but FedEx Ground guarantees a five-day delivery, and I've had a few Priority Mail packages take up to a week. FedEx Ground won't supply boxes for you, so you're on your own there. When you drop off your box at UPS, you can get four-day service for $14.95.

You can find the FedEx home page at www.fedex.com/us. The link for rates is conveniently located at the top of the page.

Getting the right (packing) stuff

You can never think about packing materials too early. If you wait until the last minute, you won't find the right-size box, approved tape, or the labels you need. Start thinking about shipping even before you sell your first item.

Before you pack, give your item the once-over. Here's a checklist of what to consider about your item before you call it a wrap (gotta love Hollywood lingo):

- ✔ **Is your item as you described it?** If the item has been dented or torn somehow, e-mail the winning bidder immediately and come clean. And if you sell an item with its original box or container, don't just check the item; make sure that the box is in the same good condition as the item inside. Collectors place a high value on original boxes, so make sure that the box lives up to what you described in your listing. Pack to protect it as well.

- ✔ **Is the item dirty or dusty, or does it smell of smoke?** Some buyers may complain if the item they receive is dirty or smelly, especially from cigarette smoke. Make sure that the item is fresh and clean, even if it's used or vintage. If something's dirty, check to make sure that you know how to clean it properly (you want to take the dirt off, not the paint), and then give it a spritz with an appropriate cleaner or just soap and water. If you can't get rid of the smell or the dirt, say so in your item description. Let the buyer decide whether the item is desirable, aromas and all.

If the item has a faint smell of smoke or is a bit musty, a product called Febreze may help. Just get a plastic bag, give your item a spritz, and keep it in the bag for a short while. *Note:* This is not recommended for cardboard; in that case, spray the Febreze on a folded paper towel and put the towel in a big, open plastic bag so it doesn't come into physical contact with the item. And, as with any solvent or cleaning agent, read the label *before* you spray. Or, if you're in a rush to mail the package, cut a 2-x-2-inch piece of sheet fabric softener and place it in an open plastic bag enclosed with the product.

When the item's ready to go, you're ready to pack it. The following sections give you suggestions on what you should consider using and where to find the right stuff.

Storing bags of recycled packing materials

By now, you may have realized that I have commandeered a large chunk of my home for my eBay business, and you might think that I live in a giant swamp of packing materials. Not really. But I do have to store *loads* of packing peanuts, bubble wrap, and air pillows. They're not heavy, but they sure are bulky!

If you have a house with a garage, you're set! Bear with me, now — my plan isn't as crazy as it seems. Go to your local store and purchase some large screw-in cup hooks. Then purchase the largest *drawstring* plastic bags you can find. (I'm partial to 39-gallon Lawn & Leaf bags.)

Screw the cup hooks into strategic locations on the ceiling rafters of your garage. Now fill the drawstring bags to capacity with packing peanuts or recycled bubble wrap, and hang. When you've finished, your garage will look like some bizarre art installation, but it gets the packing materials off the floor and out of your hair. I even set up a packing-peanuts barricade so I don't hit the end of my garage when I park!

Packing material: What to use

This may sound obvious, but you'd be surprised how many miss this: Any list of packing material should start with a box. But you don't want just any box — you want a heavy cardboard type that's larger than the item. If the item is extremely fragile, I suggest you use two boxes, with the outer box about 3 inches larger on each side than the inner box that holds the item, to allow for extra padding. And if you still have the original shipping container for such things as electronic equipment, consider using the original, especially if it still has the original foam inserts (they were designed for the purpose, and this way they stay out of a landfill a while longer).

As for padding, Table 12-2 compares the most popular types of box void-filler material.

Table 12-2	Box Void-Filler Materials	
Type	*Pros and Cons*	*Suggestions*
Bubble wrap	**Pros:** Lightweight, clean, cushions well **Cons:** Cost	Don't go overboard taping the bubble wrap. If the buyer has to battle to get the tape off, the item may go flying and end up damaged. And for crying out loud, don't pop all the little bubbles, okay?

Type	Pros and Cons	Suggestions
Newspaper	**Pros:** Cheap, cushions **Cons:** Can be messy, adds weight to the package	Seal fairly well. Put your item in a plastic bag to protect it from the ink. I like shredding the newspaper first. It's more manageable and doesn't seem to stain as much as wadded-up paper. I spent about $30 at an office-supply store for a shredder. (Or find one on eBay for much less.) Best use is in Flat-Rate boxes.
Cut-up cardboard	**Pros:** Handy, cheap **Cons:** Transmits some shocks to item, hard to cut up, heavy	If you have some old boxes that aren't sturdy enough to pack in, this is a pretty good use for them. Again, this adds weight.
Styrofoam peanuts	**Pros:** Lightweight, absorb shock well, clean **Cons:** Environmentally unfriendly, annoying	Your item may shift if you don't put enough peanuts in the box, so make sure to fill the box. Also, don't buy these; recycle them from stuff that was shipped to you (plastic trash bags are great for storing them). And never use plastic peanuts when packing electronic equipment, because they can create static electricity. Even a little spark can trash a computer chip.
Air pillows	**Pros:** Extra lightweight **Cons:** Not quite enough protection for delicate breakables	Air packing pillows are perfect for filling in the area around smaller boxed items that you want to double box. They are also handy if you have breakables that you've prewrapped in bubble wrap; just use the pillows to fill out the box. Most are crushproof and can support about 150 pounds without a blowout.

(continued)

Table 12-2 *(continued)*

Type	Pros and Cons	Suggestions
Air-popped popcorn	**Pros:** Lightweight, environmentally friendly, absorbs shock well, clean (don't use salt and butter, but you knew that), low in calories **Cons:** Cost, time to pop	You don't want to send it anywhere there may be varmints who like it. The U.S. Postal Service suggests popcorn. Hey, at least you can eat the leftovers!

Whatever materials you use, make sure that you pack the item well and that you secure the box. Many shippers will contest insurance claims if they feel you did a lousy job of packing. Do all the little things that you'd want done if you were the buyer — using double boxes for really fragile items, wrapping lids separately from containers, and filling hollow breakables with some kind of padding. Here are a few other items you need:

- **Plastic bags:** Plastic bags protect your item from moisture. I once sent a MIB doll to the Northeast, and the package got caught in a snowstorm. The buyer e-mailed me with words of thanks for the extra plastic bag, which saved the item from being soaked along with the outer box. (Speaking of boxes, if you send an item in an original box, bag it.)

  For any small items, such as stuffed animals, you should always protect them in a lunch baggie. For slightly larger items, go to the 1-quart or 1-gallon size. Be sure to wrap any paper or cloth products, such as clothing and linens, in plastic before you ship.

- **Bubble-padded mailers:** The shipping cost for a package that weighs less than 13 ounces (First-Class mail) is usually considerably cheaper than Priority. Many small items, clothing, books, and so on, will fit comfortably into the many available sizes of padded envelopes. You can find them made of kraft paper or extra-sturdy vinyl. A big plus is that they weigh considerably less than boxes — even when you use extra padding. See Table 12-3 for standard sizes.

Table 12-3 **Standard Bubble-Padded Mailer Sizes**

Size	Measurements	Suggested Items
#000	4" x 8"	Collector trading cards, jewelry, computer disks, coins
#00	5" x 10"	Postcards, paper ephemera
#0	6" x 10"	CDs, DVDs, Xbox or PS2 games
#1	7¼" x 12"	Cardboard sleeve VHS tapes, jewel-cased CDs and DVDs

Size	Measurements	Suggested Items
#2	8½" x 12"	Clamshell VHS tapes
#3	8½" x 14½"	Toys, clothing, stuffed animals
#4	9½" x 14½"	Small books, trade paperbacks
#5	10½ x 16"	Hardcover books
#6	12½" x 19"	Clothing, soft boxed items
#7	14¼" x 20"	Much larger packaged items, framed items, plaques

✔ **Address labels:** You'll need extras because it's always a good idea to toss a duplicate address label inside the box, with the destination address and a return address, in case the outside label falls off or becomes illegible.

✔ **Shipping tape, 2 or 3 inches:** Make sure that you use a strong shipping tape for the outside of the box. Clear plastic will do just fine. There is also box-color tape that works very well for recycling boxes (taping over old shipping information). Remember not to plaster every inch of box with tape; leave space for those *Fragile* and *Insured* rubber stamps.

✔ **Hand-held shipping tape dispensers:** It's quite a bit easier to zzzzzip! tape from a tape dispenser than to unwind it and bite it off with your teeth. Have one dispenser for your special shipping tape and one for your clear tape.

✔ **Lightweight 2-inch clear tape:** For taping the padding around the inside items. I also use a clear strip of tape over the address on the outside of the box so it won't disappear in the rain.

✔ **Scissors:** A pair of large, sharp scissors. Having a hobby knife to trim boxes or shred newspaper is also a good idea.

✔ **Handy liquids:** Three that I like are Goo Gone (which is available in the household supply section of most retail stores and is a wonder at removing unwanted stickers and price tags); WD-40 (the unstick-every-thing standby that works great on getting stickers off plastic); and Un-Du (the best liquid I've found to take labels off cardboard). Lighter fluid also does the trick, but be *very* careful handling it and be sure to clean up thoroughly to remove any residue.

✔ **Rubber stamps/stickers:** Using custom rubber stamps or stickers can save you a bunch of time when preparing your packages. I purchased some "thank you" self-inking rubber stamps to give my parcels some pizazz.

✔ **Thermal label printer:** Once I thought this was a flagrant waste of money, but now I wouldn't be without one (I have two). When you begin shipping several packages a week, you'll find it far more convenient to use a separate label printer for addressing and delivery confirmations. Dymo offers one of the best deals; you can find them on eBay for about $100. If you want to get industrial, try one of the Zebra thermal printers (I use the LP2844). These printers can print labels for FedEx and UPS as well as USPS (you can also get deals on these on eBay). There's a great deal for my readers on these printers, bundled with Endicia software, at www.endicia.com/coolebaytools/.

✔ **Black permanent marker:** These are handy for writing information ("Please leave on porch behind the planter") and the all-important "Fragile" all over the box or "Do Not Bend" on envelopes. I like the big, fat Sharpie markers.

If you plan to sell on eBay in earnest, consider adding a 10-pound weight scale (for weighing packages) to your shipping department. I'm using a super-small 13-pound-maximum scale, which I bought on eBay for only $29.95.

When it comes to fragile items, dishes, pottery, porcelain, china — anything that can chip, crack, or smash into a thousand pieces — *double-box the item*. The boxes should be about 3 inches different on each side. Make sure that you use enough padding so that the interior box is snug. Just give it a big shake. If nothing rattles, ship away!

Packing material: Where to find it

The place to start looking for packing material is the same place you should start looking for things to sell on eBay: your house. Between us, I've done thousands of eBay transactions and never once paid for void fill. I make most of my personal purchases from online vendors (I love e-commerce) and save all the bubble wrap, padding, and packing peanuts I get in the boxes with my orders. Just empty the boxes of void fill and place it into large plastic trash bags — that way, they don't take up much storage space. If you recently got a mail-order shipment box that was used only once — and it's a good, sturdy box with no dents or dings — there's nothing wrong with using it again. Just be sure to completely cover any old labels so the delivery company doesn't get confused.

Beyond the ol' homestead, here are a few other suggestions for places where you can rustle up some packing stuff for your beginning eBay sales:

✔ **Your local supermarket, department store, or drugstore:** You won't be the first person pleading with a store manager for boxes. (Ah, fond memories of moving days past.) Stores like giving them away because it saves them the work of compacting the boxes and putting them in the trash or recycling bin.

I have found that drugstores and beauty-supply stores have a better variety of smaller boxes. But make sure you don't take dirty boxes reeking of food smells.

✔ **The inside of your local supermarket, department store, or drugstore:** Places like Kmart, Walmart, Target, and office-supply stores often have good selections of packing supplies.

✔ **Shippers such as UPS, FedEx, and the U.S. Postal Service:** These shippers offer all kinds of free supplies as long as you use these supplies to ship things with their service.

The Postal Service also ships free boxes, labels, and shipping forms for Express Mail, Priority Mail, and Global Priority Mail to your house. In the United States, you can order by phone (800-222-1811) or online (shop.usps.com). Here are a few rules for USPS orders:

- Specify the service (Priority Mail, Express Mail, or Global Priority Mail) you're using because the boxes and the labels all come with the service name printed all over them, and you can use them only for that specific service.

- Order in bulk. For example, address labels come in rolls of 500 and boxes in packs of 25.

- The boxes come flat, so you have to assemble them. Hey, don't look a gift box in the mouth — they're free!

✔ **eBay and online sellers:** Many terrific eBay sellers are out to offer you really good deals. (You can't beat eBay sellers for quality goods, low prices, and great service.) I recommend the following family-run eBay stores:

- **BubbleFAST** — an eBay seller from the Chicago area — sells tons of reasonably priced bubble wrap, mailers, and more. Find them on eBay or on the website www.bubblefast.com.

- **Royal Mailers** is where lots of folks buy their padded paper envelope mailers for eBay sales. This company also sells Tyvek envelopes, vinyl bubble mailers, zipper-lock plastic bags, air pillows, box sealing tape, and lots more. They offer *free shipping* and a discount of 5 percent to my readers if you use this code: COOLEBAY. Visit their website at www.royalmailers.com.

- **Uline** is where I buy all my shipping boxes for items that do not fit into free Priority Mail boxes. They have shipping boxes for almost any size package and because they ship from several locations in the United States, the cost (and time) of shipping is kept to a minimum. Find them at www.uline.com.

Notice that I mention where these vendors are located. When ordering a large shipment, the distance it has to travel from the vendor's place to yours can tack on quite a bit of cash (and time) to your shipping costs!

Buying Postage Online

Isn't technology great? You no longer have to schlep to the post office every time you need stamps. What's even better, with the new print-it-yourself postage, you can give all your packages directly to your mail carrier. When you install your Internet postage software, you apply for a USPS postal license that allows you to print your own *Information-Based Indicia* (IBI) for your postage. IBI is a barcode printed either on labels or directly on an envelope; it has both human- and machine-readable information about where it was printed, along with some security-related elements. IBI provides you, and the post office, with a much more secure way of getting your valuable packages through the mail.

You can print postage for First Class, Priority, Express, and Parcel Post, and additional postage for delivery confirmation and insurance. If your printer mangles a sheet of labels or an envelope, you can send the printed piece to your Internet postage provider for a refund. Several vendors of Internet-based postage exist, but Endicia.com and Stamps.com are the most popular.

Printing your postage electronically gives a real benefit: the commercial base price reduction, which is available for Priority Mail and Express Mail. For Priority Mail packages weighing 10 pounds or less, commercial base prices average 13 percent lower than retail (at the post office) prices, and are based on zone and weight. For Express Mail, the commercial base prices are 3.5 percent lower than the retail prices.

For international shipping, you'll get 5- and 8-percent discounts on Priority Mail International and Express Mail International.

Preparing Postage with Endicia

In the early '90s, a couple of guys came up with new software to enable people to design direct-mail pieces from the desktop. Wow! What an innovation. With the inexpensive software, you could also produce your own barcoding for the Postal Service. I used that software then, just as I use DAZzle now.

DAZzle — combined with the patented Dial-A-Zip — became the basis for the software that comes free with the Endicia Internet Postage service. There isn't a more robust mailing program on the market.

Endicia has all the basic features and more:

> ✔ **Prints postage for all classes of mail, including international:** From Anniston, Alabama, to Bulawayo, Zimbabwe, the DAZzle software not only prints postage but also lists all your shipping options and

applicable rates. For international mailing, Endicia advises you about any prohibitions (no prison-made goods can be mailed to Botswana), any restrictions, any necessary customs forms, and areas served within the country.

✔ **Provides free tracking numbers for Priority Mail, First Class, and Standard Post:** You can print electronic tracking for Media Mail for only $0.20 additional (a substantial savings from the Postal Service counter purchase).

✔ **Packaging Advisor:** The Endicia software gives you options for your package. After pasting in the recipient's address, you can click to compare the costs of various USPS options based on the ZIP codes provided. I checked one of today's shipments in Figure 12-4.

Figure 12-4:
DAZzle
software,
showing
my shipping
options and
costs.

Packaging Advisor

	Mail Class	Package Type	Price
Origin ZIP:	Priority Mail	Small or Medium Flat Rate Envelope	$5.05
91325-3816	Priority Mail	Small Flat Rate Box	$5.15
	Priority Mail	Legal Flat Rate Envelope	$5.25
	Priority Mail	Flat Rate Padded Envelope	$5.70
Destination ZIP:	Priority Mail	Package (Rectangular)	$6.51
06010-3203	Priority Mail	Package (Non-rectangular)	$6.51
	Priority Mail	Large Envelope (flat)	$6.51
Zone: 8	Priority Mail	Regional Box A (15 lbs max)	$9.88
	Priority Mail	(Medium) Flat Rate Box	$11.30
Weight: 1 lbs	Priority Mail	Large Flat Rate Box	$15.30
	Priority Mail	Regional Box.B (20 lbs max)	$16.13
	Express Mail	Legal Flat Rate Envelope	$18.11
	Express Mail	Flat Rate Padded Envelope	$18.11
	Express Mail	Small or Medium Flat Rate Envelope	$18.11
	Express Mail	Package (Non-rectangular)	$27.68
	Express Mail	Package (Rectangular)	$27.68
	Express Mail	Large Envelope (flat)	$27.68
☐ Only selected class	Express Mail	(Medium) Flat Rate Box	$39.95
	Priority Mail	Regional Box C (25 lbs max)	$47.01
☐ No Flat Rate Envelopes			
☐ Automatically show Packaging Advisor		Close	Help

✔ **Fetches your eBay orders from PayPal:** After connecting your eBay account, the premium version of the service will import your sales and allow you to print in bulk — or one by one and automatically send the tracking number back to eBay.

✔ **Print customs forms:** You no longer have to go to the post office with your international packages. Just print the customs form from the DAZzle software (some are integrated into the label) and give the package to your letter carrier.

✔ **Enables you to design mail pieces:** The software enables you to design envelopes, postcards, and labels with color graphics, logos, and text messages. You can print your labels with postage tracking on anything from plain paper (tape it on with clear tape) to 4" x 6" labels in a label printer.

✓ **Integrates with U-PIC private insurance:** If you're saving time and money by using a private package insurer, you can send your monthly insurance logs electronically to U-PIC at the end of the month.

Endicia offers two levels of service. All the preceding features come with the standard plan for $9.95 a month. The premium plan adds special features, customizable e-mail, enhanced online transaction reports and statistics, business reply mail, return shipping labels (prepaid so your customers won't have to pay for the returns), and stealth indicias for $15.95 a month.

For a free 60-day trial (30 days longer than offered to anyone else) for my readers, go to

http://www.endicia.com/coolebaytools

Shipping directly from eBay

I consider printing labels from eBay or PayPal to be required for all beginning sellers. By using their service, a seller can streamline the buyer's shopping experience, making it simple to buy, click, and pay. Those out in the eBay world who haven't used it find the service to be a life-changing experience. Because you don't need to use additional software or sign up with an additional service, shipping with eBay is a convenient system for those who don't have to ship many packages each week.

eBay shipping services work great when you're just starting out in your business — but after you get rolling, you need a mailing service that includes recordkeeping, such as Endicia or Stamps.com. The issue connected with using eBay for shipping is important: When you process your shipping (UPS or USPS), the shipping amount is deducted from your PayPal (sales revenue) balance. This can cause a bookkeeping nightmare when you're selling on eBay in earnest. Best practices for any business is to keep all expenses separate in the bookkeeping process.

Chapter 13

Troubleshooting Transactions

There's no getting around it: The more transactions you conduct on eBay, the more chances you have of facing some potential pitfalls. In this chapter, I give you pointers on how to handle an obnoxious or difficult buyer as if he or she is your new best friend (for a little while anyway). In addition, I explain how to keep an honest misunderstanding from blowing up into a vitriolic war. You find out how to handle a sale that's (shall I say) on a road to nowhere, how to get some attention, and if it all goes sour, how to sell to the next highest bidder legally and relist the item, and get back the Final Value Fee you paid eBay. There's no way that all of what I mention here will happen to you, but the more you know, the better prepared you'll be.

Dealing with a Buyer Who Doesn't Respond

Most of the time, the post-transaction between buyers and sellers goes smoothly. However, if you have difficulty communicating with the winner of your auction or fixed-price sale, you should know the best way to handle the situation.

You've come to the right place if you want help dealing with potential non-paying buyers. Of course, you should start with good initial post-transaction communication; see Chapter 12 for details. (For more information on how to deal with a fraudulent seller, see Chapter 16.)

Requesting immediate payment

One convenient way to avoid payment issues with a buyer is to request an immediate payment upon purchase. When you list an item for sale, you get the option on fixed-price sales (and auctions with a Buy It Now option) to request an immediate payment from the buyer. When buyers click the Buy It Now button, they are presented with a PayPal payment window requesting immediate payment. In this scenario, the item is not considered sold until the buyer completes the PayPal payment.

Setting buyer requirements

In your My eBay Account area, under Seller Account > Buyer Requirements, there's an area where you can specify who can bid on or buy your items. In this area, you can require that anyone who buys or bids on one of your items falls into some safe categories on eBay. You can require several things from your buyer, including

- ✔ Has an existing PayPal account.
- ✔ Has no Unpaid Item strikes in a set prior period.
- ✔ Has a minimum feedback score.
- ✔ Has a shipping address only in the countries where you state you will ship.

I recommend that you check out this area and select requirements that make you feel more comfortable that you will get paid.

Going into nudge mode

Despite my best efforts, sometimes things fall through the cracks. Buyers should pay for the item without delay through PayPal — or at least pay within the next 24 hours after the close of the sale. Sometimes winners contact sellers immediately, and some use Checkout and pay for the item immediately, which saves you any hassle. However, if you don't hear from the buyer within three business days of your initial contact, my advice is *don't panic.*

People are busy; they travel, they get sick, their computers crash, or sometimes your item simply slips the winner's mind. After three days of no communication (allow for weekends), you can go to your My eBay page and send a payment reminder message. You find the Contact Buyer link on the item's transaction on the My eBay Sold page, as shown in Figure 13-1.

Figure 13-1: The Contact Buyer link in the item's transaction.

If a few more days pass and you still haven't heard from the winner, you need to get into big-time *nudge-nudge mode* — as in, "*<insert userID here>*, remember me and your obligation to buy the Tiffany lamp you purchased on eBay last week?"

Send a polite-but-firm message letting <random eBay user> know that when he/she won or bought your item, they became obligated to pay and complete the transaction. If Mr. (or Ms.) X doesn't intend to buy your item for any reason, he needs to let you know posthaste.

Don't threaten your buyer. The last thing you want to do is add insult to injury in case the buyer is facing a real problem. Besides, if the buyer goes to sleep with the fishes, you'll *never* see your money.

Here's what to include in your nudge-nudge e-mail:

- ✔ A gentle admonishment, such as, "Perhaps this slipped your mind," or "You may have missed my e-mail to you," or "I'm sure you didn't mean to ignore my first e-mail."

- ✔ A gentle reminder that eBay's policy is that every bid is a binding contract. You can even refer the buyer to eBay's rules and regulations if you want.

- ✔ Ask the buyer if there was a problem. Did the buyer order the item by mistake?

- ✔ A date by which you expect to see payment. Gently explain that if the deadline isn't met, you'll have no other choice but to consider the deal invalid.

Technically, you can nullify the transaction if you don't hear from a buyer within three business days. However, eBay members are a forgiving bunch under the right circumstances. I think you might give your buyer a one-week grace period after the listing ends to get in touch with you and set up a payment plan. If, at the end of the grace period, you don't see any real progress toward closing the deal, say goodnight, Gracie. Consider the deal kaput and go directly to the section "Going Badly? Cut Your Losses" (later in this chapter) to find out what recourse you have.

Do a little sleuthing

I'd like to say that history repeats itself, but that would be a cliché. (All right, you caught me, but clichés are memorable because they're so often true.) After you send your polite and gentle nudge-nudge e-mail, but before you decide that the transaction is a lost cause, take a look at the bidder's Feedback as a Buyer history. Figure 13-2 shows you what that feedback looks like.

Figure 13-2:
You can get a good idea of whether a buyer will complete a sale by looking at his or her feedback as a buyer.

To check a bidder's feedback (starting at your item page), do the following:

1. **Click the number in parentheses next to your winner's User ID.**

   This action takes you to the member's feedback profile page.

2. **Click the Feedback as a Buyer tab.**

3. **Scroll down the feedback profile page and read the comments.**

   Check to see whether the bidder has received negative feedback from previous sellers. Make a note of it in case you need some support and background information (should you be chastised at a later date for blocking an unwanted bid).

Blocking a customer

If you've had a bad experience with a particular customer and you don't want that person to be able to bid or buy your items in the future, you can set up a bidder block for his or her User ID. If you block bidders, they can't bid; eBay tells them that they have to contact you by e-mail before their bids will be accepted. You can add or delete bidders from your list at any time. eBay has managed to make the page a little hard to find; try going directly to the Buyer/Bidder Management area at

pages.ebay.com/services/buyandsell/biddermanagement.html

If the buyer's feedback profile provides any indication that the buyer has gone AWOL in the past, start thinking about getting out of the transaction before too much time passes. If the buyer looks to be on the level, continue to give him or her the benefit of the doubt.

Stepping things up a notch

If the item is a large transaction and you really want it to go through, your next course of action is to contact the winner by phone. To get the contact information of an eBay member for transaction purposes only, do the following:

1. **Click the Advanced Search link, which is next to the Search box on the top of most eBay pages.**

   You arrive at the Advanced Search area.

2. **Click the Find Contact Information link, which is under the Members area in the left-side link box.**

3. **In the Contact Info box, type the User ID of the person you're trying to contact and the item number of the transaction in question.**

4. **Click the Search button.**

   eBay e-mails you the registered contact information of the person with whom you want to be in touch and also sends your contact information to that person.

Wait a day before calling the person. I like sending a last-chance e-mail after seven days that says you want to put the item back up on eBay if the buyer is no longer interested. Also mention that you want to apply for any credits you can get from eBay due to an incomplete transaction. If enough money is involved in the transaction, and you feel it's worth the investment, make the call to the winner. eBay automatically sends your request and your information to the bidder, and that may be enough of a nudge to get some action.

If you do get the person on the phone, keep the conversation like your e-mail — friendly but businesslike. Explain who you are and when the auction closed, and ask if any circumstances have delayed the bidder's reply. Often the buyer will be so shocked to hear from you that you'll receive payment immediately — *or* you'll know this person is a complete deadbeat.

Other Possible Auction Problems

I'm not quite sure why, but where money is involved, sometimes people act weird. Buyers may suddenly decide that they can't purchase an item after they've made a commitment, or there may be payment problems or shipping problems. Whatever the problem, look no further than this section to find out how to make things better.

Buyer back out? Try Second Chance offer

Every time eBay members place a bid or click the Buy It Now button, they make a commitment to purchase the item in question — in theory, anyway. In the real world, people have second thoughts, despite the rules. You have every right to be angry that you're losing money and wasting your time. Remind the buyer that making a bid is a binding contract. But, unfortunately, if the winner won't pay up, you can't do much except apply for a Final Value Fee refund and lick your wounds. Jump to Chapter 6 to find out more about buyer's remorse.

A seller's nightmare

I was on Facebook, messaging with some other eBay sellers (feel free to find me on Facebook https://www.facebook.com/MarshaCollierFanPage — all my readers are my friends!) and one was bemoaning a recent transaction. A seller always wants to sell a product, and a cooperative buyer makes the entire process pleasant. This particular seller was having a problem receiving payment from a buyer. Here's what she said:

"The buyer first said her boss opened a PayPal account for her under his e-mail address and she couldn't access it and now her daughter used her credit card so she can't pay me. I tried to tell her she can add another e-mail address to the PayPal account and make it the primary but..."

Is this fair? I recommended to the seller that she offer to mutually close the deal through eBay so she'd be free to resell the item to someone else. A buyer has a responsibility to carry out his or her part of the transaction as seamlessly as we expect service from the seller when we buy.

You can also sell additional merchandise by making a Second Chance offer when you have multiples of the same item in stock and wish to accept any of the underbidders' final bids.

Keeping your cool

By all means, if the buyer of your item tells you that the transaction can't be completed, no matter what the reason, remain professional despite your anger. For one thing, at least such a would-be buyer has the heart to break the news to you instead of ignoring your e-mail and phone calls.

When Plan A fails, try Plan B, or even C — Second Chance offer

You have several options if the winner backs out:

- ✔ **You can make a *Second Chance offer*: Offer the item to another bidder from the auction.** eBay offers a little-known feature called Second Chance offer, which protects buyers just as if they were the winner of the auction. This is a great feature that turned the *previously eBay-illegal* practice of side deals into fair and approved deals. You can make a Second Chance offer to any underbidder from your auction (at the amount of that bidder's high bid) for up to 60 days after the auction's end. The steps that follow this list detail how to make a Second Chance offer.

- ✔ **You can request a full or partial Final Value Fee credit and then relist the item and hope it sells again.** (I give you more information on requesting a Final Value Fee credit and relisting your item later in this chapter.) Who knows? This bidder may actually *earn* you money in the long run if you relist the item and get a higher winning bid.

You can make a Second Chance offer in two ways. Just follow these steps:

1. **Go to the completed auction page.**

   On the top of the page, you'll see some transaction-related links, as shown in Figure 13-3.

Figure 13-3:
After an auction is completed, you find a bunch of handy links on the page.

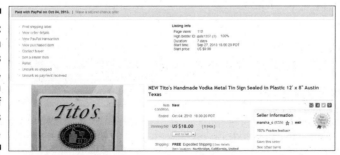

2. **Click the Make a Second Chance offer link.**

   You're taken to the Second Chance Offer page, which has the auction number already filled in.

3. **Click Continue.**

   A page appears, showing all your underbidders and their high bids.

4. **Select an underbidder (or more than one underbidder if you have multiples of the item) to offer the item to; then click the Review Second Chance Offer link.**

   When you make a Second Chance offer, you can give the recipient one, three, five, or seven days to take you up on the offer. You are not charged a listing fee for the item, but you are responsible for Final Value Fees if the transaction is completed.

5. **Check over the offer and then click Submit to send it to the underbidder.**

Alternatively, you can go to your My eBay Sold area and click the drop-down menu next to the item listing on the page. Choose Second Chance Offer, and you'll arrive at the decision-making page from there, as shown in Figure 13-4.

Figure 13-4: Here's where you may get out of a difficult situation by offering your item to one of the underbidders in the unsuccessful auction.

The item you send is busted — and so are you

Uh-oh! Could it be true? Could you have sent the wrong item? Or is it possible that the crystal vase you thought you packed so well is a sad pile of shards at the bottom of a torn box? If so, read Chapter 12 as soon as you take care of this catastrophe so that you can get some hints on packing and insurance.

Leaving feedback after an imperfect auction experience

If a buyer never materializes, backs out, bounces a check, or moves slower than a glacier to send your payment (but wants the item sent overnight from Boston to Khartoum at your expense), you need to think about how you want to word your feedback. As a seller, you can no longer leave negative feedback, but you can still write in a comment for other sellers to take heed. But if you do that, remember to stick to the facts and don't get personal. You can always leave *no* feedback.

Here are a few feedback tips:

✔ If the transaction was shaky but everything turned out all right in the end, go ahead and leave positive feedback, but gauge it, depending on how tough things went.

✔ If a blizzard stopped planes out of Chicago for three days and that's why it took a long time to get online to pay, take a deep breath, blame the fates, and leave positive feedback with a fair comment.

✔ If the buyer was a living nightmare, take a long break before getting nasty — and have someone you love and trust read it before you send something into the virtual world that you can't take back.

For more information on leaving feedback, check out Chapters 4 and 6.

It's time to do some serious problem-solving. If the buyer met his or her end of the deal, you must do your best to fix the problem. Your communication skills are your number-one asset in this situation, so get to work.

Picking up the pieces

No matter how carefully you pack an item, sometimes it arrives on the buyer's doorstep mangled, broken, or squashed. News of this unfortunate event travels back to you fast. Shortly after opening the package, the buyer will let you know — hopefully in a message, versus filing a complaint — how unhappy he or she is. (Sometimes such missives aren't very polite, but stay calm.)

When you send an item of value to a customer, it's best to insure the package. eBay holds you responsible for seeing that the item arrives as described when it reaches the customer, so it's best to insure irreplaceable or high-value items. (See Chapter 12 for more on shipping insurance).

If a package is lost, you'll know it because the tracking number never shows delivery, and the buyer tells you the package is a no-show. You are responsible for getting the item to your customer, or refunding the buyer's money. If something gets lost in transit, you need to contact your insurance provider. If your item isn't located in 30 days, it's declared lost, and there's a round of paperwork and processing to do before you get your money.

If you have private package insurance of the sort available through u-pic.com, the process is much simpler than dealing with the USPS or UPS. You don't have to contact the shipper; you merely have to contact the insurance company and place a claim.

Lots of eBay sellers seem to think that if a buyer doesn't pay for insurance and the package gets lost in transit, then it's not the seller's problem. They couldn't be more wrong. The Federal Trade Commission has a strict rule covering mail-order merchandise delivery. The short version is that if your item doesn't get to the buyer within 30 days, you must refund the payment. The long version can be found at the FTC website:

```
http://business.ftc.gov/documents/bus02-business-guide-
mail-and-telephone-order-merchandise-rule
```

Boxed out of a claim

In my experience, neither UPS nor the U.S. Postal Service will pay on an insurance claim if they feel you did a lousy job of packing. Always use good packing products, wrap carefully, and get ready to plead your case.

Every shipping company has its own procedure for complaints. But here's the one thing they do have in common: No procedure is hassle-free. If you have insured through your shipper, contact those folks just as soon as a problem arises — and have your value documentation at the ready.

You have regrets — seller's remorse

You've undoubtedly heard about buyer's remorse. Here's a new one for you — *seller's remorse.* If you're selling your velvet Elvis footstool because your spouse said, "It's me or that footstool!" and then decide that your spouse should have known how much you revered the King when you went to Graceland on your honeymoon, you can end the listing. Read "Making changes or canceling bids" and "Ending your listing early," later in this chapter.

Going Badly? Cut Your Losses

So your auction is cruising along just fine for a couple of days when you notice that the same eBay user who didn't pay on a previous auction is your current high bidder. You don't want to get burned again, do you? Of course not; *cancel* this deadbeat's bid before it's too late (perhaps you should have put that person on your Blocked Bidder list?). Although canceling bids — or, for that matter, entire auctions — isn't easy (you have a load of explaining to do, pardner), eBay does allow it.

If you feel that you have to wash your hands of a listing that's given you nothing but grief, it doesn't mean that you have to lose money on the deal. Read on to find out the protocol for laying a bad auction to rest and beginning anew.

Many of these functions are also available from the drop-down menus on the right side of the item's listing on the My eBay Sell page.

Making changes or canceling bids

Face the facts: Oftimes things don't go as planned. You did your very best, and things didn't work out. Before you kill an auction completely, if there are no bids, see whether you can improve it by improving your description or reducing your opening bid. You may also cancel a bid, which removes a bidder from your auction, but the auction continues running.

When you cancel a bid, you need to provide an explanation, which goes on record for all to see. You may have a million reasons for thinking your auction is a bust, but eBay says your explanation had better be good. Here are some eBay-approved reasons for canceling a bid (or even an entire auction):

- ✔ A bidder informs you that he or she is retracting a bid, or asks you whether it's okay to back out.

- ✔ Despite your best efforts to determine who your high bidder is, you can't find out — and you get no response to your e-mails or phone calls.

- ✔ You decide, mid-auction, that you can't sell your item because you've learned it was already sold in an outside venue — or the dog ate it. (You must cancel all bids and end the listing in this instance.)

I can't drive this point home hard enough: *Explain why you're canceling a bid, and your explanation had better be good.* You can cancel any bid for any reason you want, but if you can't give a good explanation of why you did it, you will be sorry. Citing past transaction problems with the current high bidder is okay, but canceling a bidder who lives in Japan because you don't feel like shipping overseas — after you said you'd ship internationally — could give your feedback history the aroma of week-old sushi.

To cancel a bid, do the following (you can also reach the Bidder Cancellation Form by going to `http://offer.ebay.com/ws/eBayISAPI.dll?CancelBidShow` and typing in the item number):

1. **Go to the listing page.**

2. **Click the Bid History link.**

   You're taken to the Bid History page.

3. **Scroll to the bottom of the bidding history and click the Cancel Bids link.**

   You'll be brought to a page outlining eBay's policies on bidding.

4. **Scroll down to the Canceling Bids area and click the Canceling Bids link.**

   You arrive at the Canceling Bids page, as shown in Figure 13-5.

Figure 13-5: Use this form to remove a bidder from one of your auctions.

Canceling bids placed on your listing

Bids should only be canceled for good reasons (see examples). Remember, canceled bids cannot be restored.

Enter information about your listing below and click Cancel Bid.

[   ]
Item number

[   ]
User ID of the bid you are canceling

Reason for cancellation:

[   ]
(80 characters or less)

[cancel bid]   [clear form]

5. **Type the item number, the User ID for the bid you're canceling, and the reason for canceling the bid.**

6. **Click the Cancel Bid button.**

   Be sure that you really want to cancel a bid before you click the Cancel Bid button. Canceled bids can never be reinstated.

Canceling bids means that you removed an individual bidder (or several bidders) from your auction, but the auction itself continues running. If you want to end the auction completely, read on.

Blocking bidders

If you have a bidder who just doesn't get the message and continually bids on your auctions despite the fact that you've e-mailed and told him or her not to, you can block the bidder from ever participating in your auctions. You can create a list of such bidders to prevent them from bidding temporarily or permanently, and you can edit the list at any time. You can find the page from the same page as described in the preceding section. Click Block Bidders and then create your list. Alternatively, you can go directly to this address:

```
pages.ebay.com/services/buyandsell/biddermanagement.html
```

Ending your listing early

If you put your auction up for a week and the next day your boss says you have to go to China for a month, or your landlord says you have to move out immediately so he can fumigate for a week, you can end your auction early. But ending an auction early isn't a decision to be taken lightly. You miss all the last-minute bidding action.

Also know that sellers are not allowed to cancel bids and end listings early in order to avoid selling an item that did not meet the desired sale price. That would be a violation of eBay's reserve-price policy. (**Hint**: You should have put a reserve price on the item.)

There are only two circumstances in which eBay will allow you to cancel a listing without violating policy:

- ✔ The item is lost, broken, or otherwise no longer available for sale.
- ✔ You made a mistake when creating the listing, or entering the starting price or reserve price.

You may also not end a listing if there are less than 12 hours to go before the item's auction ends. If there is a bid on your item, you are bound to sell it to the high bidder for his or her bid price.

eBay makes it clear that ending your auction early does not relieve you of the obligation to sell this item to the highest bidder. To relieve your obligation, you must first cancel all the bids, and then end the auction, and you will be charged a Final Value Fee for the amount of the highest bid. Of course, if no one has bid yet, you have nothing to worry about.

When you cancel an auction, you have to write a short explanation that appears on the bidding history section of your auction page. Anyone who bid on the item may message you for a written explanation. If bidders think your explanation doesn't hold water, don't be surprised if your inbox becomes nasty.

Bidding on your own item is against the rules. Once upon a time, you could cancel an auction by outbidding everyone on your own item and then ending the auction. But some eBay users abused this privilege by bidding on their own items merely to boost the sales price. Shame on them.

To end an auction early, go to your My eBay Active Selling page and in the drop-down menu next to the listing, choose End Item. You will be required to sign in again. You can also go directly to `http://offer.ebay.com/ws/eBayISAPI.dll?CancelBidShow`.

Then follow these steps:

1. **Click the appropriate link: either Cancel Bids and End Listing Early or Sell Item to High Bidder and End Listing Early.**

2. **On the next page, select a reason for ending your listing.**

3. **Click the End Your Listing button.**

    An Ended Listing page appears, and eBay sends an End of Listing Confirmation e-mail to you and to the highest bidder.

Filing an Unpaid Item case

If closing a successful auction is the thrill of victory, finding out that your buyer is a nonpaying bidder is the agony of defeat. Adding insult to injury, eBay still charges you a Final Value Fee, even if the high bidder never sends you a cent. But you can do something about it. You can file for a *Final Value Fee credit.*

To qualify for a Final Value Fee credit, you must prove to eBay that one of the following events occurred:

✔ The winning buyer never responded to invoices or reminders.

✔ The winning buyer backed out of the sale.

✔ The winning buyer's payment did not clear or was never received.

✔ The winning buyer returned the item to you, and you refunded the payment.

If both you and the buyer decide that it's okay not to go through with the transaction, that's okay with eBay, too. eBay will allow you to get back your Final Value Fee by going through the Resolution Center process. You'll find an option that will absolve the buyer of any wrongdoing with eBay's unpaid-item police.

The instant you open a case, eBay shoots off an e-mail to the buyer of your item (copying you on the e-mail) and warns the eBay user of his or her nonpaying status.

There are two ways to handle this situation. You can open a case manually or use eBay's automated Unpaid Item Assistant.

The Unpaid Item Assistant will open and close cases for you. Once the assistant opens a case, the buyer has four days to make payment. If the buyer pays, the case is closed. If the buyer doesn't pay, the case is automatically closed and you get a Final Value Fee credit.

To use the Unpaid Item Assistant, you will need to opt in from your My eBay page:

1. **Move your mouse pointer over the Account tab.**

2. **Click the Site Preferences link on the drop-down menu that appears.**

3. **Scroll down the page to the Unpaid Item Assistant heading.**

4. **Click the Show link (and then Edit if it appears) to the right of the heading, and then click Edit.**

   A page will open as shown in Figure 13-6.

Figure 13-6: Setting up the automated Unpaid Item Assistant.

Unpaid Item Assistant Preferences

Unpaid Item Assistant can manage the unpaid item process for you, according to your preferences. Learn more

- Yes — I want Unpaid Item Assistant to open and close cases on my behalf

   Open a case if payment hasn't been received after 8 days ▾

   (!) You are allowing buyers to make combined payments within 3 days. If you'd like cases to open sooner, please click here to lower your combined payments setting.

   Send me an email

   When Unpaid Item Assistant opens a case   Real-time   ▾

   When Unpaid Item Assistant closes a case   Real-time   ▾

   Automatically relist the item when case is closed with no payment ⓘ

   No ▾

   Automatically request for my eBay Giving Works donation refund ⓘ

   No ▾

   Exclude buyers from Unpaid Item Assistant

   If you exclude members , the assistant will not automatic open a case with them. You'll open the cases manually in the Resolution Center.

   Exclusion list:

   You can exclude up to 5,000 user IDs. Separate multiple user IDs with a comma,space,new line, or semi-colon.

- No thanks – I'll use the standard unpaid item process as needed, opening and closing cases manually.

Important:

- Changing your preference will not impact cases that are already open.
- Currently, Unpaid Item Assistant works for listings that use eBay Checkout. If you use a different checkout service, please contact the vendor to see if Unpaid Item Assistant is supported.

Save   Cancel

5. **Click the radio button next to Yes to indicate you want cases opened automatically.**

   A drop-down menu appears.

6. **Select a number of days that you want to allow your buyer to pay for the item before closing a case on the transaction.**

7. **Click the Save button.**

If you want to do this manually, and at least 7 days — no more than 45 days — have elapsed since the end of the auction, you can apply for a Full Final Value Fee credit. First, however, you must file an Unpaid Item Alert:

1. **Go to your My eBay Sold view.**

   Find the transaction in question on the list of sold items.

2. **Click the drop-down menu at the right of the listing and then choose Resolve a Problem.**

   You're taken to the Resolution Center.

3. **Select the I Sold an Item and Haven't Received My Payment Yet option and click Continue.**

4. **Sign in to your account and enter your User ID and password.**

   The Report an Unpaid Item Case form appears.

5. **Type the item number of the listing in question (if it's not already there) and then click the Continue button.**

6. **You'll be asked to select an issue from a drop-down menu that applies to your situation. After you do, click Continue.**

7. **Review everything you've entered to be sure that it's correct and then click Continue.**

   If you and the buyer mutually agreed not to complete the transaction, when you click Continue, you see the Final Value Fee Credit Request page.

You need to wait *at least* seven days after the listing ends to file a case and then another seven days before you can apply for a Final Value Fee credit. I think it's jumping the gun to label someone a nonpaying bidder after only seven days — try to contact the bidder again unless the bidder sends you a message about backing out (or you have good cause to believe that you have a deadbeat on your hands). If you still want to file for your Final Value Fee credit after seven days, do the following:

1. **On your My eBay page, hover your cursor over the Account tab. When the drop-down menu appears, choose Resolution Center.**

   You're taken to the Resolution Center.

2. **Under the Your Cases heading, find the transaction in question.**

3. **Click the View Dispute link under the status column.**

   You're now in the area where you may respond to any comments the buyer has left regarding why he or she hasn't yet paid for your item.

4. **Enter your response (if any) to the buyer in the messages area and click Submit Response, or to get your Final Value Fee refund, click Close Dispute.**

5. **Click the Close Dispute button on the bottom of the page.**

   You're taken to the Credit Request Process Completed page, which confirms that your refund is being processed by eBay.

When your listing ends, you have up to 45 days after the auction closes to request a credit. After 45 days, kiss your refund goodbye; eBay won't process it.

Anyone caught applying for a refund on a successful item transaction can be suspended or something worse — after all, such an action is a clear-cut case of fraud.

If you want to verify eBay's accounting, grab your calculator and use Table 9-2 in Chapter 9 to check the math. (Ah, calculators. Why couldn't I have had one of those in high-school algebra class?)

But is she a natural blonde?

Here's an example of an item that would have made the seller a bundle if he or she had done a little more strategizing up front:

Platinum Mackie Barbie: Beautiful Platinum Bob Mackie Barbie. MIB (removed from box once, only to scan). The doll comes with shoes, stand, booklet, and Mackie drawing. The original plastic protects her hair and earrings. Buyer adds $10 for shipping and insurance. The starting price was $9.99, and even though the bidding went to $256, the seller's reserve price was not met, and the item didn't sell. And the Second Chance offer didn't bite.

When relisting this item, the seller might do well to lower the reserve price and add much more to the description about the importance and rarity of the doll (unless, of course, $256 was far below what the seller wanted to make on the doll).

Déjà vu — relisting your item

Despite all your best efforts, sometimes your auction ends with no bids or bids that are not even close to your reserve price. Or maybe a buyer won your item, but the transaction didn't go through. eBay takes pity on you and offers you the chance to pick yourself up, dust yourself off, and start all over again.

The best way to improve your chances of selling a relisted item is by making changes to the listing. eBay says the majority of the items put up for auction should sell. If you sell your item the second time around (in most cases), eBay rewards you with a refund of your Insertion Fee. You receive your refund after at least one billing cycle. Accept this refund as a reward for learning the ropes.

In the case of an unpaid item, you may (only in this situation) qualify for an Insertion Fee credit by relisting the item. If the item sells the second time, eBay will refund the Insertion Fee for relisting.

You *must* only use eBay's Relist feature to receive the credit. After the item is filed as unpaid, you can use the Relist link on the unpaid item page or do the following:

1. **Go to your My eBay page.**

2. **On the left side of the page in the Selling area, click the Sold link.**

   You arrive at the page without Sold Listings. You will be able to find the unpaid item because it's specially marked. See Figure 13-7 for an example.

3. **Click the Relist link from the drop-down menu next to the unpaid item.**

Figure 13-7: Finding your unpaid item for relisting on the Sold items page (note that I have already relisted this item).

To be eligible for a refund of your Insertion Fee, here's the scoop:

- ✔ You must relist no more than 90 days after closing the original auction.

- ✔ You can get credit only if you got no bids in your original auction, or if the bids you got did not equal the reserve in your reserve-price auction.

- ✔ You can change anything about your auction item description, price, duration, and minimum price, but you can't sell a different item.

- ✔ If you set a reserve price in your original auction, you must set the same reserve, lower it, or cancel the reserve altogether. If you set a higher price or add a reserve, you're not eligible for a relisting credit.

If your item doesn't sell after two tries, better take a different tack. If you want to be eligible for a new Insertion-Fee refund (when your item hasn't sold twice in a row), you must use the Sell Similar option. This sets up the item in a new cycle for eBay. To get your third shot at selling, do the following (from the Unsold section of your My eBay Selling page):

1. **Click the drop-down menu next to the auction item that you want to relist and choose Sell Similar.**

   You're taken to the original listing form with all the information filled in.

2. **Make your changes to the auction (I hope major ones, as mentioned further on), launch it, and pray!**

The more specific your item title, the more you improve your odds of being profitable. If you're selling an old Monopoly game, don't just title it **Old Monopoly board game**; call it **Rare 1959 Monopoly Game Complete in Box**. For more information about listing items, see Chapter 10.

Here's a list of ideas that you can use to improve your auction's odds for success:

- ✔ **Change the item category.** See if the item sold better in another category (see Chapter 3).

- ✔ **Add a picture.** If two identical items are up for auction at the same time, the item with a photo gets more and higher bids. Zoom in on Chapter 14.

- ✔ **Spruce up the title and description.** Make it enticing and grab those search engines. Breeze on over to Chapter 10.

- ✔ **Set a lower minimum bid.** The first bidders will think they're getting a bargain, and others will want a hot item. Mosey on over to Chapter 10.

✔ **Set a lower reserve price or cancel the reserve.** A reserve price often scares away bidders who fear it's too high. See (yup) Chapter 10 for ways to make your reserve more palatable to prospective bidders.

✔ **Change the duration of the auction.** Maybe you need some more time. Go to (you guessed it) Chapter 10.

Long-time eBay veterans say that reducing or canceling your reserve price makes an auction very attractive to buyers.

Chapter 14

Increase Your Profits with Pictures and Other Strategies

You may be enjoying most of what eBay has to offer, and you're probably having some good buying adventures. If you're selling, you're experiencing the excitement of making money. But there's more. Welcome to eBay, the advanced class. Although eBay requires you to have at least one photo of your item (at least 500 pixels on the longest side), the more images you add to your listing, the more it will be noticed.

In this chapter, you go to the head of the class by discovering some insider tips on how to enhance your listings with images and descriptive text. Successful eBay sellers know that pictures (also called *images*) really help sell items. This chapter gives you the basics on how to create great images. I also give you advice on linking pictures to your items so that buyers around the world can view them.

Using Images in Your Listings

Would you buy an item you couldn't see? Most people won't, especially if they're interested in purchasing items that they want to display or clothes they intend to wear. Without a picture, you can't tell whether a seller's idea of good quality is anything like yours — or if the item is really what you're looking for.

Welcome to the cyberworld of *imaging,* where pictures are called not pictures but *images,* and your monitor isn't a monitor but a *display.* (Certainly your smartphone isn't exactly just a "phone" either.) With a digital camera or a scanner and software, you can manipulate your images — spin, crop, and color-correct — so that they grab viewers by the lapels. Even cooler: When you're happy with your creation, you can add it to your eBay listing for others to see.

Don't rule out using smartphone images on eBay. These days, pictures taken on many smartphones rival those taken on digital cameras. Consider the top phones from manufacturers like Samsung Galaxy series, Apple iPhone, and HTC. The tech news website `cnet.com` features a page that offers updated reviews and compares smartphone cameras head to head. Be sure to check out the latest before you buy.

Sellers, take heed and read these other reasons why you should use your *own* well-made digital images in your item pages, as well as eBay's stock photos (when available):

✔ If you don't have your own picture, potential buyers or bidders may wonder whether you're deliberately hiding the item from view because you know something is wrong with it. Paranoid? Maybe. Practical? You bet.

✔ Fickle shoppers don't even bother reading an item description if they can't see the item. Maybe they were traumatized in English class.

✔ Taking your own pictures shows that you actually have the item in your possession. Many scam artists take images from a manufacturer's website to illustrate their bogus sales on eBay. Why risk appearing suspect? Snap a quick picture!

✔ Everyone's doing it. I hate to pressure you, but lots of digital images are *de rigueur* for items on eBay, so if you're not using more than one, you're not reaching the widest possible number of people who would buy your item. eBay requires that you use at least one. From that point of view, you're not doing the most you can to serve your potential customers' needs if you don't use multiple images; it's just good business.

So which is better for capturing images: digital cameras or digital scanners? As with all gadgets, here's the classic answer: It depends. For my money, it's hard to beat a digital camera. But before you go snag one, decide what kind of investment (and how big) you plan to make in your eBay sales.

If you buy a digital SLR, be sure to check the manufacturer's website to see if older, traditional lenses can be used on the camera you buy. It's often the case with the major brands, although digital lenses don't have to be as "good" as the old lenses were — due to all the electronic manipulation that goes on inside the new cameras. Next, go to eBay and see what kind of deals you can find on compatible lenses.

Whether you buy new or used digital equipment on eBay, make sure that it comes with a warranty. If you *don't* get a warranty, Murphy's Law practically ensures that your digital equipment will break the second time you use it.

Choosing a digital camera

If price isn't a factor, you should buy the highest-quality digital camera you can afford, especially if you plan to use images for items that vary in size and shape. By *highest quality,* I don't necessarily mean a camera with vast amounts of megapixels; I mean a camera from a quality manufacturer that has a high-power optical zoom and a good (nonplastic) lens.

Samsung, Sony, Canon, Kodak, and Nikon all make good basic digital cameras. You can find them for about $150 (easily found on eBay for even less). Middle-of-the-road new (and quality used) digital cameras sell for between $100 and $75. Compare prices at computer stores and on the web.

Digital shooting for eBay, now with a Samsung Smart Camera

I've been on eBay since 1996, so I've taken lots of pictures to promote my online sales. I'm pretty happy with the quality of most of my own images. When I've sold paper ephemera, I usually just lay the item on a scanner — and scan away. It's still the best way to get a good image of that type of item. I started early on with an Olympus camera, but quickly changed to the Sony Mavica FD-73. The FD-73 was one of the first that had a 10X digital zoom, which helps with intricate close-ups. Then I upgraded to a used FD-92 with an 8X optical zoom (a newer model that added a memory stick). There was another Sony, a Canon, and a Nikon after that.

Recently I purchased a smart camera. A smart camera is just like a smartphone, only it turns a pocket camera into something special. I bought a Samsung WB250F — a fancy Android-powered 14+-megapixel camera with

a 18X zoom. To be honest, it's way too much camera for my eBay photo shoots, but you can buy them now for as low as $150.

One great thing about my "smart camera" is that it will send images over Wi-Fi from the camera to my SkyDrive, or even to a smartphone, which makes for easy uploading. Newer cameras not only add Wi-Fi and fantastic zoom capabilities, but *image stabilization* — which holds the camera steady when zoomed in for ultra macro close-ups. If you've ever taken a picture fully zoomed, you know that the slightest breath can jiggle the camera and blur the resulting image. The camera can also be set to Manual mode, if you don't want to use the auto-features.

Prices are getting lower for cameras that are loaded with features. Consider buying a smart camera; they are well worth the price!

A great place to buy digital cameras is (surprise!) eBay. Just do a search of some popular manufacturers, such as Canon, Samsung, Sony, and Nikon, and you will find pages of listings of both new and used digital cameras.

When shopping for a digital camera, look at the following features:

- **Resolution:** Look for a camera that has a low resolution of at least 1024 × 768 pixels. This isn't hard to find because new cameras tout their strength in *megapixels* (millions of pixels). You don't need that high a resolution for eBay because your pictures will not be printed; instead, they're shown ultimately on a monitor. A *pixel* is a tiny dot of information that, when grouped with other pixels, forms an image onscreen. The more pixels an image has, the clearer and sharper the image is; the more memory the image scarfs up, however, the slower it can show up on a screen. This lag becomes more important when you optionally add images to your description. When you upload images to eBay, they compress them for optimum viewing and loading as part of the item page.

  The minimum requirement (eBay's rules) is that your image must be 500 pixels on the longest side; they recommend images to be at least 1600 pixels for best reproduction. A 1024 × 768-pixel image may seem paltry next to the 14-million-pixel punch of today's digital cameras, but trust me: No one viewing your listings will ever know the difference. And pictures included in the description will load a *lot* faster.

  You want only high-pixel, high-resolution images for printing. The terms ppi and dpi (found when you scan photos) only affect the printed size of the final picture. The human eye sees photo prints with printer output resolutions over 240 ppi (pixels per inch) as continuous-tone images, even though the image is actually made up of slightly overlapping dots of ink.

  Digital images for the web or e-mail attachments usually run between 150 × 250 pixels for "thumbnail" images to as large as 1024 × 768 pixels. Images of 600 × 800 and smaller will fit on almost all monitors without requiring scrolling.

- **Optical zoom:** Here's where the camera manufacturers try to pull the wool over consumer's eyes. They sell cameras with an optical and a digital zoom. The *optical zoom* is a true zoom done by the camera, the lens, and its built-in CCD (computer chip in cameras that converts light into electronic data) — but a *digital zoom* is virtual; it's *interpolated* through software in the camera. That means it makes up data to fill in any holes it doesn't capture. You've seen this effect if you've ever tried to enlarge a picture from the web in a software program — it gets all blurry.

  If you ever plan on shooting close-ups, look for a high-quality optical zoom.

✔ **Storage type:** Smart card? SDHC? MicroSD card? CompactFlash card? Memory stick? (Whew.) The instructions that come with your camera explain how to transfer images from your media type to your computer. (No instructions? Check the manufacturer's website.) Most computers have card slots into which you can insert your camera's memory card; the computer reads the card like it's a teeny-tiny disk drive. I rarely take out my camera's card; I upload my images to SkyDrive via Wi-Fi, and then edit if necessary on my computer.

A versatile way to get the best images of items that require extreme close-ups (such as jewelry, stamps, currency, coins) is to use a super device called a Cloud Dome. When photographing complex items, no matter how good your camera is, you may find it difficult to capture the item cleanly and exactly (especially the colors and brightness of gems and metals). Your camera mounts to the top of this Cloud Dome, and pictures are taken inside the translucent plastic dome. Cloud Dome now also makes a Nimbus Dome, to be used with your smartphone.

The dome diffuses the light over the entire surface of the object to reveal all its intricate details. You can purchase Cloud Domes on eBay or from the manufacturer's website at www.clouddome.com. Even in black and white, you can see the difference that a Cloud Dome can make when taking pictures of jewelry, as shown Figure 14-1.

Figure 14-1: Before and after pictures of items shot through a Cloud Dome.

Choosing a scanner

If you plan to sell flat items such as autographs, stamps, books, or documents — or if you need a good piece of business equipment that can double as a copier, printer, and fax machine — consider getting an all-in-one printer that has a digital scanner. I have an HP Color Laser Pro 200 because I resent paying for ink refills continually, and it was quite reasonably priced. Whether you choose inkjet or laser, you can find used all-in-ones on eBay for around $100, or a brand-new one for about $200.

Here's what you need to look for when you buy a scanner:

- **Resolution:** As with printers and photocopiers, the resolution of digital scanning equipment is measured in *dots per inch* (dpi). The more dpi, the greater the resolution.

  Some scanners can provide resolutions as high as 12800 dpi, which looks awesome when you print the image, but all the rez you need to dress up your eBay listings is (are you ready?) 72 or 96 dpi (dots or pixels per inch)! That's it. Your images will look great and won't take up much storage space on your computer's hard drive. Basic scanners can scan images at resolutions of up to 1200 dpi, so even they are far more powerful than you need for your eBay images.

- **Flatbed:** If you're planning to use your scanner to scan pictures of documents (or even items in boxes), a flatbed scanner is your best bet. Flatbeds work just like old-school copiers: You simply lay your item or box on the glass and scan away.

Making Your Picture a Thing of Beauty

The idea behind using images in your listings is to attract tons of potential buyers. With that goal in mind, you should try to create the best-looking images possible, no matter what kind of technology you're using to capture them.

Get it on camera

Point-and-shoot may be okay for a group shot at some historical monument, but illustrating your sale is a whole different idea. Your digital camera might be best used in manual mode (versus auto) so you can make adjustments to your images. Now that we have digital cameras, experimenting takes a whole lot less time. However you use your camera, there are some basic photographic guidelines that can give you better results.

For more on using scanners, read ahead to the next section, "Yes, I scan." Then c'mon back to these dos and don'ts to ensure that your digital image is a genuine enhancement to your online sale:

✔ **Do** take the picture of your item outside, in daylight, whenever possible. That way the camera can catch all possible details and color.

✔ **Do** forget about fancy backgrounds; they distract viewers from your item. Put small items on a neutral-colored, nonreflective towel or cloth; put larger items in front of a neutral-colored wall or curtain. You might even buy an *infinity board* on eBay to use as a background. You'll cut out almost all the background anyway when you crop your images. (This chapter explains how to prepare your picture.)

✔ **Do** use extra lighting. You can do this with your camera's flash mode or with extra photo lighting on stands. Use extra lighting even when you're taking the picture outside. The extra lighting acts as *fill light* — it adds more light to the item, filling in some of the shadowed spots.

✔ **Don't** get so close to the item that the additional light washes out (over-exposes) the image. The easiest way to figure out the best distance is by trial and error. Start close and keep moving farther away until you get the results you want. Digital cameras make this easy: You can see the picture seconds after you shoot it, keep it and modify it, erase it, and start again.

✔ **Do** take two or three acceptable versions of your image; you can choose the best one later on your computer.

✔ **Don't** use incandescent light bulbs or fluorescent kitchen lighting to illuminate your photos. Incandescent lighting can make items look yellowish, and fluorescent lights lend a bluish tone to your photos. Some sellers use GE Reveal incandescent bulbs; they throw a good-quality light which, when combined with natural daylight, produces an even tone. My favorites are the 5,000-degrees-Kelvin compact fluorescent bulbs. They have come down in price and take a special fixture, but with a 10,000-hour lifespan, they should have you taking pictures into the next decade. (*Hint:* You can find 5,000-K portable lamps on eBay for just a little more.)

✔ **Do** take a wide shot of the entire item, if your item relies on detail (for example, an engraved signature or detailed gold trim). Then take a tight close-up or two of the detailed areas that you want buyers to see and include them in your description.

✔ **Do** make sure that you focus the camera; nothing is worse than a blurry picture. Most cameras today are auto-focus, so holding the camera still is (as ever) the biggest challenge for a shutterbug.

Taking pictures of your item from different angles gives the prospective buyer more information. When you have several images to upload to eBay, you can also use your photo-editing program to put them in a single composite image for your description, as shown in Figure 14-2.

Figure 14-2:
Take several pictures from different angles to give the buyer a better idea of how your item looks.

Some eBay miscreants, whether out of laziness or deceit, steal images from other eBay members. (They simply make a digital copy of the image and use it in their own listings. This is bad form because then the copied image doesn't represent the actual item being sold.) This pilfering has happened to me on several occasions. To prevent picture-snatching, eBay lets you watermark your User ID to all your photos when you upload them. Then the next time somebody lifts one of your pictures, it has your name on it. Don't forget to report the jerks who lightfinger images; use the Report Item link at the right of their Description tabs on the offending listing — *using other sellers' photos is against eBay rules!*

Yes, I scan

If you use a scanner and traditional (that is, nondigital) camera to create images for your eBay items, you've come to the right place. (Also check out the tips in the preceding section.) Here's how to get crisp scans of your items:

✔ Select items to scan on glossy paper if you have an option; it scans best.

✔ When you take traditional photos for scanning, get as close to your item as your camera allows. Enlarging photos in the scanner will only result in blurry (or worse, jagged) images.

✔ Scan the box that the item came in by laying it on the flatbed, or if there's a photo of the item on the box, scan that portion of the box.

✔ If you're scanning a three-dimensional item (such as a doll, jewelry item, or box) and you can't close the scanner lid, drape a black or white T-shirt over the item after you place it on the scanner's glass plate; that way you get a clean background and good light reflection from the scanner.

✔ If you want to scan an item that's too big to put on your scanner all at once, scan the item in sections and assemble the digital pieces with your image-editing software. The instructions that come with your software should explain how to do this.

Software that adds the artist's touch

After you take the picture (or scan it) and transfer it into your computer according to the manufacturer's instructions, the next step is to edit the picture. You have to approach the image like a book or magazine editor: Cut, fix, resize, and reshape your picture until you think it's good enough to be seen by the public. If you're a non-techie type, don't get nervous; many of the programs have one-button magical corrections that make your pictures look great.

The software program that comes with your digital camera or scanner puts at your disposal an arsenal of editing tools that help you turn a basic image of your item into something special. Although each program has its own collection of features, a few basic tools and techniques are common to all:

✔ **Image quality:** Enables you to enhance or correct colors, sharpen images, remove dust spots, and increase or reduce brightness or contrast.

✔ **Size:** Reduces or increases the size or shape of the image.

✔ **Orientation:** Rotates the image left or right; flips it horizontally or vertically.

✔ **Crop:** Trims your picture to show the item, rather than extraneous background.

✔ **Create an image format:** Gives your edited picture a specific format, such as .JPG, .GIF, or others when you save it. The best format for putting photos on the web (and thus the preferred format on eBay and the one I strongly recommend) is .JPG (pronounced "JAY-peg").

Copying another business's text or images without permission can constitute copyright infringement, which may result in a very unfriendly "Cease and Desist" letter. If the copyright holder alerts eBay through the VeRO program, that action may end your listing.

Quick and easy editing with Pixby

Every image-editing software program has its own system requirements and capabilities. Study the software that comes with your camera or scanner. If you feel that the program is too complicated (or doesn't give you the editing tools you need), investigate some of the other popular programs. A simple-to-use program called Pixby Fast Photos was developed by an eBay seller with us in mind. It's incredibly simple to use, and the learning curve is small. I use it and love its simplicity and speed.

It has convenient one-click edit commands, built-in image browser, image uploader, unlimited undo and redo, and previewing uploaded images in web browser to check size and verify links. When it comes to editing, the Fast Photos tools let you Resize, Rotate, JPEG Optimize, Sharpen, Add a Text Watermark, Add a Border, create a Gallery Thumbnail, Enhance, and Upload an image with one mouse click. It costs only $24.95, and you can get a free 21-day trial at www.pixby.com/marshacollier.

Making Your Images Web-Friendly

Because digital images are made up of pixels — and every pixel has a set of instructions that has to be stored someplace — you have two difficulties facing you right after you take the picture:

- ✔ Digital images contain computer instructions, so bigger pictures take up more memory.

- ✔ Very large digital images take longer to *build* (appear) on the buyer's screen, and time can be precious on a web page.

Keep in mind that when you upload an image to eBay for your Gallery pictures (the ones that appears at the top of your listing and next to your item's title in search results), you really don't need to worry about size. eBay will standardize their size after you upload them, but they must be a minimum of 500 pixels on the longest side. That said, images shouldn't be larger than 7MB.

To get around both these problems when you add additional photos to your description, think small. Here's a checklist of tried-and-true techniques for preparing your elegantly slender, fast-loading images to display on eBay:

- **Set your scanner image resolution at 72 pixels per inch.** You can do this with the settings for your scanner. Although 72 ppi may seem like a low resolution, it only nibbles computer memory (instead of chomping), shows up fast on a buyer's screen, and looks great on eBay.

- **When using a digital camera, set the camera to no higher than the 1024×768 format.** That's custom made for a monitor. You can always crop the picture if it's too large.

- **Make sure description images are no larger than 480 pixels wide.** When you size your picture in your image software, it's best to keep it no larger than 300×300 pixels or 4 inches square, even if it's a snapshot of a classic 4×4 monster truck. These dimensions are big enough for people to see without squinting, and the details of your item show up nicely.

- **Crop any unnecessary areas of the photo.** You need to show your item only; everything else is a waste.

- **Use your software to darken or change the photo's contrast.** When the image looks good on your computer screen, the image looks good on your eBay item page.

- **Save your image as a .JPG file.** When you finish editing your picture, save it as a .JPG. (To do this, follow the instructions that come with your software.) .JPG is the best format for eBay; it compresses information into a small file that builds fast and reproduces nicely on the Internet.

- **Reduce the size of an image used in your description if it's larger than 50K.** Small is fast, efficient, and beautiful. Big is slow, sluggish, and dangerous: Impatient eBay users will move on to the next listing if they have to wait to see your image. Software like Pixby, mentioned earlier in this chapter, can reduce images easily.

The Image Is Perfect — Now What?

Now that your masterpiece is complete, you want to emblazon it on your item page for all the world to see. When most people first get the urge to dazzle prospective buyers with a picture, they poke around the eBay site looking for a place to put it. You can upload your images to eBay, but they will only be kept on the site for 90 days — then poof!

Trade secret: Keep an archive of your pictures. Should you ever want to use them again (or to link to them from your description), you need to store the originals off eBay. This way you have your original images no matter what; meanwhile, eBay makes optimized copies of your images to use in your listing — and stores them for the requisite 90 days.

To help eBay find your image, all you have to do is type its URL address. In the Add Photos section of the listing form, click Copy Your Photos from a Web Address link, and then type the address in the URL text field. Then, by clicking the Import button, you tell eBay to go ahead and copy your photos into your listing.

If you use eBay's photo uploader, your photo will reside on eBay's servers and will upload once, directly from your computer. I talk more about that in just a minute.

You can highlight your image's URL with your cursor, right-click your mouse, and copy it to your computer's clipboard. Then go to the item page you're filling out on eBay, put your cursor in the Picture URL box, and paste the address into the box.

A typical address (for someone using AOL) looks something like this:

```
members.aol.com/ebay4dummy/rolexwatch.jpg
```

Because your image needs an address, you have to find it a good home online. You have several options:

- **Your own website:** If you have a website, why not set up a separate folder for eBay pictures? Web hosts give you so much space that there's generally plenty to spare. You're already paying for the space, so you can park pictures there at no extra charge.

- **An image-hosting website:** Websites that specialize in hosting pictures are popping up all over the Internet. Some charge a small fee; others are free. The upside here is that they're easy to use.

- **Your server:** If you have your own server (those of you who do, well, you know who you are) can store those images right in your own home.

- **eBay Picture Services:** You can find out about using eBay's photo-hosting service later in this chapter.

Using your website to store your images

If you have a website, you can easily upload your images from there. A simple website where you can blog and post promotions to your eBay images can be as inexpensive as $3 to $4 a month from hosts like Network Solutions and Hostgator. All you need to do is set up an eBay folder for your item's pictures and get FTP (file transfer protocol) login information from your webhost.

To get your eBay images up to your website, use a free app like FireFTP in a Firefox browser, free from Mozilla at

```
https://addons.mozilla.org/en-US/firefox/addon/fireftp/
```

After you've uploaded your images to your website folder, get the address of your item's location and type it in the Picture URL box of eBay's Sell an Item form. You can use the uploaded images for your main eBay pictures or within descriptions. The pictures will appear whenever someone views your item pages. Figure 14-3 shows you a description with an embedded video.

Figure 14-3:
Mission Belt
Company
(of Shark
Tank fame)
embedded
a video
in their
description.

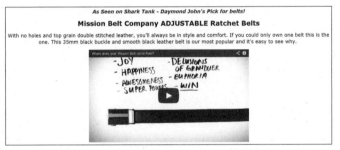

Using image-hosting websites to store images

Okay, realistically, many people are combing cyberspace looking for the next great thing. eBay's success has entrepreneurs all over the globe coming up with different kinds of e-commerce-support businesses. As usual, a lot of junk pops up on the Internet in the wake of trends — but a promising development caught my attention — *image-hosting* websites.

Perfecting your picture in LunaPic

You need to know that I am lazy — sometimes I don't even want to open a program. When it comes to editing my images for eBay, I'm still looking for a magic wand. So I browsed the Internet and found a *free* online photo-editing website, www.lunapic.com.

Although I prefer to use a program on my computer, LunaPic works great for quick, on-the-fly editing that I often need. You can even edit pictures on someone else's computer because there's no need to install software. It's a website that makes photo editing as easy as getting a burger at the drive-through window. Register on the site, and you have full photo-editing capabilities. Upload photos from your computer (or webcam) to the site, perform your touch-up, and then save and download! LunaPic has a full-featured toolset on the site; in it, you find tools to adjust brightness, contrast, color, and sharpness.

Image-hosting websites have changed from one-stop shops to mega-markets loaded with tons of services for your listings. Some image-hosting sites let you post your pictures without requiring you to use their management software. Not that I think such software is a bad thing — it's great! — I just like to choose what I use. (Flip to Chapter 20 for more about eBay-management software.)

Here are a few convenient image-hosting sites that allow you to post a few of your images for *free*:

- ✔ FreePictureHosting.com (www.freepicturehosting.com)
- ✔ ImageShack (www.imageshack.com)
- ✔ PhotoBucket (www.photobucket.com)

Using eBay's photo uploader

eBay hosts up to 12 images per listing for free (you pay a fee on eBay Motors vehicle listings). The first photo (you can change the order once you have uploaded them) appears as your main Gallery photo in Search results and the featured photo on the listing page. Under the featured photo, there is a viewer where the buyer can scroll and click to enlarge your other images: The enlarged views magically appear in the larger photo area.

When you upload photos to eBay, you need to keep these tips (rules) in mind:

- ✔ Any listing on eBay is required to have at least one image to display the item.

- ✔ Photos *must* be a minimum of 500 pixels on the longest side. eBay recommends that they be at least 1600 pixels.

- ✔ You can choose from several image types: JPG (JPEG), PNG, TIF (TIFF), BMP or GIF. Most sellers use photos with the .jpg file extension.

- ✔ Do not get fancy. Images with borders, text, or graphics embedded in them are a violation of policy (plus they're supposed to be pictures of your items, not ads).

- ✔ When you export your JPG images for eBay, and your software gives you a choice, select an image quality of 90 or more. Then eBay will optimize it for viewing on the site.

When you prepare to list an item for sale, you will be asked whether to add photos. If you don't want to upload from your computer — and have product images on your website — you have the option to have eBay copy your website images. Just input the URL of your picture in the tab entitled Copy Web Files (in the Classic uploader) or Import from Web in the enhanced photo uploader. To upload your image from your computer to eBay to be used with this listing, follow the directions onscreen.

To post your photo, you have options:

1. **Click the Add/edit photos to use the enhanced photo uploader, or click the Classic Uploader link.**

2. **After clicking the classic uploader link, click the Browse box.**

   An Open File dialog box appears.

3. **Find your image on your computer and click Open.**

   The name of the image appears in the Pictures list. Figure 14-4 shows the upload page — which is where you upload your image to the Sell Your Item page. (If your upload on the Sell Your Item page doesn't look like Figure 14-4, click the link shown on the right to go to Basic where you can make minor edits to your images.)

4. **Add more pictures if you want and click Upload.**

Standard | Basic

Select photos for upload — Try the new time-saving features in the Standard Uploader

Add up to 12 photos. (All 12 photos are free.)

Browse — Recommended size: For the best quality, use photos that are more than 1600 pixels in height or width.

	Photos	Status	
1	white infinity.jpg	Pending	Remove
2	infiniti.jpg	Pending	Remove

Copied 2 / Pending 2 / Available 8

Select optional photo upgrades

Gallery Plus ($0.35)
☐ Display large photos in search results — capture special details or different views for buyers.

Upload Cancel

Figure 14-4:
Click Upload and you're on your way.

Here are a couple things to keep in mind:

✔ eBay keeps an image online for the duration of your listing and for up to 90 days (as long as you have the link available to access the page). After that, the image disappears (unless you relist the item).

✔ You can always post the image again if you need it later; be sure to leave a copy of the image on your computer.

Multiple pictures in your descriptions

Here's the answer to *the most-asked* question when I teach a class on eBay. Many sellers have additional pictures within the listing description area. This isn't magic; you can easily do it, too. Just add a tiny bit of HTML code in your description. Here is the HTML code to insert one picture in your description area:

```
<img src="http://www.yourserver.com/
    imagename.jpg">
```

Be sure to use the brackets to open and close your code (they're located above the comma and the period on your keyboard). This code reflects the URL of your picture and the coding `img src=` to tell eBay's server to insert a picture.

When you want to insert two pictures, just insert code for each picture, one after the other. If you want one picture to appear below the other, use the HTML code for line break, `<BR>`. Here's how to write that:

```
<img src="http://www.yourserver.com/
    imagenumber1.jpg"> <BR>
<img src="http://www.yourserver.com/
    imagenumber2.jpg">
```

When you use your own photo hosting on eBay, you can use a different photo for your Gallery image.

Putting On the Hits

Okay, you have a well-written description on eBay and great images to go with it. Now all you need to do is track the number of users peeking at your items and attract even more people to your listing.

Your item is up and running on eBay, and you're dying to know how many people have stopped by to take a look. To easily monitor your *hits* — the number of times visitors stop to look at the goods — you can use eBay's free visitor counter (one of your options when listing the item). A counter is a useful marketing tool; for example, you can check the number of times people have looked at but not bid on your items.

I assume eBay will be removing this feature in the near future, as they have made this information publicly viewable on the listing page. Figure 14-5 shows an example.

Figure 14-5:
This item is pricy; per-haps that is why there are more views than buys.

> Nimbus CLOUD DOME Smartphone MOBILE Photography Diffuser Photo Light Box iPhone
> 1 sold | 4 watching | ⌂ 74 views

If you have lots more lookie-loos than bids, you may have a problem.

If your counter indicates that you're not getting many hits, consider the following potential problems so you can resurrect your sale:

- ✔ Does the picture take too long to load?
- ✔ Is the opening bid/selling price too high?
- ✔ Are those neon-orange-and-lime-green bell-bottoms just too retro to sell?

Counters are available when you're listing your item on the eBay Sell Your Item form. You can also view the number of views — as well as how many people have marked your item to "watch" on your My eBay: All Selling page.

Tell Your Story on Your About Me Page

Want to know more about the people behind those User IDs? Thousands of eBay members have created their own personal web pages on eBay (called *About Me pages*). About Me pages are easy to create — and are as unique as each eBay member. eBay users with active About Me pages have a special ME icon next to their User IDs.

Take your time when you create your About Me page. A well-done About Me page improves your sales because people who come across your auctions and check out your About Me page can get a sense of who you are and how serious you are about your eBay activities. They see instantly that you're no fly-by-night seller.

Before you create your About Me page, I suggest that you look at what other users have done. eBay members often include pictures, links to other web-sites (including their personal or business home pages), and links to just about any web location that reflects their personalities, which is why they're so entertaining. If your purpose is to generate more business, I recommend that you keep your About Me page focused on your item listings, with a link to your website.

Sellers with many sales running at once often add a message to their About Me pages that indicates that they're willing to reduce shipping charges if buyers purchase multiple items. This direct tactic may lack nuance, but it increases the number of people who look at (and bid on) your sales.

To create your About Me page, do the following:

1. **Go to any eBay user's About Me page, scroll to the very bottom and click the Create My About Me Page link. If you can't find the link, go to**

   `cgi3.ebay.com/ws/eBayISAPI.dll?AboutMeLogin`.

   You're taken to About Me: Create Your Own eBay Personal Page.

2. **If you haven't signed in, type your User ID and password in the appropriate boxes.**

3. **Click the Edit Your Page button.**

4. **Select Use Our Easy Step-by-Step Process.**

You're taken to the About Me layout page. You have a couple layout options, which eBay is kind enough to show you:

- Newspaper Layout
- Centered Layout

5. **Click the button that corresponds to the layout option you want.**

You're taken to a second About Me creation page.

6. **Enter the following information:**

- *Page Title:* Type the title of your About Me page (for example, *Larry's Lunch Boxes*).

- *Paragraph 1:* Type a personal attention-grabbing headline, such as *Welcome to Larry Lunch's Lunch Box Place.*

- *Text:* Type a short paragraph that greets your visitors (something like *Hey, I like lunch boxes a lot,* only more exciting).

- *Paragraph 2:* Type another headline for the second paragraph of the page, such as *Vintage, Modern, Ancient,* or *I Collect All Kinds of Lunch Boxes.*

- *Text:* Type another paragraph about yourself or your collection (such as, *I used to stare at lunch boxes in the school cafeteria . . .* only more, you know, *normal*).

- *Picture:* If you're adding a picture, type a sentence describing it, for example: *This is my wife Loretta with our lunch box collection.*

- *URL:* Type the website address (URL) where people can find your picture. See the section earlier in this chapter that shows you how to upload digital images.

- *Feedback:* Select how many of your feedback postings you want to appear on your About Me page. (You can opt not to show any feedback, but I think you should put in a few comments, especially if they're complimentary, as in, *Larry sent my lunch box promptly, and it makes lunchtime a blast! Everybody stares at it . . .*)

- *Items for Sale:* Select how many of your current listings you want to appear on your About Me page. If you don't have any items for sale at the moment, you can select the Show No Items option.

- *Label:* Type a caption to introduce your items, for example: *Lunch Boxes I'm Currently Selling.*

- *Favorite Links:* Type the names and URLs of any websites you want visitors to see; for example, a website that appraises lunch boxes (*It's in excellent condition except for that petrified ham sandwich . . . .*)

7. **Click the Continue button. (Or, if you don't like your current layout, click the Back button to go back to Step 1.)**

   You're now looking at your final About Me page. At the bottom of the page, you see a group of buttons.

   - *Edit Some More:* Returns you to Step 2.

   - *Save My Page:* Saves your About Me page so that you're one step closer to publishing it on eBay.

   - *Edit Using HTML:* If you know HTML code, you can customize your About Me page. (For example, you can insert pictures with the code I give you in the "Multiple pictures in your descriptions" sidebar, earlier in this chapter.)

   - *Start Over:* Takes you to a link page where you can delete what you created and begin again.

8. **When you're happy with your masterpiece, click the Save My Page button.**

   Yes, you did it; now anybody in the world with access to the Internet can find your personal About Me page on eBay.

Don't forget to update your About Me page often. A good About Me page makes prospective buyers eager to know more about your items. An out-of-date About Me page turns off potential bidders. If you choose to update, you need to edit it by using HTML. If you don't use HTML, you have to create a whole new page.

You can link to your About Me page from your website or from your e-mail because all About Me pages have their own personal URLs. The address ends with your User ID. For example, here's the URL for my page:

```
members.ebay.com/aboutme/marsha_c
```

Tell the World on Your Profile Page

If staying social is the key to the new web, your eBay profile is the hub of your eBay user interaction. Your About Me and your profile pages are there for customers and the eBay community. People like to know about other people, and your eBay pages let folks know with whom they are transacting.

Although my editors would love for me to give you a long, drawn-out, step-by-step list to show you how to get to your My World page, I won't. It's all too simple: To get to your profile page, click your User ID on your My eBay page — or any eBay page for that matter — even when you click your User ID after clicking "Hi" at the top right of any page.

This page will be pre-populated with items you're selling, your reviews (if you've reviewed an item on eBay), and your bio and profile picture if you've previously uploaded them to a My World page. (My World is now defunct.)

When you click your name or User ID, you arrive at your own profile page. Your profile page contains basic information about you as a seller, your recent feedback, your eBay Store (if you have one), as well as:

- **Items for sale:** Images and links to your current listings.

- **Collections:** Links to items you have chosen to "add to your collections" from eBay item pages. You may make many collections, and set them to be private or public from your profile page.

- **Following:** When you chose to follow an item search, or an eBay seller, they will show up here.

If you are following a search or seller for your own personal research, you can choose to make those selections private by clicking on the word Public under the image on the profile page.

Take an opportunity to edit the page. Here's the lowdown on what you can do to personalize your page after clicking the Edit Profile button under your User ID. When you click that button, small pen icons appear, showing you where you can edit the page:

- **Upload a profile photo:** Click the pen icon in the corner of the square next to your User ID. The page will prompt you to upload your profile image. Choose a profile photo that portrays you and your personality. There are no set requirements for size at this point, so I suggest using a close-to-square headshot. If you do not select a headshot, your face might be too small for folks to see.

- **Upload a cover photo:** Just as on Facebook, you may upload a photo for the top of your page. Keep in mind that text covers a good deal of the cover photo, so don't select a picture where the most important spot is at the bottom. When you're selecting (or cropping) an image for use as a cover photo, keep in mind eBay's recommended 1200 pixels x 270 pixels size for best viewing. Also eBay prefers image files to be smaller than 5MB.

- **Add content:** Here you have 250 characters to talk about yourself, your eBay life, or the items you enjoy selling or buying.

It is easy to share a link to your profile or find other buyers and sellers by typing an eBay ID into an eBay URL, like this: `www.ebay.com/usr/<UserID>`. My profile page, for example, is `http://www.ebay.com/usr/marsha_c` and is pictured in Figure 14-6. I can't wait to see your creativity on *your* eBay profile page!

Figure 14-6:
Welcome
to my eBay
profile
page!

Part IV

Even More of eBay's Special Features

In this part...

- ✔ Handling privacy concerns
- ✔ Resolving buying and selling issues
- ✔ Having fun with the eBay community
- ✔ Using charity auctions to bid on great items for a good cause

Chapter 15

Privacy: Protecting Yourself Online

*O*n the Internet, as in real life, you should never take your personal privacy for granted. Sure, you're ecstatic that you can shop and sell on eBay from the privacy of your home, but remember: Just because your front door is locked doesn't mean that your privacy is being protected. If you're new to the Internet, you may be surprised to find out what you reveal about yourself to the world, no matter how many precautions you take. (Yes, we all know about that neon-green facial you wear when you're shopping online . . . just kidding . . . honest.)

All moves across the Internet have become part of the "big data" movement. You have most likely heard of *data mining,* which takes enormous amounts of data from every Internet citizen's posts, movements, and clicks. This data is even collected from your smartphone. There is so much information available that specialists have to go in and pull sets and subsets to decipher the data. Once they have this information, they can spot business trends, plan cities, discover crime, and more.

In 2012, President Obama announced the Big Data Research and Development Initiative, which explored how big data could be used to address important problems faced by the government. To further that goal, the NSA will lead operations when the Utah Data Center goes online in 2014.

Needless to say, the amount of information eBay gets from you is infinitesimal compared to the personal information collected by the NSA. In this chapter, you find out how much eBay knows about you and who eBay shares your information with. I explain what you can do to protect your privacy and tell you some simple steps you can take to increase not only your Internet privacy but also your personal safety.

What eBay Knows about You

The irony of the Internet is that although you think you're sitting at home working anonymously, third parties such as advertisers and marketing companies are surreptitiously getting to know you.

While you're busy collecting Winter Olympic memorabilia or buying that hot new Kate Spade purse, eBay is busy collecting nuggets of information about you. eBay gets some of this information from you and some of it from your computer. All the data eBay gets is stored in the mammoth eBay data bank.

What you tell eBay

eBay gets much of what it knows about you *from* you. When you sign up, you voluntarily tell eBay important and personal information about yourself. Right off the bat, you give eBay all or some of these basic tidbits:

- ✔ Name
- ✔ E-mail address
- ✔ Snail-mail address
- ✔ Phone number
- ✔ Your date of birth
- ✔ Password

"Okay, that's no big deal," you say, but if you're using your credit card to settle your eBay fees (and using PayPal), you're also giving the following personal financial information:

- ✔ Credit card number
- ✔ Expiration date
- ✔ Bank account number
- ✔ Credit card billing address
- ✔ Credit card history

Don't worry about giving this information to eBay or PayPal. The bottom line is that *every time* you pay by check or with a credit card in the real world, you give away personal info about yourself. The eBay companies carefully lock up this information (in a high-security area on their servers), but other companies or individuals may not be so protective. eBay has a vested interest in your safety.

What cookies gather

Websites collect information about you by using *cookies*. No, they don't bribe you with oatmeal-raisin goodies. Cookies are nothing more than tiny pieces of data that companies (such as eBay) put in your web browser to store data about your surfing and item-viewing habits.

Most web designers install cookies in the site code to help you navigate their sites. Sometimes the cookie becomes sort of an "admission ticket" so that you don't need to register or log in every time you land on the site.

Cookies can't steal information from other files on your computer. A cookie can access only the information that you provide to its website.

eBay has partnerships with companies that provide page-view and data-tracking technology and advertisers who display the ads on eBay pages, whether you want to see them or not. If you click a banner, a cookie from that particular advertiser *may* go onto your computer, usually to prevent you from seeing it again.

The ads you see on eBay are served up by Ad Choice. If do not wish to participate in eBay's ad-customization programs, you can opt-out at the Ad Choice program page:

```
http://cgi6.ebay.com/ws/eBayISAPI.dll?AdChoiceLandingPage&
partner=0
```

Note that if you opt out, you will still see ads, but they will not be relevant to your online searches, since no data is collected.

Another example, DoubleClick, a subsidiary of Google, is a major player in the cookie-tracking field. They say that it uses your information to limit the number of times that you see the same advertisement. DoubleClick also measures the kinds of ads that you respond to — and tracks which member websites you visit and how often. The bottom line is that DoubleClick is just trying to sell you stuff with ads based on your personal interests. The upside is that you get to see stuff that you may like.

These cookies, wherever they come from, target various criteria. Targeting is accomplished by using IP addresses or by reference to information about users stored within other cookies on your computer. Common information picked up by some cookies is

- What web browser you are using
- Which operating system your computer uses

- ✔ Who is your Internet service provider
- ✔ Your bandwidth
- ✔ The time of day you viewed the advertiser's cookie

If you want to keep your browsing information private, you can remove your-self from the cookie system or adjust your privacy settings by going to this website:

http://www.google.com/policies/technologies/ads/

Your eBay sign-in cookie

There are several types of cookies; the most common ones you will encounter are:

- ✔ **Session:** This cookie type remains on your computer as long as your browser is open or until you log out of the site. When you close your Internet browser (Internet Explorer, Firefox, Safari, or Chrome), the cookie disappears as completely as if you snarfed it up with icy-cold milk.

- ✔ **Persistent (tracking):** This flavor of cookie is perfect if you don't share your computer with anyone else; it permits your computer to always remain signed in to a particular website. Generally, these cookies have a timer that will expire within a pre-prescribed period of time (say, a year). Each time you visit a site with such a cookie, it pings the server's owners to let them know you are a repeat visitor. They may also record from where you came to the website. For this reason, persistent cookies are also called *tracking cookies.*

Some third-party service providers may also leave cookies when you visit eBay.

eBay's "keep me signed in" sign-in cookie is a good thing. It prevents the repetitive task of typing your User ID and password at every turn. This cookie simplifies your participation in bidding, watching items, viewing completed listings, and so on. Because you don't have to sign in every moment that you're doing business on eBay, it's a real timesaver.

Web beacons

Web beacons are clear, 1-pixel-x-1-pixel images that are placed in the HTML (or Internet page code) for individual pages. They are also commonly called *tracking bugs* or *pixel tags.* Web beacons, like cookies, are used mainly for collecting marketing information. They track the traffic patterns of users from one page to another.

Web beacons are also often used in e-mails. Ever wonder how someone knows you've received an e-mail? Or why you may receive an e-mail from a company whose website you've just visited? Blame the sneaky-but-harmless beacons.

Web beacons are invisible as cookies and are incorporated into web pages without your knowing. Turning off cookies on your browser won't disable beacons, but this action does protect your anonymity. Web beacons are not as ominous as they may seem; the information collected is not personally identifiable; they just track your passage along the site.

What web servers collect

Every time that you log on to the Internet, you leave an electronic trail of information; it's just like when you're on a scavenger hunt. eBay, like millions of other websites, uses *servers,* which are immense pieces of hardware that do nothing but collect and transfer bits (and bytes) of information day and night. Your Internet connection has a special address (IP address) that iden-tifies you to all servers when you surf the Net. This is called an *IP (Internet Protocol) address* and is often used by law enforcement to track those whose shenanigans wreak havoc on websites — or on other users.

Web servers all over the Internet track some or all of the following information:

- ✔ What website you came in from
- ✔ The ISP (Internet service provider) that you use
- ✔ The items that you're selling or viewing on eBay
- ✔ The websites you linked your listings to
- ✔ Your favorite websites (if you link them to your About Me page)

eBay collects the following information while you visit the eBay site:

- ✔ What you do while logged on to the site
- ✔ Which categories you tend to browse
- ✔ Which items you've viewed recently
- ✔ What times you log on and log off

Like incredible Internet archivists, eBay's servers keep a record of everything you bid on, win, and sell — which is great news if you have a problem with a transaction and need eBay to investigate. Also, eBay couldn't display feedback about you and other users if its servers didn't store all the feedback you write and receive. Have you ever sent an e-mail to eBay? eBay's servers record it and keep it in some murky recess of eBay's memory. Remember, we live in the age of electronic commerce, and the people on eBay run a serious business that depends on e-commerce. They have to keep everything in case they need it later.

To see a chart on what personal information is accessible by third parties through data sharing, check out this address:

```
http://pages.ebay.com/help/policies/privacy-appendix.html
```

Be sure to visit the page; you may be surprised by the amount of information that exists on the eBay servers about you and your habits.

For current examples of how this type of information can be used against you as you surf the Internet, visit this website:

```
www.anonymizer.com/consumer/threat_center/
```

eBay's Privacy Center has all the legalese in an easy-to-read fashion at this page:

```
http://www.ebayprivacycenter.com/privacy
```

 You *can* also surf the Internet free of cookies and tracking if you use Google's Chrome browser, Firefox, Safari, or a recent version of Internet Explorer. These browsers have an option that allows you to visit the web without giving off a trace of who you are. It's called *Incognito, private browsing,* or *invisible* mode. You can get into this mode easily, after you've installed the browser, by typing Ctrl+Shift+N.

Cookie-removal-ware

I got a call from a friend who complained that her laptop computer was getting slower and slower. She brought it over to my house and when I had a look at it, I also noticed that it was opening extra pop-up windows and accessing the Internet spuriously. After checking to see whether she had a virus (no, she didn't), I went to the Internet to get her some spyware-removal software. Perhaps her problem was that too many people had inserted information-gathering cookies on her computer.

That was certainly the case. After installing and running the software, I found that she had over 350 cookies pulling information from her computer as she surfed. After those were deleted, her computer ran much faster.

She certainly didn't give these people permission to spy on her comings and goings on the Internet. These cookies were placed on her computer without her knowledge. If you want to purge these uninvited spies from your computer, download any of the free antispyware or antimalware software from a reliable source. If you are on a PC on Windows 7, you can learn more about spyware and download Microsoft Security Essentials from

```
http://www.microsoft.com/security/pc-security/
spyware-remove.aspx.
```

If you are using Windows 8, antispyware is built in with an antivirus program, Windows Defender.

If you're apprehensive about all the information that web servers can collect about you while you innocently roam the Internet, I understand. But before you start looking out for Big Brother watching over your shoulder, consider this: On the World Wide Web, *everybody's* collecting information — and very little is private anymore.

The odds are excellent that all the information that eBay knows about you is already in the hands of many other folks, too — your bank, your grocer, the staff of any magazines you subscribe to, clubs you belong to, any airlines you've flown, and any insurance agencies you use. That's life these days. And if you're thinking, "Just because everybody knows all this stuff about me, that doesn't make it right," all I can say is, "You're right." But maybe you'll sleep better knowing that eBay is a place where the privacy issue is taken seriously. See the next section for details.

eBay's Privacy Policy

eBay had a Privacy Policy for all its users before privacy policies were even in vogue. eBay maintains the safety standards set forth by the pioneer in online safeguarding: TRUSTe.

TRUSTe (www.truste.com) sets a list of standards that its member websites have to follow to earn a certification. The thousands of websites that subscribe to this watchdog group must adhere to its guidelines and set policies to protect privacy. eBay has been a member of TRUSTe since the privacy watchdog group was founded.

Do seals bite back?

Because eBay pays to display the TRUSTe mark, some online critics say that the seal is nothing more than windowdressing. These critics wonder whether it would be in the web watchdog's best financial interest to bite the hand that feeds it all those display fees. Critics complain that the seal offers a false sense of security — and suggest that you view the seal as nothing more than a disclaimer to be careful in your Internet dealings.

The truth is, TRUSTe can pull its seal whenever a website becomes careless in its handling of privacy issues. However, the critics make a good point: _Always be careful in your Internet dealings,_ no matter how much protection a site has. If you ever feel your personal information has been compromised, file a complaint at the TRUSTe website:

```
https://feedback-form.truste.com/watchdog/request
```

To review the policy that's earned eBay the TRUSTe seal of approval, visit

```
http://pages.ebay.com/help/policies/privacy-policy.html
```

In addition to setting and displaying a privacy policy, eBay follows these guidelines as well:

- ✔ eBay must make its Privacy Policy links easily accessible to users. You can find the link on eBay's home page in the Legal & More area at the bottom. Next to the copyright date (at the very, very bottom of the page), click the Privacy Policy link. Take advantage of this opportunity to find out how your data is being protected.

- ✔ eBay must disclose what personal information it collects and how it's using the info.

- ✔ Users must have an easy way to review the personal information that eBay has about them.

- ✔ Users must have an _opting out_ option that lets them decline to share information.

- ✔ eBay must follow industry standards to make its website and database secure so that hackers and nonmembers have no access to the information. eBay uses Secure Sockets Layer (SSL), which is an encryption program that scrambles data until it gets to eBay.

Unfortunately, no website, including the CIA's website, is completely secure, so you still have to be on your guard while you're online.

Grateful Dead cookie jar

In 1999, an auction description read: "This is one of the grooviest jars I have ever come across — a real find for the die-hard Grateful Dead fan or for the cookie jar collector who has it all. Made by Vandor, this Grateful Dead bus cookie jar looks like something the Dead *would* drive. Beautiful detailing on the peace signs; the roses are running lights. Painted windows. You have just got to see this piece. Only 10,000 made, and I have only seen one other. Comes with box that has Grateful Dead logos on it. Buyer pays all shipping and insurance."

The cookie jar started at $1 and sold on eBay for $102.50. When I updated this book in 2002,

it sold on eBay for $125; when I updated again in 2004, it went for $150. Today, there's one for sale at $250. The Grateful Dead's bus cookie jar is riding the tracks these days; in 2009 an auction closed with the final bid at $125. Perhaps the Baby Boomer Deadheads are feeling the economic crunch. Still, the price of the original has skyrocketed from the original issue price, so much so that Vandor just came out with a 40th anniversary replica. Buy it now for your Deadhead friends — and buy it quick. Only 1,200 were made, and the price is edging past the $200 mark.

What Does eBay Do with Information about Me, Anyway?

Although eBay knows a good chunk of information about you, it puts the information to good use. The fact that it knows so much about you actually helps you in the long run.

Here's what eBay uses personal information for:

- **Upgrading eBay:** Like most e-commerce companies, eBay tracks members' use and habits to improve the website. For instance, if a particular item generates a lot of activity, eBay may add a category or a subcategory.

- **Clearing the way for transactions:** If eBay didn't collect personal information such as your e-mail address, your snail-mail address, and your phone number, you couldn't complete the transaction you started after an auction was over.

- **Billing:** You think it's important to keep track of your merchandise and money, don't you? So does eBay. It uses your personal information to keep an eye on your account and your paying habits — and on everybody else's. (Call it a gentle encouragement of honest trading habits.)

✔ **Policing the site:** Never forget that eBay tries to be tough on cyber-crime; if you break the rules or regulations, eBay will hunt you down and boot you out. Personal information is used to find eBay delinquents, and eBay makes it clear that it cooperates with law enforcement and with third parties whose merchandise you may be selling illegally. For more about this topic, read up on the VeRO program in Chapter 9.

Periodically, eBay runs surveys asking specific questions about your use of the site. It uses your answers to upgrade eBay. In addition, eBay asks whether it can forward your information to a marketing firm. eBay says that it does not forward any personally identifiable information, which means that any info you provide is given to third parties as raw data. However, if you're nervous about privacy, I suggest that you make it clear that you don't want your comments to leave eBay should you decide to participate in eBay surveys. If you don't participate in the surveys, you won't have any hand in creating new eBay features, though, so you can't complain if you don't like how the site looks and works.

What Do Other eBay Members Know about Me?

eBay functions under the premise that eBay's members are buying, selling, working, and playing in an honest and open way. That means that anyone who's surfing the site can immediately find out some limited information about you:

✔ Your User ID and history

✔ Your feedback history

✔ All the auctions and fixed-price sales you run

✔ Sellers you have purchased from in your feedback profile

eBay clearly states in its policies and guidelines that e-mail addresses should be used only for eBay business. If you abuse this policy, you can be suspended or even ousted from eBay for good.

eBay provides limited eBay member registration information to its users. If another member involved in a transaction with you wants to know the following facts about you, they're available:

✔ Your name (and business name if you have provided that information)

✔ Your e-mail address

✔ The city, state, and country data that you provided to eBay

✔ The telephone number that you provided to eBay

Following the transaction, buyers and sellers exchange some real-world information. As I explain in Chapters 6 and 12, the exchange of merchandise, money, and information is all part of an eBay transaction. Make sure that you're comfortable giving out your home address. If you're not, I explain alternatives in this chapter.

Spam — Not Just a Hawaiian Delicacy

Although you can find plenty of places to socialize and have fun on eBay, when it comes to business, eBay is . . . well, all business. eBay's policy says that requests for registration information can be made only for people with whom you're transacting business on eBay. The contact information request form requires that you type the item number of the transaction you're involved in as well as the User ID of the person whose contact info you want. If you're not involved in a transaction, as a bidder or a seller in the specified item number, you can't access the user information.

When it comes to e-mail addresses, your secret is safe. The PayPal transaction page contains your e-mail address so that the person on the other end of the transaction can contact you. Using eBay messages is a far more efficient way to check on a transaction since the messages are recorded by eBay. After the other user has your e-mail address, eBay rules state that the user can use it only for eBay business.

Here's a list of "business" reasons for e-mail communication, generally accepted by all on eBay:

✔ Communicating with sellers or buyers during and after transactions

✔ Suggesting items to friends that they may be interested in, using the Share feature (on the item page)

✔ Discussing common interests with other members, such as shared hometowns, interesting collections, and past or current listings.

Sending spam versus eating it

Sending e-mail to other members is a great way to do business and make friends. But don't cross the line into spam. *Spam,* a Hormel canned meat product (I give Spam its own sidebar), now has an alternate meaning. When you spell it with a small *s, spam* is unsolicited e-mail — most often, advertising — sent to multiple e-mail addresses gleaned from marketing lists. Eventually, it fills up your inbox the way "Spam, Spam, Spam, and Spam" filled up the menu in an old *Monty Python* restaurant skit.

Spam I am

Spam, the unwanted electronic junk mail, is named after Spam, the canned meat product. (Spam collectibles on eBay are another matter entirely.) According to the Spam website, more than 6 billion cans of Spam have been consumed worldwide. (By the way, Hawaiians eat more Spam than residents in any other state in the Union.) Spam is made from a secret recipe of pork shoulder, ham, and special spices. It was first produced in 1937 and got its name from the *SP* for *spice* and the *AM* from *ham*.

It's widely believed that spam (junk e-mail) got its name from the old *Monty Python* sketch because the refrain "Spam-Spam-Spam-Spam" drowned out all other conversation, and one of the participants kept saying, "I don't want any Spam. I don't like Spam." Others say that it came from a bunch of computer geeks at USC who thought that junk e-mail was about as satisfying as a Spam sandwich. Perhaps they've never enjoyed a Spam luau in Hawaii under the moonlight — aloha! For more Spam fun facts, visit www.spam.com.

Think of spam as the electronic version of the junk mail that you get via the U.S. Postal Service. The original Spam may be okay for eating (if you're into that kind of thing), but sending the electronic variety can get you banned from eBay.

If you send an e-mail that advertises a product or service to people who haven't agreed (opted in) that they wanted this sort of e-mail, you're guilty of spamming.

You are not allowed to add any eBay user, even a user who has purchased an item from you, to your mailing list (e-mail or physical mail) without their express consent.

Trashing your junk mail

Sometimes spam can come in the form of mail from people you know and expect mail from. Your closest friend's computer may have been abducted by some weird Internet virus that replicated the virus to everyone in his or her e-mail address book. Obviously, this is not a good thing for those who receive and open the e-mail.

Don't open e-mail from anyone you don't know, especially if a file is attached to it. Sometimes, if a spammer is really slick, it's hard to tell that you've received spam. If you receive an e-mail with no subject line, however — or if the e-mail has an addressee name that isn't yours, or is coming from someone you never heard of — delete it. You never know; it could be just annoying spam — or worse, it could contain a computer virus as an attachment, just waiting for you to open and activate it.

Speaking of e-mail, if you're new to the technology, I recommend getting a good antivirus program that can scan e-mail attachments and rid your system of some annoying and increasingly dangerous computer bugs.

For some interesting general anti-spam tips, drop in at `spam.abuse.net`. This website offers helpful advice for doing battle with spam artists. Also, I've been using a handy software program for years called MailWasher, which allows me to preview my e-mail before it's downloaded to my computer. It even bounces spam back to the sender on command — as if your e-mail address didn't exist. Best of all, this program is free and available from `www.mailwasher.net`.

E-mail spoofing

E-mail spoofing has become the bane of the online community and can wreak havoc. *Spoofing* is accomplished when crafty techno-geeks send e-mail and make it appear to come from someone other than themselves — someone you know and expect e-mail from. Most often, this type of e-mail is programmed to invade your privacy or, even worse, bilk you out of confidential information.

A spate of e-mails has purportedly been sent from eBay, PayPal, and other major e-commerce sites, claiming that your membership has been suspended or that your records need updating. The opportunistic e-mail then asks you to click a link to a page on the site, which then asks you to input your personal information. Don't do it!

My Messages safeguard your privacy

Being the conscientious company it is, eBay has set up a private area, accessible only through one of the links on your My eBay page, called Messages. Messages enables you to communicate with other eBay members without revealing your e-mail address. All your missives with other members, such as Contact the Seller communications, appear in this area. You can answer mail, send new mail, and delete communications from this area, just as if it was your own e-mail software.

This service can protect you from most of the most dangerous forms of spam. For safety's sake, whenever you receive an e-mail sent (in reality or purportedly) from eBay or an eBay member, don't click the e-mail link to Respond Now. Open your Internet browser and go directly to your Messages area. If the e-mail is legitimate, it will appear there. Merely click the e-mail to open it, read it, and reply. Your privacy (in the form of your e-mail address) isn't exposed to the receiving party.

Most sites will *never* ask you to provide sensitive information through e-mail, so don't do it. If you receive an e-mail saying your "account has been suspended," close the e-mail and go directly to the site in question — *without* using the supplied link in the e-mail. You'll know soon enough if there is a problem with your account.

If you get this sort of e-mail from eBay and want to confirm whether it is really from eBay, visit this eBay security page:

```
http://pages.ebay.com/help/account/recognizing-spoof.html
```

To help eBay in its investigation of these information thieves, send a copy of the e-mail (along with all identification headers) to spoof@ebay.com. When forwarding the e-mail, do not alter it in any way.

I Vant to Be Alone — and Vat You Can Do to Stay That Vay

The Internet has a long reach. Don't be surprised if you furnish your personal information freely on one website, and it turns up somewhere else. If you don't mind people knowing things about you (your name, your hobbies, where you live, and your phone number, for example), by all means share. But I personally think you should give only as much information as you need to do business on the site.

Privacy is not secrecy. Don't feel obligated to reveal anything about yourself that isn't absolutely necessary. (Some personal facts are in the same league as body weight — private, even if hardly a secret.)

Although you can't prevent privacy leaks entirely, you can take some precautions to protect yourself. Here are some tips to keep your online information as safe and secure as possible:

- ✔ **User ID:** When eBay first started, members used their e-mail addresses to buy and sell. Today, users appear on the site with a *nom de plume* (okay, User ID, but *nom de plume* sounds oh, so chic). Your first line of defense against everyone who surfs the eBay site is to choose a User ID that doesn't reveal too much about you — unless you want to promote an existing business. Chapter 2 gives you some pointers on how to choose your User ID.

- ✔ **Password:** Guard your password as if it were the key to your home. Don't give any buyers or sellers your password. If a window requesting your password pops up in an auction, skip it — it's somebody who is up to no good. Use your password *only* on official eBay screens. (See Chapter 2 for tips on choosing passwords.)

Fighting back

Robbin was minding her own business, selling software on eBay, when she ran into one of the world's nastiest eBay outlaws. He was a one-stop-shopping outlet of rule-breaking behaviors. First, he ruined her auctions by bidding ridiculously high amounts and then retracting bids at the last legal minute. (This couldn't happen today because eBay changed their bidding policies due to these nefarious practices). He e-mailed her bidders, offering the same item but cheaper. He contacted Robbin's winning bidders to say he was accepting her payments. Then he started leaving messages on her answering machine. When she finally had enough, she contacted Trust & Safety, which suspended him.

But like a bad lunch, he came back up — with a new name. So Robbin fought back on her own. She got his registration information and sent him a letter. She also informed the support area at his ISP about what he was doing, and because he used his work e-mail address, she also contacted his boss.

Her efforts must have done the trick. He finally slipped out of eBay and slithered out of her life. The lesson: Don't rely completely on eBay to pick up the pieces. If you're being abused, stand up for your rights and fight back through the proper channels!

In the virtual world, as in the real world, cyberstalking is scary and illegal. If you think someone is using information from eBay to harass you, contact eBay immediately — as well as your local police. Chapter 16 gives you the ins and outs of contacting eBay's security team.

If you're concerned that someone may have your password, change it immediately:

1. **Go to your My eBay area and hover your cursor over the Account tab. From the drop-down menu, click Personal Information.**

2. **On your arrival in the Personal Information area, find the Password line and click the Edit link.**

3. **Follow the instructions to change your password.**

   Your password is immediately changed.

If some dastardly evildoer has changed your password, and you can't sign in to your account, go to the eBay home page. Click the Customer Support link at the top of the page. Then you can choose the Contact eBay tab on the resulting page. You'll be in touch with a live human being who can help you secure your account before damage can be done.

✔ **Credit card information:** Whenever you use your credit card on eBay, you can make sure that your private information is safe. Look for an SSL (SSL stands for *Secure Socket Layer*) link or check box. SSL is an encryption program that scrambles the information so that hackers have almost no chance of getting your information. (I explain more about SSL in Chapter 2.)

When buying from a listing that accepts credit cards, check the seller's feedback and carefully weigh the risks of giving your credit card number to someone you don't know versus paying through PayPal. PayPal is the safest way to pay because your credit card number is not released.

Never give anyone your Social Security number online. Guard yours as if it were the key to the Crown Jewels.

✔ **Registration information:** When you first register, eBay requests a phone number and address for billing and contact purposes. I've never had a problem with anyone requesting my registration information and then misusing it. However, many people want an added measure of anonymity. You can give eBay the information it wants in several ways without compromising your privacy:

• Rather than your home phone number, provide eBay with a cell-phone number, a work phone number, Google Voice, or a SkypeIn number. Screen your calls with an answering machine.

• Use a post office box rather than your home address.

• Start a bank account solely for eBay transactions. Make it a DBA (doing business as) account so you can use an alternate name. Your bank can help you with this process.

Never say anything online that you wouldn't feel comfortable saying to the next person who passed you on the street. Basically, that's who you're talking to. You can find stories of romances blossoming in the eBay community — and I'm delighted for the happy couples, I swear — but come on, that doesn't mean that you should lose your head. Don't give out any personal information to strangers; too often that's asking for trouble. Have fun on eBay but hang on to your commonsense.

✔ **Check feedback:** Yep, I sound like a broken record (in case you don't remember, *records* were the large, black, prone-to-breaking vinyl disks used by people to play music on electric turntables before iPods and CDs were invented), but here it is again: *Check feedback*. eBay works because its participants police it. The best way to find out about the folks whom you're dealing with is to see how others felt about them. If you take only one thing away from this book, it's to check feedback *before* you bid or buy!

Chapter 16

Staying Safe and Getting Help

· ·

In This Chapter

▶ Keeping eBay members safe

▶ Staying current with the rules

▶ Getting the buyer's or seller's phone number

▶ Knowing your items through authentication

▶ Saving yourself: Where to go when eBay can't help

· ·

Millions of people transact business every day on eBay. If you're new to the this sort of commerce, you may need a reality check. With hundreds of millions of items for sale worldwide, and millions of new listings every day, the law of averages dictates that you're bound to run into some rough seas eventually. If you do, know that you can get the answers you need from eBay's Customer Support department. In this chapter, I take you through the security resources — from reporting abuses to resolving insurance issues. This chapter explains how eBay enforces its rules and regulations and points out how to go outside eBay for help if you run into some really big-time problems.

Keeping eBay Safe with eBay Security

The Security Center is the eBay area that focuses on protecting eBay buyers and sellers from members who aren't playing by the rules. Through this department, eBay issues warnings and policy changes — and in some cases, it gives eBay bad guys the heave-ho.

You should know about two important safety areas on eBay:

> ✔ **Security Center:** You reach the Security Center from a small link found at the bottom of almost every eBay page. From here you can find and report safety violations. If eBay ever moves this link, just type `http://pages.ebay.com/securitycenter/` into your browser and you're there.

✔ **Resolution Center:** Find this link from the Legal & More tab at the bottom of the eBay home page; just put your cursor over the Customer Support link and choose Resolution Center from the drop-down menu. This is where you report transactional issues: unpaid items, items received not as described, and more. Find it directly at `http://resolutioncenter.ebay.com/`.

The Security Center (shown in Figure 16-1) is more than just a link to policies and information. You get the latest tips on staying safe on the Internet. It also connects you with a group of eBay staffers who handle complaints, field incoming tips about possible infractions, and dole out warnings and suspensions. These dedicated employees investigate infractions and send e-mails in response to tips. eBay staffers look at complaints on a case-by-case basis, in the order they receive them. Some common complaints they receive are about these problems:

✔ Shill bidders (see the section on "Selling abuses" in this chapter)

✔ Feedback issues and abuses (see the section on "Feedback abuses" in this chapter)

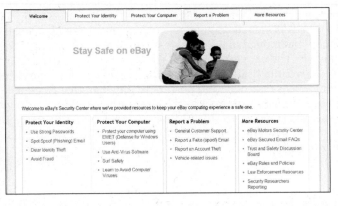

Figure 16-1:
The Security Center as it appears when you click the Security Center link.

Keep in mind that eBay is a widely varied community of people, most of whom have never met each other. No matter what you buy or sell on eBay, don't expect eBay transactions to be any easier than buying or selling from a complete stranger. Whatever the personality of the seller, know your purchase is covered by eBay's Buyer Protection.

If you've read previous chapters in this book, you probably know about eBay's rules and regulations. For a closer online look at them, click the Policies link `http://pages.ebay.com/help/policies/everyone-ov.html` (which is at the bottom of most eBay pages), and then check the User Agreement `http://pages.ebay.com/help/policies/user-agreement.html`. The agreement is revised regularly, so check it often.

Buyers Are Safe When Shopping on eBay

One of the reasons people flock to the United States eBay marketplace is the eBay Buyer Protection policy. Under this policy, all purchases (with some exclusions listed below) are covered, and the buyer can get a full refund through their PayPal account. Even shipping costs are refunded.

The way it works is that eBay hosts a *resolution* process (somewhat like mediation) when buyers may claim that their item was not received, or the item they received was different from what was described in the listing.

Items that are not eligible for resolution are

✔ Items that are covered for businesses under eBay's Business Equipment Purchase Protection

✔ Items that are listed (or belong) in these categories:

- Vehicles (for which there is the eBay Vehicle Purchase Protection)

- Real Estate

- Classified listings on eBayclassifieds.com or eBay.com

- Items purchased on half.ebay.com

- Items purchased on the eBay Digital Music Center

- eBay Wholesale Deals

- Items shipped to another location after being received at the buyer's address as specified in the PayPal transaction

There are defined steps that the buyer has to go through to make a claim. Buyers should first contact the seller through eBay messages and attempt to resolve the issue. If the buyer doesn't hear from the seller or can't resolve the issue with the seller, he or she can then file a case with eBay. Buyers who don't hear back, or don't otherwise resolve the issue after contacting the seller, can file a claim at the Resolution Center. eBay reviews the case, checks to be sure that there is no fraud history on the part of the buyer, and contacts the seller. Before contacting the seller, eBay reviews the transaction information and any messages sent between the buyer and the seller through eBay Messages, as well as checking on package transit time.

As a seller, you can protect yourself by following the tips in this book. Additionally, when shipping an item that sells for over $250, get proof of delivery in the form of a Signature Confirmation. PayPal requires a signature to prove delivery for expensive items.

Abuses You Should Report

Before you even consider blowing the whistle on someone by reporting him or her to eBay, make sure that what you're encountering is actually a misuse of eBay. Some behavior isn't nice (no argument there), but it *also* may not be a violation of eBay rules — in which case, eBay can't do much about it. Note that the reporting system is monitored, and abuse by an eBay member may result in a range of unpleasant actions. The following sections list the primary reasons you may start an investigation.

Selling abuses

If you're on eBay long enough, you're bound to find an abuse of the service. It may happen on an auction you're bidding on; or a seller whose listings compete with your items may do something really, really wrong. Be a good community member and be on the lookout for the following:

- ✔ **Shill bidding:** A seller uses multiple User IDs to bid, or has accomplices place bids to boost the price of his or her auction items. eBay investigators look for six telltale signs, including a single bidder putting in a really high bid, a bidder with really low feedback but a really high number of bids on items, a bidder with low feedback who has been an eBay member for a while but who's never won an auction, or excessive bids between two users.

- ✔ **Payment interception:** An unscrupulous user, pretending to be the actual seller, contacts the winner to set up terms of payment and shipping in an effort to get the buyer's payment. You can easily avoid this situation by paying directly through the eBay site with PayPal.

- ✔ **Fee avoidance:** A user reports to eBay a lower-than-actual final price or illegally submits a Final Value Fee credit, or both. Final Value Fee credits are explained in Chapter 13.

- ✔ **Hot bid manipulation:** A user, with the help of accomplices, enters phony bids to make an auction appear to have a lot of bidding action. Let the experts at eBay decide on this one; but you may wonder if you see loads of bids come in rapid succession, but the price moves very little.

Bidding abuses

If you want to know more about bidding in general, see Chapter 6. Here's a list of bidding abuses that eBay wants to know about:

- **Bid shielding:** Two users working in tandem. User A, with the help of accomplices, intentionally bids an unreasonably high amount and then retracts the bid prior to the 12-hour cancellation deadline of the auction — leaving a lower bid (which the offender or an accomplice places) as the winning bid.

- **Bid siphoning:** Users send e-mail to bidders of a current auction to offer the same merchandise for a lower price elsewhere.

- **Auction interference:** Users warn other bidders through e-mail to stay clear of a seller *during a current auction,* presumably to decrease the number of bids and keep the prices low.

- **Bid manipulation (or invalid bid retraction):** A user bids a ridiculously high amount, raising the next highest bidder to maximum bid. The manipulator then retracts the bid and rebids *slightly* over the previous high bidder's maximum.

- **Nonpaying bidder:** People call them deadbeats; the bottom line is that these people win auctions but never pay up. Your bid on eBay is a legal contract to buy if you win — it is *not* a game.

- **Unwelcome bidder:** A user bids on a specific seller's auction despite the seller's warning that he or she won't accept that user's bids (as in the case of not selling internationally and still receiving international bids). This practice is impolite and obnoxious. If you want to bar specific bidders from your auctions, you can exclude them. See Chapter 13 for the scoop on how to block bidders.

Feedback abuses

All you have on eBay is your reputation, and that reputation is made up of your feedback history. eBay takes any violation of its feedback system very seriously. Because eBay's feedback is transaction related, unscrupulous eBay members now have less opportunity to take advantage of this system. Here's a checklist of feedback abuses that will get you into trouble. These can all be reported through the Security Center:

- **Feedback extortion:** A buyer threatens to post reputation-destroying feedback if the seller doesn't follow through on some unwarranted demand. Typical extortion attempts include demanding a refund or a generous discount after the bad buyer has won the item.

✔ **Personal exposure:** A member leaves feedback for a user that exposes personal information that doesn't relate to transactions on eBay.

✔ **Malicious feedback:** Writing malicious feedback is a sick game played by those who have very little to do with their time but upset upstanding eBay sellers. These sickies register on eBay with a new User ID and use the Buy It Now function to buy many items from a seller who has a high positive feedback rating. A few hours later, they leave dastardly negative feedback. The only goal of this action is to ruin the seller's reputation.

✔ **–4 Feedback:** Any user reaching a Net Feedback score of –4 is subject to suspension.

After you post feedback, your words are out there. They become part of cyber-space — effectively forever — and are there for all to see. Your words are a reflection of your online persona.

Know that eBay wields its power on a case-to-case basis. If the Customer Support representative doesn't see things your way, you might just be out of luck. It's happened to me more than once.

Identity abuses

Who you are on eBay is as important as what you sell (or buy). eBay moni-tors the identities of its members closely — and asks that you report any great pretenders in this area to Customer Support. Here's a checklist of iden-tity abuses:

✔ **Identity misrepresentation:** A user claims to be an eBay staff member or another eBay user, or he or she registers under the name of another user.

✔ **False or missing contact information:** A user deliberately registers with fraudulent contact information or an invalid e-mail address. If you come across someone on eBay who has false information registered on eBay, that member can be suspended.

✔ **Under age:** A user falsely claims to be 18 or older. (You must be *at least* 18 to enter into a legally binding contract.)

✔ **Dead/invalid e-mail addresses:** When e-mails bounce *repeatedly* (single bounces are almost a fact of life on the Internet) from a user's registered e-mail address, chances are good that the address may be dead — and it's doing nobody any good.

✔ **Contact information:** One user publishes another user's contact infor-mation on the eBay site.

When there is any form of contact information violation, eBay puts a squeeze on the wrongdoing member(s). When such members attempt to log on to the eBay site, they are faced with a message that lets them know they can't proceed onto the site without correcting their information.

Operational abuses

If you see someone trying to interfere with eBay's operation, eBay staffers want you to tell them about it. Here are two roguish operational abuses:

- ✔ **Hacking:** A user purposely interferes with eBay's computer operations (for example, by breaking into unauthorized files). If someone attempts to alter any of the eBay-generated information in a listing, such as a feedback rating or User ID, that person is violating important eBay rules.

- ✔ **Spamming:** The user sends unsolicited e-mail to eBay users. Just because you are in a transaction with someone doesn't give you the right to e-mail the person after the auction is over to solicit future business. You're not allowed to send a newsletter or solicitations unless your recipients have expressly opted in to your list. No one has the right to send you e-mail unrelated to your transaction without your permission.

Miscellaneous abuses

The following are additional problems that you should alert eBay about:

- ✔ A user is threatening physical harm to another eBay member.
- ✔ A person uses racist, obscene, or harassing language in a public area of eBay.

For a list of trading offenses and how eBay runs each investigation, go to `http://pages.ebay.com/help/buy/report-trading.html`.

Reporting Abuses to eBay Security

If you suspect a seller of abusing eBay's rules and regulations, you can report him or her directly on the item page. Look to the far right of tabs above the description on the page of the item in question and click the Report Item link, as shown in Figure 16-2.

Figure 16-2:
You'll find
the Report
Item link just
above the
description.

Click here to report an item.

When you click that link, you'll come to the only area on eBay where you can report listing violations. Select the reason for your report and further information from the drop-down menus. After you make your selections, click Continue.

If your issue is connected to a transaction that you're currently involved in with another eBay member, click the Report a Problem link on the Security Center page discussed earlier. You're presented with a page that suggests answers to the various questions you may have. To actually reach eBay, click the link on this page to the Customer Support Team. You'll land on the Customer Support page, which presents you with some of the most basic questions about eBay, as well as clickable links to find answers. To *really* (this time I promise) contact eBay, click a question that resembles your issue, and click the Call Us (or Call Me) link on the right of the page, as shown in Figure 16-3.

Figure 16-3:
Here's
where you
get to the
heart of the
issue.

When you become a PowerSeller or have an eBay store, you see a slightly different page from the one shown to non-PowerSellers and have considerably more contact options. (More reason to finish this book and get started selling!)

If you encounter any of the abuses outlined in this chapter, be sure to report the problem. Community policing is what makes eBay work.

The Security Center offers a wealth of good general information that can help you prevent something from going wrong in a future transaction. Be sure to use these pages as a resource to help prevent problems.

If you're involved in a troubled transaction and need to launch a report, follow these steps:

1. **Read all the information on the Investigations page (**`http://pages.ebay.com/help/buy/report-trading.html`**) before filing a new complaint.**

2. **Click any of the many informational links.**

   No matter which link you click, you're taken to an area that instructs you further and provides answers about what offenses eBay can and cannot investigate.

3. **If you find that you have a legitimate case that should be investigated, you are supplied a link to the proper reporting area.**

   Alternatively, you can click the Report Item link on the transaction page.

If you file a report, make your message clear and concise by including everything that happened — but don't editorialize. (Calling someone a "lowdown mud-sucking cretin" may make you *feel* better, but it doesn't provide any useful info to anyone who can help you; it doesn't make you seem very uncretinlike, either.) Keep it businesslike — just the facts. Do include all pertinent documentation, such as e-mails and receipts — and don't forget the transaction number.

Here's a checklist of what you should include in your report to Customer Support:

- ✔ Write only the facts as you know them.
- ✔ Attach any pertinent e-mails with complete headers if required.

   Headers contain all the information that precedes an e-mail message. eBay uses the headers to verify how the e-mails were sent and to follow the trail back to the originator of the messages. See the sidebar "Finding the hidden headers in an e-mail message" to locate this information.

- ✔ Be sure that the subject line of your report precisely names the violation.

After eBay receives your report via the Customer Service form, you usually get an automatic response that your e-mail was received — although in practice, several days may go crawling by before eBay investigates your allegations. (The Customer Service department must look at a *lot* of transactions.)

Finding the hidden headers in an e-mail message

Most of the time, your e-mail program hides the headers in an e-mail message. If you're using Outlook (a Windows e-mail program), here's how you find them:

1. **Open an e-mail message by double-clicking the Subject line.**

2. **In the open e-message, choose File⇨Properties.**

   The Properties dialog box appears.

3. **Click the Details tab.**

   Bingo! The headers appear. Copy and paste these into the eBay form whenever you need to report any spurious e-mail.

If you're using Gmail as an e-mail provider, try this:

1. **Open the message you'd like to view headers for, by clicking on the Subject.**

2. **In the open e-message, click the down arrow next to Reply, at the top of the message pane and select Show Original.**

   The Properties dialog box appears.

3. **The full headers appear in a new window.**

For users of Hotmail:

1. **Log in to your Hotmail account.**

2. **Select Inbox from the left-side menu.**

3. **Right-click the message you'd like to view headers for and select View Message Source.**

   The full headers appear in a new window.

This information is vital not just to eBay, but to any online entity to which you might need to report an e-mail abuse.

Depending on the outcome of the probe, eBay may contact you with the results. If your problem becomes a legal matter, eBay may not let you know what's going on. The only indication you may get that some action was taken is that the eBay member you reported is suspended.

If your complaint doesn't warrant an investigation by the folks at eBay, they may pass it along to someone at the overworked Customer Support staff, who then contacts you. (Don't bawl out the person if the attention you get is tardy.)

Unfortunately, suspended members can show up again on the eBay site. Typically, nefarious sorts like these just use a different name and credit card to register back on the site. In fact, this practice is common, so beware! If you suspect that someone who broke the rules once is back under another User ID, alert Customer Support. If you're a seller, you can refuse to accept bids from that person. If the person persists, alert Customer Support with e-mail.

Although slow (or no) response can get frustrating, avoid the temptation to initiate a reporting blitzkrieg by sending reports over and over until eBay "can't ignore" you. This practice is risky at best and inconsiderate at worst; it just slows the process for everyone — and it won't endear the e-mail bombardier to the folks who could help. It's better to just grin and bear it and wait for action to be taken.

Stuff eBay Won't Do Anything About

People are imperfect everywhere, even online. (Ya think?) You probably won't agree with some of the behavior that you run into on eBay (ranging from slightly annoying to just plain rotten). Although much of that conduct is just plain nasty, it can (and does) go on as long as it doesn't break eBay rules.

In some cases, you may need to bite your tongue and chalk up someone's annoying behavior to ignorance of the unwritten rules of eBay etiquette. Just because people have computers and some things to sell or buy doesn't mean that they possess grown-up social skills. (But you knew that.)

Here's a gang of annoying issues that crop up pretty regularly but that *aren't* against eBay's rules and regulations:

- ✔ **A seller sets astronomical shipping costs.** eBay policy says that shipping costs must be reasonable. Basically, eBay is wagging its finger and saying, "Don't gouge your buyers." When sellers gouge their buyers with high shipping fees, eBay penalizes them in their Best Match search results. Some sellers try to avoid fees or may be disappointed that a sale didn't make enough money, so they think that jacking up shipping costs will increase their profit.

   Under the rules, eBay will stop someone from charging excessive amounts for shipping. For more information on eBay's Excessive Shipping policy, go to `http://pages.ebay.com/help/policies/selling-practices.html`.

   One should always check shipping terms on the item page. Buyers must decide whether to agree to those terms *before* they bid or buy. The best way to protect yourself from being swindled is to buy only from a seller whose shipping costs feel fair to you.

- ✔ **A seller or buyer refuses to meet the terms that you mutually set.** eBay has the power only to warn or suspend members. It can't make anyone do anything — even someone who's violating a policy. If you want to make someone fulfill a transaction, you're more or less on your own. I heard one story of a seller who refused to send a product after being paid. The seller said, "Come and get it." The buyer happened to be in town on business — and did just that!

But if your item never arrives, you can apply to eBay for a refund under the Buyer Protection plan. Information on how to file is further on in this chapter.

Often, reluctant eBay buyers just need a nudge from eBay in the form of a warning to comply. So go ahead and file a case report to get a Final Value Fee credit request (I explain how to do this in Chapter 13).

✔ **An eBay member sends unwanted e-mail messages (spam).** In fact, members can send spam by using eBay's own tools. All the user has to do is access the Contact a Member Form by clicking a member's User ID. eBay sees non-transaction–related communication as spam; you need to report any member who abuses this system. (You'll see a reporting link on any e-mail sent through the eBay system). Although the items spammers are selling may be perfectly good, eBay won't offer you any protection if you participate in off-the-site deals. I suggest that you ignore these deals and avoid doing business with those who offer them in the future.

New eBay users are often the unwitting perpetrators of annoying behavior, but you're ahead of the pack now that you know what *not* to do. You can afford to cut the other newbies some slack and help them learn the ropes before you report them.

Knowing the Deeds That Can Get You Suspended

Playing by eBay's rules keeps you off the eBay's Security radar screen. If you start violating eBay policy, the company is going to keep a close eye on you. Depending on the infraction, eBay may be all over you like jelly on peanut butter. Or you may safely lurk in the fringes until your feedback rating is lower than the temperature in Nome in November.

Here's a docket of eBay no-no's that can get a member's permanent record damaged — and the member possibly *suspended:*

✔ Feedback rating of –4

✔ Three instances of deadbeat bidding with three different sellers

✔ Repeated warning for the same infraction

✔ Feedback extortion

✔ Bid shielding

✔ Unwelcome bidding after a warning from the seller

- ✔ Shill bidding
- ✔ Auction interception
- ✔ Fee avoidance
- ✔ Fraudulent selling
- ✔ Identity misrepresentation
- ✔ Bidding when younger than age 18
- ✔ Hacking
- ✔ Physical threats

If you get a suspension but think you're innocent, respond directly to the person who suspended you to plead your case. Reversals do occur. Don't broadcast your suspicions online. If you're wrong, you may regret it. Even if you're right, it's bad form.

Be careful about accusing members of cheating. Unless you're involved in a transaction, you don't know all the facts. *Law & Order* moments are great on television, but they're fictional for a reason. In real life, drawing yourself into a possible confrontation is senseless. Start the complaint process, keep it businesslike, and let eBay's staff figure out what's going on.

eBay Motors Vehicle Protection Program

Another beneficial eBay venture is eBay's Vehicle Purchase Protection, which offers a *free* limited warranty to anyone who purchases a car on eBay. Look for the Vehicle Protection Program Shield above the description area to see whether the vehicle you're interested in is covered. Qualified cars are identified in the listing description in the Item Specifics box, with the words *Vehicle Protection Program up to $50,000.*

Your vehicle purchase is protected for up to $50,000 or the vehicle purchase price, whichever is lower. You can find more information at eBay Motors:

```
http://pages.motors.ebay.com/buy/purchase-protection/
index.html
```

PayPal Purchase Protection

In addition to offering a safe way to purchase, PayPal offers an even better reason to pay through its service. If you purchased your item on the website of a PayPal-verified seller, you're covered for your original purchase price, plus shipping. This protection covers you only for nondelivery of tangible items and tangible items that are received significantly not as described — not if you are just disappointed with the item.

If you paid for an eBay purchase with a credit card through PayPal, be sure to make a claim with eBay first. Do *not* make a claim with your credit card company. PayPal Purchase Protection is for PayPal purchases, and you're not covered if you've made a claim with your credit card company.

For the latest information on this program, go to

    http://pages.ebay.com/help/buy/paypal-buyer-protection.html

Launching a Report

The second that you complain about a seller who's taken money but hasn't delivered the goods, an investigation team gets in gear. The Resolution Center is where you can go to file a formal complaint when you run into trouble with a transaction.

The first step is to get in touch with the seller and see if he or she will work things out with you. You can e-mail your seller through eBay's Message Center, or call the person directly.

When you're in a transaction with someone, eBay will give you that person's registered phone number. Go to Advanced Search and in the Members area, select Find Contact information. After you input the other person's eBay ID and the item number, eBay e-mails you the person's phone number.

To get to the Resolution Center, click the Customer Support link in the eBay navigation bar. You can get to the Resolution Center also from your listing in My eBay, in which case your item number will be filled in on the form for you:

1. **Go to your My eBay page.**

2. **In the Purchase History area, click the link to take you to the items you've purchased.**

3. **Scroll down the page to find the item in question and choose Resolve a Problem from the pull-down menu at the far right (as shown in Figure 16-4).**

   The Resolution Center's Resolve a Problem form appears.

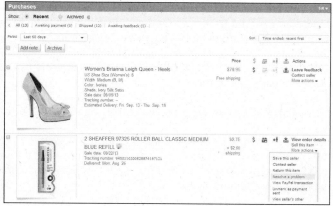

Figure 16-4:
Resolve
problem
transactions
through
eBay's
Customer
Support
here.

4. **Choose the problem you're having in your transaction and click Continue.**

   Now you get to the Report an Item Not Received or Not as Described form. If you arrived at the Resolution Center from your item listing, your item number is already filled in.

5. **If needed, enter the item number.**

6. **Click Continue.**

7. **Tell eBay how you paid for this item.**

   If you paid by PayPal, you are sent to the Resolution page.

8. **Review your case details and then click Open Case.**

   The Your Case Is Now Open page appears and tells you that your trading partner has been notified and has ten days to respond. From here on, you can continue your dealings in the Resolution Center.

To file a claim with eBay, you must initiate the complaint process no sooner than 7 days and no later than 45 days after the close of the listing. Be careful not to jump the gun and register a complaint too soon. I suggest waiting about 2 weeks before you register your complaint about an Item Not Received (an item lost in the mail can often take as long as 30 days to arrive); double-check first to make sure that your e-mail is working and that you have the correct contact information of the person with whom you're having difficulties. After all, neither eBay nor your ISP is infallible.

After you register a complaint, eBay informs the other party that you're making a claim. eBay says that it will try to contact both parties and help reach a resolution. *Registering* the complaint is not the same thing as *filing* an insurance complaint. Registering starts the process; filing for a refund comes after a grace period if the situation isn't resolved.

If you've clearly been ripped off, use the Item Not Received or Significantly Not as Described process to file a complaint. Just scroll to the Links area at the bottom of the page and click the Security Center link.

For a shortcut to file for an Item Not Received or Significantly Not as Described, go directly to the form at

`http://feedback.ebay.com/ws/eBayISAPI.dll?InrCreateDispute`

If the accusation you're registering is a clear violation, eBay gives you information on the kind of third-party assistance you can get to help resolve the problem. If eBay deems the problem a violation of the law, it reports the crime to the appropriate law enforcement agency.

Getting the Real Deal? Authentication and Appraising

Despite eBay's attempts to keep the buying and selling community honest, some people just refuse to play nice. After the New York City Department of Consumer Affairs launched an investigation into counterfeit sports memorabilia sold on the website, errant online outlaws experienced some anxious moments. I can always hope that they mend their ways, while at the same time advising you *don't bet on it.* Fortunately, eBay offers a proactive approach to preventing such occurrences from happening again.

Topmost among the countermeasures is easy member access to several services that can authenticate specific types of merchandise. The good news here is that you know what kind of item you're getting; the bad news is that, as does everything else in life, it costs you money.

Have a good working knowledge of what you're buying or selling. Before you bid, do some homework and get more information. And check the seller's or bidder's feedback. (Does this advice sound familiar?) See Chapters 5 and 9 for more information about conducting research.

Before you spend the money to have your item appraised and authenticated, ask yourself a few practical questions (regardless of whether you're buying or selling):

> ✔ **Is this item quality merchandise?** Am I selling or buying merchandise whose condition is subjective but important to its value — as in, *Is it really "well-loved" or just busted?* Is this item graded by some professionally accepted standard that I need to know?

✔ **Is this item the real thing?** Am I sure that I'm selling or buying a genuine item? Do I need an expert to tell me whether it's the real McCoy?

✔ **Do I know the value of the merchandise?** Do I have a good understanding of what this item is worth in the marketplace at this time, considering its condition?

✔ **Is the merchandise worth the price?** Is the risk of selling or buying a counterfeit, a fake, or an item I don't completely understand worth the cost of an appraisal?

If you answer "yes" to any of these questions, consider calling in a professional appraiser.

As for *selling* a counterfeit item — otherwise known as a knock-off, phony, or fake item — that's a no-brainer: No way. Don't do it.

If you need items appraised, consider using an appraisal agency. You can access several agencies by going to the overview page at `http://pages.ebay.com/help/buy/authentication.html`. eBay offers links to various appraising agencies that *may* offer their services at a discount to eBay members. These are my tried-and-true favorites:

✔ **ThePCGS** (Professional Coin Grading Service), **NGC** (Numismatic Guaranty Corporation), **ANACS** (American Numismatic Association Certification Service), and **IGC** (Independent Coin Graders) serve coin collectors, by encapsulating and grading coins for sale (shown in Figure 16-5). Visit `www.pcgs.com`, `http://www.icgcoin.com`, `http://www.anacs.com/`, and `www.ngccoin.com/`.

When selling coins on eBay, you cannot put a grade within the title unless the coin has been graded by an authorized grading service.

Figure 16-5:
Graded and serial numbered coins bring in much higher process.

- ✔ **PSA/DNA** (a service of Professional Sports Authenticators) and **Global Authentics** authenticate your sports autographs. Both keep online databases of thousands of certified autographs for you to compare your purchases against. Their respective online addresses are www.psacard.com and http://www.globalauthentics.com/.

- ✔ **Global Authority** is run by specialists in authenticating autographs and memorabilia from the sports world. See www.globalauth.com.

- ✔ **APEX** (American Philatelic Expertizing Service) authenticates your postal stamps: http://stamps.org/stamp-authentication.

- ✔ **CGC** (Comics Guaranty) grades and restores comic books. Visit www.cgccomics.com/.

- ✔ **IGI** (International Gemological Institute) grades, authenticates, and identifies loose gemstones and jewelry. Visit http://igionline.com.

- ✔ **PSA** (Professional Sports Authenticators) and **SGC** (Sportscard Guaranty) help guard against counterfeiting and fraud with sports memorabilia and trading cards. You can connect with these services to grade and authenticate your trading cards. You can visit the respective addresses of these agencies at www.psacard.com and www.sgccard.com/.

Even if you use an appraiser or an authentication service, do some legwork yourself. Often two experts can come up with wildly different opinions on the same item. The more you know, the better the questions you can ask.

If a seller isn't sure whether the item he or she is auctioning is authentic, you may find an appropriate comment (such as *Cannot verify authenticity*) in the item description. Knowledgeable eBay gurus always like to share what they know, and I have no doubt that someone on the Internet may be able to supply you with scads of helpful information. But be careful — some blarney artist (one of *those* is born every minute, too) may try to make a sucker out of you.

If It's Clearly Fraud

After filing either a fraud report or a Final Value Fee credit request, you can do more on your own. If the deal involves the post office in any way — if you mail a check or the seller sends you merchandise that's completely wrong and refuses to make good — file a mail-fraud complaint with the postal inspector.

In the United States, you can call your local post office or dial 800-275-8777 for a form to fill out. After you complete the form, the USPS sends the eBay bad guy a notice that you've filed a fraud complaint. Perhaps that *will* get his or her attention.

In addition to the post office, you can turn to some other agencies for help:

- **The National Fraud Information Center:** NFIC has an online site devoted to combating fraud on the Internet. NFIC works closely with legal authorities. File a claim at `www.fraud.org/complaint` or call toll free at 800-876-7060.

- **Law enforcement agencies:** Contact the local district attorney (or state Attorney General's office) and the local and state Consumer Affairs Department in the other person's state and city. (Look online for contact information or try your local agencies for contact numbers.)

- **Federal Trade Commission:** The FTC accepts complaints and investigates repeated cases of fraud. File a claim at

    `https://www.ftccomplaintassistant.gov`

- **Internet service provider:** Contact the member's ISP. You can get this bit of info from the person's e-mail address, just after the @ symbol. (See? This easy access to information does have its advantages.) Let the ISP know whom you have filed a complaint against, the nature of the problem, and the agencies that you've contacted.

Any time you contact another agency for help, keep eBay up to date on your progress by writing to its representatives the old-fashioned way — yep, on paper, with stamped envelope (you might want to keep some Forever stamps around for just such occasions). Address your letter to eBay ATTN: Fraud Prevention, 2145 Hamilton Ave., San Jose, CA 95125.

A very thin line separates alerting other members to a particular person's poor behavior and breaking an eBay cardinal rule by interfering with an auction. Don't make unfounded or vitriolic accusations — especially if you were counting on them never getting back to the person they were about (or, for that matter, if you hoped they *would*). Trample the poison out of the gripes of wrath *before* you have your say.

Communication and compromise are the keys to successful transactions. If you have a difference of opinion, write a polite e-mail outlining your expectations and offer to settle any dispute by phone. See Chapters 12 and 13 for tips on communicating after the auction ends — and solving disputes *before* they turn wicked, aggressive, or unprintable.

Chapter 17

Social Media and the eBay Community

*e*Bay is more than just an Internet destination for buying and selling great stuff. eBay wants the world to know that it has created a community. When eBay first began, the community was very strong, with thousands of eBay users; Customer Service representatives attended the boards (mostly to keep everyone in line) and they were a fun place to be. As in real-life communities, you participate as much as works for you. With the advent of social media and the eBay community, you can get involved in all sorts of neighborhood activities, or you can just sit back, and watch the world go by.

As you've probably heard by now, one of the main ways to participate in the eBay community is through transaction feedback (which I explain in detail in Chapters 4 and 6). In this chapter, I show you some other ways to become part of the community. You can socialize (making friends who live in your community or who live across the planet), gain knowledge from other members, post messages, or just read what everybody's talking about on Facebook, Twitter, eBay's discussion boards, groups, and the corporate Announcements Board. I include tips on how to use all these places to your benefit, and then give you a change of scenery by surfing through some off-site social media sites that can help you with your buying and selling.

Joining eBay's Community

On the bottom of every eBay page is a group of links: Click Community to connect to other eBay members; or click the Announcement link to check proposed changes to the site on the Announcements page. But there's a whole lot more to the Community area of eBay. Take a little time to explore it for yourself.

News and chat, this and that

It's not quite *The New York Times,* but you can find all the announcements, groups, and discussion board links from the Community Overview page. Figure 17-1 shows you what the page looks like. (eBay is continually making changes to the community, so note that this page will change with regularity.)

Figure 17-1:
The main Community page features links to informative places on eBay, including areas to ask questions and post messages.

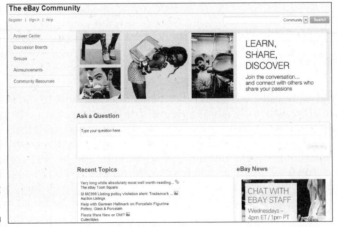

The eBay Community

Register | Sign in | Help

Answer Center
Discussion Boards
Groups
Announcements
Community Resources

LEARN, SHARE, DISCOVER

Join the conversation...
and connect with others who
share your passions

Ask a Question

Type your question here.

Recent Topics

Very long while absolutely most well worth reading...
The eBay Town Square
[*] MC999 Listing policy violation alert: Trademark ...
Auction Listings
Help with German Hallmark on Porcelain Figurine
Pottery, Glass & Porcelain
Fiesta Ware New or Old?
Collectibles

eBay News

CHAT WITH EBAY STAFF
Wednesdays –
4pm ET / 1pm PT

Here's a list of the core headings of the main Community page. Each heading offers you links to the specific eBay areas:

- **Answer Center:** Questions can be asked on almost any topic. Everyone may have an opinion, and you may get a solid answer.

- **Discussion Boards:** Click the links in this section to be whisked to eBay's discussion boards.

- **Groups:** Are you a joiner? There are lots of folks with special interests on eBay that want to share. Here's where you will find them.

✔ **Announcements:** This area covers general news, policy changes, technology updates, system announcements, and more. You can also find links to eBay events, including Town Hall meetings, eBay Radio, and Online Workshops.

✔ **Buying Guides:** Here you will find community-generated content. Want to read other eBay members' opinions on products? Read their reviews? Click this area and you can also search for Guides (short product-related posts). From the Reviews pages, you will find links to items selling the product and for what price it is being sold on eBay.

✔ **Community Resources:** Here you will find links to policies, Security Center, and the Feedback Forum.

There are many places to connect with other eBay community members. Many are active on social media networks. You can find me on Twitter (@MarshaCollier) `http://twitter.com/MarshaCollier` or through `Facebook`. If you have a quick question, ping me (tech-speak for *contact*), and I will try to answer ASAP.

Filling in your eBay Profile and creating Collections

Did you know that if you click your User ID on any eBay page, you arrive at your very own profile page? (You also have a link on your Feedback profile page.) Unlike the About Me page, which you have to choose to set up yourself, every eBay member has a profile page. Yours is ready and waiting for you to embellish.

In Chapter 14, I show you the basics of how to set up your own. You can also add custom features to this page to share your other community moments.

Your profile page reflects your many varied interests. From here, eBay gives you other ways to express yourself (links to all these pages are also on the main Community page):

✔ **Collections:** Have a hobby? Maybe enjoy an old series of TV shows or a movie? (No cracks about my collection of the rare *Star Trek* collectibles `www.ebay.com/cln/marsha_c/The-Most-Rare-Star-Trek-Collectibles/59087095010%20`). You can curate your own online image collection of items to share with the community. Anytime you see a Star icon you can click to add to a collections page (see Figure 17-2). Take my word for it; you'll enjoy putting one together.

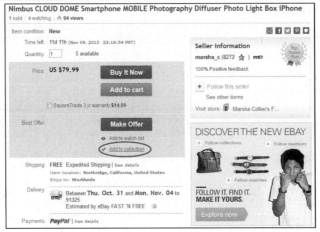

Figure 17-2:
Look for
this link to
add your
favorites to
a collection
to share.

✔ **Reviews:** Wondering what other eBay members think of a particular product, book, or movie? Visit eBay's Reviews to find out. Better yet, contribute one of your own. Reviews you have posted show up when a search is made on an item for which eBay users have posted reviews. Figure 17-3 shows a review written by eBay member eclecticcollectit for my most recent book. You can also visit the Reviews home page for more information `http://www.ebay.com/crw`.

Figure 17-3:
eBay mem-
bers review
books. Note
the three
clickable
tabs that
show you
the listings,
product
details, and
reviews.

Reviews & Research

Customer Reviews

★★★★★
Average review score based on
1 user reviews

100%
of customers
recommend
this product

Rating distributions

5 star	▬▬▬▬▬	1
4 star		0
3 star		0
2 star		0
1 star		0

See all reviews

Write a review

Sorted by Relevance   View all customer reviews (1)

Must-Have Tool for the Serious eBay Seller   Created: 08/12/13

by: eclecticcollectit (977 ⭐)   See all reviews by eclecticcollectit

★★★★★ **Yes,** I would recommend this product to a friend.

The 3rd Edition of Marsha Collier's eBay Business All-in-One for Dummies takes your eBay business to the next level.
All the way from the basics of selling on eBay to sourcing merchandise to the legal aspects of having a home-based
business - this book has it all!
Broken down into nine mini-books, it's easy to find the answers you're looking for. If you're serious about selling on eBay this is the tool you'll want
to keep on hand.
eBay Business All-in-One for Dummies gives you the information you need to be a success on eBay!

✔ **Guides:** Do you have a special talent? Maybe you're an expert on antique linens and want to share that knowledge. Here's the place. Go to the Guides area and post your guide to help other eBay members. There's a link on the home page in the Legal & More area, or just go to `http://www.ebay.com/gds` and you'll see the page shown in Figure 17-4.

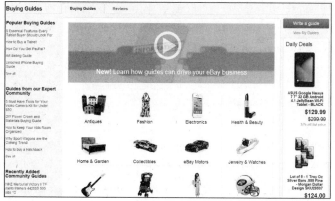

Figure 17-4: The Buying Guides page is where you can contribute knowledge to the community.

Hear ye, hear ye! eBay's Announcements Board

If you were living in the 1700s, you'd see a strangely dressed guy in a funny hat ringing a bell and yelling, "Hear ye, hear ye!" every time you opened eBay's announcements boards. (Then again, if you were living in the 1700s, you'd have no electricity, computers, fast food, or anything else you probably consider fun.) In any case, eBay's Announcements Board is the most important place to find out what's going on (directly from the home office) on the website. And no one even needs to ring a bell.

The Announcements Board is where eBay lists any news that affects buyers and sellers, new features, and policy changes. Visiting this page is like reading a morning eBay newspaper because eBay adds comments to this page almost every week. You find out about upcoming changes in categories, new promotions, and eBay goings-on. eBay also uses it to help users become aware of critical changes in policies and procedures. Reach this page at `http://announcements.ebay.com/`. Figure 17-5 shows you eBay's Announcements Board with information that could affect your sales.

Figure 17-5:
Keep up
to date on
what's new
at eBay by
visiting the
General
Announce-
ments
Board.

If you feel there is a site issue, or want to know when server maintenance occurs, click the link to the right of this page to go to System Announcements. Any current issues will be posted there.

eBay has millions of active users globally — a bigger population than some countries — but it can still have that small-town feel through groups, discussion boards, and announcements.

Help! I need somebody

If you ever have specific eBay questions to which you need answers, click the Answer Center link in the Community.

These boards work differently from eBay's old chat rooms. Chat rooms are full of people who are hanging out and talking to each other all at the same time, whereas users of discussion boards tend to go in, leave a message or ask a question, and pop out again. Also, in a discussion board, you need to start a thread by asking a question. Title your thread with your question, and you'll no doubt get a swift answer to your query.

These boards cover almost any topic regarding selling and buying on eBay. Just post your question, and some kind eBay member will probably suggest an answer (but remember to double-check your answer, just as you would any advice from someone with unknown credentials). Keep in mind that the Answer Center is to answer questions; if someone tries to sell you something on there, I'd turn the other way.

One of the best solutions is to find one of the eBay Social Media sellers on Twitter (more about that later in this chapter); many are very active on the site, and you'll probably get an answer tout de suite. (I'm on there, Facebook, and Google Plus — daily — and answer whatever questions I can.)

User-to-user discussion boards

eBay has some other boards that take a different tack on things. They're *discussion* boards as opposed to *chat* boards, which basically means that the topics are deliberately open-ended — just as the topics of discussions in coffeehouses tend to vary depending on who happens to be in them at any given time. Check out these areas and read ongoing discussions about eBay's latest buzz. It's a lot of fun and good reading. Post your opinions to the category that suits you. You can find tons of discussion boards on various topics relating to doing business on eBay, but my favorites are in the General Discussion area. Each discussion board carries many topics in subcategories, as you can imagine.

Keeping up with the business of eBay

There's a place on the eBay site that buyers and sellers don't often visit. I recommend that you go to the bottom of almost every eBay page and click the link, *About eBay*. Clicking here will give you great insights as to where the company is going — and news of developments that may influence you as a buyer or seller.

You'll find continually updated topics on eBay news, sustainability, eBay's blogs, investment information, and jobs (should you be interested in working at eBay). There's a fun section that graphically illustrates eBay's history, and the first edition of *eBay For Dummies* is listed as an integral turning point in their history.

You will find these boards:

- Community Help Boards (28 subcategories)
- Category-Specific Boards (52 subcategories)
- eBay News & Information Boards (4 subcategories)
- General Discussion Boards (12 subcategories)
- PowerSellers (4 subcategories)
- Seller Tools Boards (7 subcategories)
- Special Discussion Boards (8 subcategories)

There's one cardinal rule for eBay boards: no business. No advertising items for sale! Not now. Not ever. eBay bans any repeat offenders who break this rule from participating on these boards.

Remember that you're visiting eBay and that you're a member. It's not Speakers' Corner — that spot in London's Hyde Park where protesters are free to stand on a soapbox and scream about the rats in government. If you feel the need to viciously complain about eBay, take it outside, as the bar bouncers say.

Category-specific discussion boards

Want to talk about Elvis, Louis XV, Sammy Sosa, or Howard the Duck? Currently over 20 category-specific discussion boards enable you to tell eBay members what's on your mind about merchandise and auctions. You reach these boards by clicking Community and then clicking Discussion Boards.

Of course, you can buy and sell without ever going on a discussion board, but you can certainly benefit a lot from one. Discussions mainly focus on merchandise and the nuts and bolts of transactions. Category-specific discussion boards are great for posting questions on items that you don't know much about.

On eBay, you get all kinds of responses from all kinds of people. Take a portion of the help you get with a grain of salt; some of the folks who help you may be buyers or competitors.

Don't be shy. As your second-grade teacher said, "No questions are dumb." Most eBay members love to share their knowledge of items.

eBay groups

If you're the friendly type and would like an instant group of new friends, I suggest that you click the link in the Connect area to eBay Groups. Here you can find many user groups, hosted on eBay but run by eBay community members. They may be groups consisting of people from the same geographic area, those with similar hobbies, or those interested in buying or selling in particular categories.

Currently, we can find Groups with a large amount of categories and even further subcategories:

- Collectors Clubs (18 Categories)
- Groups for Groups (2 Categories)
- Mentoring Groups (3 Categories)
- News & Events (1 Category)
- Regional (53 Categories)
- Seller Groups (6 Categories)
- Special Interest Groups (32 Categories)

eBay Groups may be public groups (open to all) or private clubs with their own private boards. Only invited members of a private group can access a private board.

Joining a group is easy: Just click any of the links on the main Groups page and you're presented with a dizzying array of groups to join. Your best bet, though, is to participate in chats or discussions and find other members that you'd like to join up with.

Learning and Selling through Social Media

Social media is in its infancy; it reminds me of the point at which eBay was in 1997. The burgeoning number of social media sites draw many eBay sellers and buyers because they are generally a computer-savvy group. All cultural changes began with words — and the experts predict that social media will be the marketing tool of the future. It's well on its way there right now.

Social media sites have grown well beyond their initial role as tools of social contact. Following and friending like-minded people on social media networks (and connecting with them) not only builds a sense of community but also gives you a built-in support group.

When I say to connect, I mean to converse. You don't have to sit on the sites regularly; you need to drop by and respond to people who have commented to you. You also need to reach out and comment to others. Marketing can be a natural next step — if you handle it right. But keep this distinction in mind . . . .

Social media discussion is *not* the same as advertising. You will see many online sellers promoting their goods, one after the other, as their sole "conversation." That's actually more broadcasting — like commercials on TV in the old days. Everyone skipped over commercials then — and they skip over them now. Ads-as-faux-conversation is old school and not very interesting to *anyone* who's following you online.

Many small businesses on social media try to get hundreds of followers for their social media pages. A multitude of friends and followers does not equate to producing massive sales. The quality of your conversation and the people you connect with is what draws people to you.

eBay's official blog can be found at `http://blog.ebay.com` (as shown in Figure 17-6). If you are interested in the business of e-commerce, it's a worthwhile visit.

Figure 17-6: The official eBay corporate blog.

In this chapter, I give you a brief overview of social media. If you're interested in this form of marketing, you might want to check out my book, *Social Media Commerce For Dummies*. I also wrote a book on online customer service; there's a preview of it on my site `http://theultimateonlinecustomerserviceguide.blogspot.com`.

Finding friends and customers on Facebook

You have a Facebook page, right? You share fun thoughts and ideas with your family and friends, right? Well, when you set up an eBay business, you can have a page for your small business. I'm not suggesting that you'll be directly selling from your Facebook page (although you can), but having a page is an efficient way to meet people online and interest them in what you're selling.

Your initial base for building a business page comes from your friends. When you get over 25 people to "like" your business page, you can get a custom URL from Facebook for the page. Mine is `http://www.facebook.com/MarshaCollierFanPage` (because it was established a long time ago — when they were called "fan" pages). The page is different from my personal page `http://www.facebook.com/marsha.collier`. I try to treat each page differently, encouraging more intimate contact on my personal page, and posting business information and conversation on my business page. Even my pictures are selected for a different style.

Unless your political and religious views reflect your core self and/or your business, it's best to stay away from making public statements on these topics. Whatever you put on the Internet is indexed and recorded somewhere — and your prospective customers may be put off if they do not hold the same views as you.

As a subtle touch on my business page, I use an application (see Figure 17-7) called *Auction Items* (despite the name, the app also posts your fixed-price listings). Applications such as this can only be used on business pages. The application will be listed in the links on the left side of your business page. I find this app gives my items punch, and yet isn't as "in-your-face" as other marketing programs. You can find it to put on your page at `https://www.facebook.com/AuctionItems`.

Figure 17-7:
The eBay
Auction
Items
applica-
tion on my
Facebook
business
page has
clickable
links that
directly go
to a page
with my
eBay
listings.

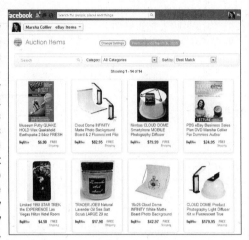

The publishers of the app also offer other free tools. They enable eBay sellers to embed their listings into their websites by inserting a short HTML code into the website or via a WordPress plug-in. You can learn more about these at http://apps.esoftie.com.

Another example is my friend (and fellow eBay seller — *dnasupplies*) Anita Nelson. She has two Facebook pages as well, one personal and one for her business, Model Supplies (see Figure 17-8). She is also @ModelSupplies on Twitter.

Figure 17-8:
The Model
Supplies
page (note
the Auction
Items app)
builds her
eBay busi-
ness on
Facebook.

For a more detailed explanation of how to best use Twitter and Facebook, you might like my *Facebook and Twitter For Seniors For Dummies* (even if you're not a senior)!

Connecting in 140 characters on Twitter

At this writing, Twitter has 500 million total (more than 215 million active users) and serves up over 500 million tweets a day. What's a *tweet?* Not just a sound effect from a parakeet anymore. Now it's a short online comment from one Twitter user to another; tweets often flit back and forth between users who follow each other. Tweets are not only comments, but also other quick notes that can be quotes, links to news stories, and the occasional self-promotion.

If you like to chat, comment, and read news stories, I'll bet you'll like Twitter. You don't have to be there all day, because when people "talk" to you there, you will see it in your "Connect" column (you can see that on my Twitter page in Figure 17-9). To answer, you just click the Reply link.

Figure 17-9:
When I talk to folks on Twitter, they appear on my Twitter page.

You'll find that your conversations on Twitter will engage you — but only if you engage with your followers. Those who are constantly broadcasting are just trying to build follower numbers — but it's been proven that this practice will not increase sales.

So if you go to Twitter.com and sign up, you need to give your Twitter stream a name. I suggest that you use your real name — for several solid reasons:

✔ Friends will find you easier.

✔ If you change businesses down the line, you won't have to start over with a new name.

✔ On the Internet, you are the face of your business — and everything you post is archived somewhere. Your tweets on Twitter are archived in the National Archive (no joke).

✔ If it's good enough for @MichaelDell (founder of Dell), @SteveCase (founder of AOL), @RichardBranson (founder of Virgin Group), I'd say it's a good idea for you too.

After you sign in, you need to put up a picture and fill out a short bio. The first thing you need to do is put up a picture — preferably yours. People like to see what you look like when they find you on Twitter. Do everyone a favor and describe yourself clearly, as best you can, in the allotted 160 characters. Take a look at Figure 17-10 for a good example. Although Anita is a big seller on eBay, you'll meet lots of small businesses just like you. Figure 17-11 shows you @nanettestore.

Figure 17-10: eBay seller dnashop-per (Anita Nelson) shows an informative bio in fewer than 160 characters.

Anita Nelson
@AnitaNelson FOLLOWS YOU
Anita Nelson @ModelSupplies skin care & ingredients on Amazon + eBay PowerSeller. Blogger, Radio Host, LOA, Social Media Guide, Love Comedy, Music & Animals ♥

Detroit, MI USA · iModelSupplies.com

In the account setting page, scroll down and put a check mark in the box next to Always Use HTTPS. This will cause Twitter to use a secure connection where possible to encrypt your account information.

After you fill out all the cyber-paperwork, you'll see your very own Twitter page. It will be a very blank page. Don't be sad and lonely — you can begin by following me, @MarshaCollier. Say Hi and I'll follow you back.

When you visit my Twitter page, you'll see a tab that, when clicked, reveals Lists that I've made of people on Twitter. I've made one full of eBay Social Sellers that lists eBay sellers who participate in social media and are fun to follow. Just click on the link or go to `http://twitter.com/MarshaCollier/ebay-social-sellers`. On the list page, just click the link and you will automatically be following everyone on the list.

Figure 17-11: Here's an eBay seller also on Twitter. Can you get any ideas from this?

When you see their tweets in your stream, click the Reply link to say hello — or share something interesting. No doubt they will follow you back.

To find other people to follow, I suggest that you go to the website `www.tweetfind.com`. Here you can type in keywords that reflect your interests, and you will be presented with a list of people who have indicated to TweetFind what their interests are. I put in a search for eBay and found the people shown in Figure 17-12.

Figure 17-12: A built-in list of people who have a passion for eBay on Twitter.

Type in your hobbies and your interests. You'll find a bunch of people to follow, and your Twitter home page will become far more interesting.

You can also search to find like-minded folks on `klout.com`. This is a website that measures social media influencers and allows searches by category. Figure 17-13 shows the current influencers in the topic of eBay.

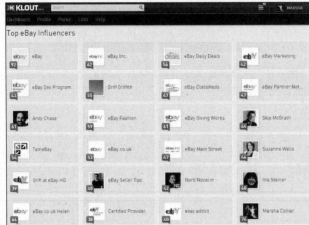

Figure 17-13: Klout measures social media influencers across the major platforms.

Search Twitter with keywords like eBay, and you can find (by clicking All) folks who tweet about eBay. You can search Twitter for mentions of keywords and find people with like ideas, but the websites I mentioned are the best places to begin.

Chapter 18

Mobile eBay Apps and Fun Features

Although eBay is a site where we buy and sell, there are a few extras that make participating on the site a whole lot more fun. In this chapter, I familiarize you with my favorites.

The Loyalty Program for Shoppers: eBay Bucks

Personally, I'm a fan of loyalty programs; they keep my attention as a customer. For the uninitiated, a loyalty program is a cashback, discount, or bonus program designed by a brand to reward their loyal customers — to keep you coming back. Usually the more you spend, the better the bonuses.

That's how it works with *eBay Bucks*. If you begin to spend regularly on the site and pay through PayPal, no doubt you'll come up on eBay's radar and they'll send you an invitation; see Figure 18-1. If you're not at that point (yet), drive your browser to the eBay Bucks FAQ (Frequently Asked Questions) at `http://pages.ebay.com/rewards/faq.html` and discover all the ins and outs.

Figure 18-1:
Enroll to
save two
percent,
right here!

Even if you're not a big shopper on the site, getting two percent back for your purchases is still not a bad deal (especially these days). Your two percent back can be used on eBay purchases during a pre-designated time span after you earn it.

Your qualified purchases, after you sign up, are totaled by each calendar quarter. Then eBay sends you an eBay Bucks Certificate to apply to purchases in the next calendar quarter. You can't save up the certificates, though; they expire after 30 days.

The Perfect Gift? An eBay Gift Certificate

If you're like me, you face dozens of birthdays, anniversaries, and holidays each year. I don't like giving gift cards generally, but eBay gift cards (or certificates) allow the recipients to shop for anything they want on eBay — from millions of sellers all over the world. They don't have to purchase the entire amount at one time. When a cardholder makes a purchase, the balance is applied to his or her PayPal account for future buying sprees.

If you're in a hurry, you don't have to hunt down a store; just go to the eBay home page, click the Legal & More tab at the bottom, and you'll see the Gift Center. You may also go directly to http://giftcard.ebay.com and click the link to give an eBay gift certificate via e-mail, U. S. Mail, or print one on the spot. When you select the e-mail option, the certificate will be instantly e-mailed and your recipient can start spending right away.

I give eBay gift cards often. I can't think of anyone who wouldn't enjoy them.

Go Mobile — for Buying and Selling

I use the eBay mobile app (Figure 18-2) when I'm out looking for items to resell on eBay. It's especially helpful at a garage sale to see how much I can sell an item for — and to find out how many people are selling an item. eBay smartly incorporated their newly acquired RedLaser app, so you can find pricing by just scanning a barcode.

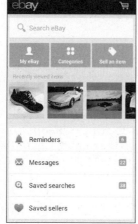

Figure 18-2: After I sign in, this is the home page of the eBay app on my Android phone.

The eBay mobile app is available on many smartphones: iOS (for the iPhone, iPad, and iPod touch), Android, Windows Phone 7, and BlackBerry. If you don't have one of those operating systems on your smartphone, you can always type the address http://m.ebay.com into your mobile browser (or, if you're reading this as an e-book, use the link in this sentence).

With the mobile app, you can do just about anything you can on the eBay site . . . almost. The smaller screen doesn't give you the robust experience that you get on eBay, but it has many powerful built-in features.

Access your My eBay page to check up on items you're watching or the progress of auctions you're running (or bidding on), or your Purchase History as shown on the left in Figure 18-3.

If you're out and about and find an item you think might do well on eBay, you can easily search for the item by tapping the magnifying glass on the app.

Figure 18-3:
Access your
My eBay
page and
see any
view.

Inside secret: Tap in the text field on the eBay mobile app and eBay's RedLaser scanner will pop up. Just tap the scan option to scan a barcode on an item to see the items being sold on eBay, as shown on the right in Figure 18-4. Then refine your search to Sold items only to see at what price that item is currently selling.

Figure 18-4:
Search for
items by
typing key-
words or tap
the text field
to activate
the barcode
scanner.

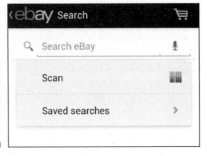

If you're into apps, eBay has a bunch to choose from. I only use the eBay app because I rarely need the others on the run. Some that I like are

✔ **eBay Fashion:** Aside from searching and visiting the Fashion vault, you can use the See It On augmented-reality feature. (iPhone only).

✔ **eBay Motors:** The Motors app is very useful. If you're out and about, you can compare prices. You also get access to free Vehicle History reports from Experian Auto Check and best of all? Use the Map feature to mark your location and find where you parked your car. (iPhone only)

✔ **RedLaser:** With this app, you can visit stores, scan barcodes, and find the best deals on eBay, online or in your local area. You can also see coupons from local stores, buy through PayPal, and pick up your item at the store.

When you are starting out on eBay, I recommend listing your eBay items for sale from your laptop or desktop computer. The text-formatting features available on the website's Sell an Item page (like bulleted lists and boldface) are not easily done on the mobile app.

The app does have an HTML description writer, so if you learn the little bit of code as outlined in Chapter 10, you can give your descriptions a little extra character. Descriptions (currently) posted from the mobile app look like the one in Figure 18-5 when viewed on the website, although you can edit your description once you get to a computer. The app currently misses some of eBay's listing refinements.

Figure 18-5:
An eBay listing listed on the mobile app, as seen on the website.

Selling and Buying: Helping Nonprofits

Most of us have donated to charity in one form or another. But here on eBay, charities really rock. Do you need a *Jurassic Park* helmet signed by Steven

Spielberg to round out your collection (and deflect the odd dino tooth)? Post a bid on one of the charity auctions. How about a signed original photograph of Jerry Seinfeld from *People* magazine? Yup, you can get that, too. All these and more have turned up in charity auctions. In short, having a big heart for charities has gotten a whole lot easier thanks to eBay.

eBay Giving Works

November 2003 was a lucky time for this country's charities. That's the month that eBay launched the eBay Giving Works Charity auction area. eBay originally teamed up with one of the first charity-giving sites on the Internet, MissionFish, which now runs the PayPal giving fund. After 9/11, as "9/11 Auction for America" (see sidebar further on), eBay's giving program originally raised over $10 million through online charity auctions for organizations supporting the victims of the tragedy and their families. The eBay community has helped raise over $300 million.

If you're involved with a charity, you can register your charity to get on the list of beneficiaries. You can also run your own fundraising events on eBay! Just go to `http://givingworks.ebay.com/`, and you'll arrive at the Giving Works hub (as shown in Figure 18-6).

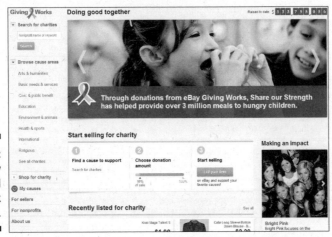

Figure 18-6: Where eBay buyers and sellers work for good.

The best part is that *you* can run an auction or fixed-price listing to benefit your favorite charity. Sellers can list items for sale and designate those items to benefit a charity from the MissionFish directory (which lists thousands of charities). The seller can also specify what percentage (from as little as

9/11 Auction for America

In late December 2001, eBay took on one of its most ambitious attempts at fundraising: the Auction for America. In responses to requests by New York Governor George E. Pataki and Mayor Rudolph Giuliani, eBay called on the community to raise $100 million in 100 days. eBay and Billpoint (eBay's payment service at the time) waived all fees, and community members gave their all, donating and buying all kinds of items to benefit the New York State World Trade Center Relief Fund, the Twin Towers Fund, the American Red Cross, and the September 11 Fund.

Community member Jay Leno sold his celebrity-autographed Harley Davidson for over $360,260; Tim Allen sold his 1956 Chevrolet Nomad for $46,000; and countless corporate sponsors joined in with the person-to-person community to raise funds. Over 100,000 sellers participated, and over 230,000 items were listed.

The auction ended on December 25, after raising $10 million. This is an amazing tribute to the eBay members and their community spirit.

10 up to 100 percent) of the auction proceeds go to the charity. You can browse to select the charity of your choice on the Giving Works page. When you list your item for sale, you can indicate — on the Sell form's Create Your Listing section — to which charity you'd like to donate proceeds, and what percentage of the final sale price to donate.

As you visit different areas of eBay, you can recognize the charity auctions by the small blue-and-gold ribbon icon next to them in searches and the Category list.

Creative charity auctions

New charities are popping up all the time on eBay. To see the sales that benefit nonprofits, go to the Giving Works page and click the link Shop for Charity. Here are some of the more creative charity auctions that have been held on eBay:

- The highest-grossing charity auction occurred in 2011. In an annual eBay fundraising auction run by Kompolt (a division of Cause Media Group), billionaire Warren Buffett donated a private lunch to benefit the Glide Foundation in New York. The 2011 auction grossed $2,626,411; in 2013, the auction netted $1,000,100 (which included lunch for 8).

✔ Oprah Winfrey has jumped onto eBay with a bang! In 2003, to fund her charity, the Angel Network, Oprah auctioned two chairs from her set. These were not just any chairs. Aside from being luxurious leather chairs designed by Ralph Lauren, they had housed the behinds of famous names such as John F. Kennedy, Jr., Halle Berry, Tom Hanks, Jim Carrey, and Michael Jordan. The 7-day auction netted the charity an amazing $64,100. In 2010, the media mogul cleaned out her own closet for her Leadership Academy for Girls.

✔ To celebrate Chivas Regal's 200th year, the company chose eBay for CHIVAS 200, the largest online charity auction in the world. From September 6 to October 31, 2001, the Chivas folks auctioned more than 200 of the world's most-wanted items and experiences — such as an opportunity to become a Russian space-station cosmonaut — all for the benefit of charity partners around the world.

✔ When I appeared on *The View* with Barbara Walters and Star Jones, all four stars of the show autographed a coffee cup that we auctioned off on eBay to benefit UNICEF. We raised over $1,000 on a single coffee cup! Now that a couple of the hosts have moved on, I wonder what that little cup's worth.

Part V
The Part of Tens

Check out www.dummies.com/extras/ebay for an additional Part of Tens chapter on navigating eBay.

In this part...

- More tips for buying and selling items
- Software programs and services that can lighten your auction load

Chapter 19

Ten (or So) Golden Rules for eBay Buyers and Sellers

*N*o matter how much experience pilots may have, they always keep numerous checklists to go over on a daily basis. The same is true on eBay (although the only crashing that you need to worry about is on your computer). No matter how many times you buy or sell, the advice in this chapter can help you survive and thrive on eBay.

Although conducting business on eBay is relatively smooth overall, any venture is bound to have a few bumps here and there. There's a certain etiquette that goes along with everything we do in life. If you follow these simple rules, your time on the site will be a whole lot more pleasant for everyone. That said, here are ten (or so) easy, important golden rules for eBay. I note which tips are geared toward buyers or sellers. Happy hunting and gathering!

After a while, posting listings and bidding become rote. You can all too easily forget the basics, so look at this book every now and again and remember: As a successful eBay member, you're part of a very special person-to-person community.

Buyer: Investigate Your Treasure Before You Buy

In the excitement of finding just what we want, many of us may develop a tendency to leap before we look. Even if the item is closing soon, carefully read the item description. Does the item have any flaws? Can you live with them if it does? Is something missing from the description that should be there? Did you read the terms of payment and shipping? (*Do you really, really want it?*)

Don't be too shy or embarrassed. If you have any questions, ask the seller a question! You're better off covering your bases before you place a bid or buy an item than you are facing disappointment when the item arrives.

Keep this in mind *before* you click the Bid or Buy button; you are *legally and morally obligated* to go through with the transaction if you win. Make sure that everything is as you want it and check for a warranty or return policy. Clarify everything up front. If the seller doesn't answer back, consider that non-response an early warning that dealing with this person may be a mistake!

Buyer: Check the Seller's Feedback

Never bid without checking the seller's feedback. You need to be able to trust the person you're buying from. Look for the Top Rated Plus Seller icon, but you may not find enough information. When it is a very pricey item, dig a little deeper. Don't just evaluate the percentage of positive and negative feedback: Investigate the seller's feedback a bit more deeply by clicking the number next to his or her User ID. Take the time to read the comments left by others who have transacted with this seller. Also, checking some of the seller's other listings, past and present, to get an idea of the seller's history can't hurt. As badly as you may want something, sending a payment to someone with a high feedback rating *who recently got a bunch of negatives* could lead to a *big* disappointment.

Buyer: Check the Price Tag and Bid Wisely

Before you bid, make sure that you have some knowledge of what to pay for the item, even if you limit your search to completed listings to get an idea of how much the item went for in the past.

If a deal sounds too good to be true, it may well be.

I love eBay — but not for every single thing that I buy (okay, almost). Make sure that you can't get the item cheaper at the store or from another online seller.

Beware of getting caught up in the frenzy of last-minute bidding: It's an easy thing to do. Whether you choose proxy bidding or sniping (see Chapter 7 for my discussion on sniping), decide how much you're willing to pay *before* you bid. If you set a limit, you won't be overcome with the urge to spend more than an item is worth — or, worse, more than you have in your bank account.

Although eBay is lots of fun, it's also serious business. Bidding is a legal and binding contract. Don't get a bad reputation by retracting bids or becoming a deadbeat.

Buyer: Leave Positive Feedback for a Good Seller

Always leave feedback after you put the finishing touches on a transaction. Leaving feedback, and thereby helping other members, is your responsibility. eBay's feedback system judges sellers on several different points. Did you get your item as described? Did the seller send you e-mails keeping you abreast of your shipment progress? Shipping times can be deceiving. Be sure to check the postmark date on the package label to see when your seller sent the item. It's not fair to ding the seller's reputation because an item rerouted itself in the mail.

Sellers are judged on your Detailed Star Ratings? a low star rating can even cost them money (eBay discounts Final Value Fees to sellers who have top service ratings in their DSRs).

Keep in mind that the transaction isn't complete until the buyer receives the merchandise and is happy with the purchase. Not all sellers leave automatic feedback, so don't expect positive feedback just because you paid for your item in a timely manner.

Buyer: Cover Your Assets

Remember that just because you're conducting transactions from the privacy of your home doesn't mean that you're doing everything you can to protect your privacy. Legitimate buyers and sellers *never* need to know your password or Social Security number. *Do not respond to e-mail that asks for that information.* See Chapter 15 about how to handle such phishing scams.

Seller: Really Know Your Stuff

Do some homework. Know the value of your item. At the very least, get an idea of your item's value by searching completed listings for similar items. If it's a new item, check out other online sites and see what your item is selling for by running a Google product search at `www.google.com/prdhp`. Knowing about your product also means that you can accurately describe what you have and never, *ever* pass off a fake as the real deal. Make sure that your item isn't prohibited, illegal, questionable, or infringing. It's your responsibility!

Before posting your listing, you should take the following actions:

- ✔ Write an honest description.
- ✔ Take a good, clear photo.
- ✔ Work out your shipping costs.

Add each of the preceding pieces of info to your item's description to avoid any unnecessary disputes later.

Seller: Polish and Shine

Make sure that your title is descriptive enough to catch the eye of someone browsing a category and detailed enough for eBay's search engine to identify. Don't just write *1960s Board Game*. Instead, give some details: *Tiny Tim Vintage '60s Board Game MIB Complete Good Cond.* Taking advantage of all 80 characters that eBay allows for your title gives you a fighting chance for your keywords to be found when prospective buyers search. The more search keywords you list, the easier it will be for someone to find your item.

Play editor and scrutinize your text for grammar mistakes and misspellings. Typos in either your title or description can cost you money. For example, a search engine will keep skipping over your *Mikky Mouce Choklit Cokie Jare.* Spelling counts — and pays. Always double-check your work!

Seller: Picture-Perfect Facts

Photos can be a boon or a bust on eBay. Double-check the photo of your item before you post it. Is the lighting okay? Does the photo paint a flattering image of the item? Crop out unnecessary backgrounds. Would *you* buy this item?

Take your picture as if you didn't have a description; be sure that it totally illustrates the item. Also, write your description as if you didn't have a photo. That way if the photo server crashes, the prospective buyer will have a good idea of what you're selling.

Be factual and honest. On eBay, all you have is your reputation, so don't jeopardize it by lying about your item or terms. Tell potential buyers about any flaws. Give as complete a description as possible, with all the facts about the item that you can include.

Seller: Communication Is Key

Respond quickly and honestly to all questions sent via eBay Messages and use the contact to establish a good relationship. Don't let more than 24 hours pass without sending a response. If a bidder makes a reasonable request about payment or shipping, going along with that request is usually worth it to make a sale. *Note:* The customer is always right! (Well, most of the time, anyway.)

Be up-front and fair when charging for sending merchandise to your buyer. You can't make much by overcharging for shipping and handling. Besides, charging outrageous fees will penalize you in eBay search and is a violation of eBay's policies; you could get yourself in trouble. After the item arrives, the buyer may realize what it cost to ship. Unreasonable charges inevitably lead to bad feelings, negative feedback, and low DSRs.

Be sure also that all tracking numbers are input into PayPal or eBay after an item ships. PayPal will send an e-mail to your buyer with that information. It's just another way to communicate and keep your buyer at ease.

Seller: Be a Buyer's Dream

Just because you're transacting through the computer doesn't mean that you can forget your manners. Live by the Golden Rule: Do unto others as you would have others do unto you. Ship the item within a day of the buyer's payment — immediately is even better. (Better yet, why not always ship the item that quickly? I try to.) And keep all your correspondence polite.

Ship the goods as soon as you can (in accordance with the shipping terms you outline in the item description, of course). An e-mail stating that the item is on its way (with the tracking number) is always a nice touch, too. That way, buyers can eagerly anticipate the arrival of their goods.

When shipping your items, use quality packing materials and sturdy boxes to prevent disaster. Broken or damaged items can lead to reputation-damaging negative feedback. Pack as if a gang of clumsy robots is out to destroy your package (or as if *you* had made this purchase). Your buyers are sure to appreciate the effort.

Seller: Listen to the Music

As I state in the golden rules for buyers, don't underestimate the power of positive feedback. Your reputation is at stake. Always generously dole out feedback when you complete a transaction. Your buyers will appreciate it and should return the favor. What should you do if you get slammed unfairly with negative feedback? Don't freak out! If you feel it's unjustly posted, do, however, contact the buyer and ask for a revision. If that doesn't work, at least post a follow-up response for others to see. Those who read your feedback can often see past a single disgruntled message, especially if they can see you handled it well.

Keep in mind that, in most cases, negative feedback results from misunderstandings. Contact the buyer the moment you smell a problem arising and see if you can work things out to your satisfaction. Always work to keep your eBay reputation pristine.

Buyers and Sellers: Keep Current, Keep Cool

You'd be surprised at how many users get suspended even though they have automatic credit card payments. Maybe they move. Or their e-mail addresses change because they change Internet service providers. Regardless, if you don't update your contact and credit card information, and that leaves eBay and other users unable to contact you, you can be suspended.

If you make any major moves (home address, billing address, ISP), let eBay know this new contact information. Click My eBay on the main navigation area at the top of eBay pages, click the Account tab, scroll down the links on the left side of the page to Personal Information, and update the appropriate data.

Chapter 20

Ten (or So) Services to Ease Your Way

*R*eady to take your sales to the next level? Are you looking for snappy-looking text or extra tools to make your sales go off the charts and make your items say, "Buy me!"? Need to slip in a bid in the middle of the night without losing sleep? Perhaps you've found a great deal on some merchandise to sell and need to pony up the cash to buy it. If so, here's a list of ten (or so) platforms to help put your sales ahead of the pack and make your bidding life easier. In this chapter, I recommend some reliable companies, and many of them offer free solutions!

As online sales grow in popularity, software developers are constantly upgrading and developing new auction and selling software to meet eBay's changes. Many of these programs automatically look for new versions of themselves — and update themselves as you start them.

You absolutely don't *have* to use any of these programs or services to run eBay sales successfully. However, when you're running more than several listings a week, the addition of a "helper" makes things go ever so much smoother (especially if it's free or very low-cost).

A large number of companies out there offer online management service and offline programs. (Let's face it, as long as people will pay, they'll be happy to have something to sell you.) I can't cover each and every one — but the software that I mention in this chapter has been tried and tested by me. You may know of other effective products — and I'd love to hear about them. I do know that these work and are good tools when you choose to expand your eBay sales.

Listed in this chapter are several options for your sales management. You find (at the end of the chapter) that eBay supplies some pretty robust tools. I mention some solid third-party alternatives, because lots of people prefer not to do everything online and exclusively on eBay. Your business is your own, and you may just want to list your items for sale on eBay and do the rest yourself. Your choice.

Be sure to check my website `www.coolebaytools.com` or my blog, `mcollier.blogspot.com` for updates on software and services pricing, as well as special discounts that are offered to my readers.

Third-Party Management Services

You're comfortable transacting your auctions online, so why not manage them online as well . . . with an extra level of privacy? The sites in this section offer useful services that save time in both posting your auctions and wrapping them up.

Auctiva

If you're new on eBay and you'd like to try a little automation to get you started, Auctiva is your entry-level choice (see Figure 20-1). Auctiva has been serving eBay sellers since my first edition of *eBay For Dummies* in 1999.

Auctiva offers online item-listing software and image hosting for eBay sellers. The easy-to-use site guides you through the process: creating auction listings, posting them on eBay, communicating with buyers, collecting payments, organizing shipments, keeping records of sales, marketing your listings, and much more.

Figure 20-1:
Auctiva's
website is
simple and
straightfor-
ward, and
they offer
free market-
ing tools.

Here are some of the site's features:

- ✔ **A one-page listing tool:** You can create your professional-looking listings with a complete one-page listing tool — and if you like variety, you can choose from hundreds of template options.

- ✔ **Image hosting:** Auctiva enables you to upload hundreds of images at a time, and you can keep your account organized by managing your images within Auctiva's online folder structure.

- ✔ **Auctiva Scrolling Gallery:** You may have noticed that at the bottom of many listings you see on eBay, there is a scrolling gallery showing other items for sale by the seller. This is an excellent tool for selling even more merchandise.

- ✔ **Profiles:** After you generate your profile information, your Auctiva profile is set to appear automatically in all your listings by default.

If you don't want to sign up for all their services, you can still get a free mar-keting tool for your listings. Auctiva Scrolling Gallery is a graphic scrolling gallery of all your listings that you can insert in the text area of your description. It's a very effective cross-promotion tool.

Their tools start for as little as $2.95 a month, which includes 500MB for host-ing your eBay images. For these features and more, visit the Auctiva website at www.auctiva.com.

inkFrog

inkFrog, shown in Figure 20-2, is a web-based service helping eBay sellers since 1999. In 2006, inkFrog bought out another respected service, SpareDollar. In its present form, inkFrog represents a super bargain in a web-based management service.

Figure 20-2:
inkFrog's super sauce is its Smart Lister that uses Terapeak data to improve your titles.

You can manage every aspect of your eBay sales, including image hosting, ad design, automated e-mail management, and report tracking. If you want to get fancy, you can design your item listing from any of its templates. Here are some more features:

- ✔ **Image hosting:** inkFrog hosts your images and has a handy uploader that allows you to insert your images with a click of your mouse.

- ✔ **Smart Lister:** Create your listings, using a simple form. Terapeak research is built in, along with inkFrog's smart-suggestion technology, to help you write titles that sell.

For more information, and even more features, visit the inkFrog website at www.inkfrog.com.

Vendio and Vendio stores

Vendio, shown in Figure 20-3, was one of eBay's first providers in 1999 and has been serving over a million sellers since. These sellers have sold over

$15 billion in merchandise to nearly 300 million buyers. Vendio is a major provider of services that help e-commerce merchants on eBay, Amazon, and many other sites reach consumers, manage transactions, and profitably grow their businesses.

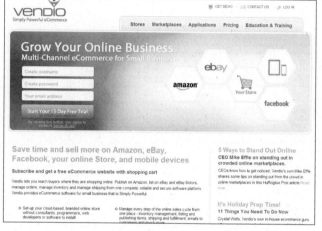

Figure 20-3:
Vendio's website offers a ton of options; it's worth the time to check out.

You can buy some or all of Vendio services (kind of like ordering in a Chinese restaurant). Here are just a few of their many applications:

✔ **Free Vendio Gallery:** Yes, you read it right, Free! This tool will insert a scrolling gallery of your other items listed on eBay within the description area.

✔ **Buyer appreciation:** This automates the process of personalized customer communication. The first time a customer bids or buys, they send a thank-you e-mail. Best of all? This service is free.

✔ **Image hosting:** Vendio's Image Hosting (included in monthly plans) includes many options. You can resize your photos, bulk upload, and apply watermarks for security.

The main Vendio service is a robust listing, inventory, and business-management platform. With its site you can manage each step of the online sales cycle: inventory management, marketing, fulfillment, customer communications, and more. To view all its offerings and current pricing, go to www.vendio.com.

Auction Wizard 2000 on your desktop

If you prefer to handle all your auction management, posting, and design on your own computer, I highly recommend Auction Wizard 2000, as shown in Figure 20-4. It's a full-service professional management software package developed by eBay sellers.

Figure 20-4:
Auction
Wizard
2000 is a
compact
program
that's a
jack-of-all-
trades.

The software is fairly simple and amazingly powerful. It expedites all the seller functions for running and completing eBay sales, including automating the following tasks:

✔ Inputting your inventory on the software's HTML templates and uploading auctions in bulk onto eBay.

✔ Image-editing software is built right in, along with FTP to send your images to your host.

✔ Automatically updating the software with the current status of your auctions — including who won, who is a runner-up, and the auction's bidding history. The preformatted e-mail and feedback files fill in the values from each auction automatically and send them to the people you do business with directly through the software.

✔ Tracking income and expenses, as well as creating a full set of reports.

If you choose to become a consignment seller — that is, sell items for other people — Auction Wizard 2000 has a separate tracking area where you can keep track of your consignment sales by consignee. It even computes the fees that you're charging for your services. Auction Wizard (also known as AW2K) charges $50 per user per year.

Download a fully functional 60-day test drive — with no inactive features and no restrictions — from `www.auctionwizard2000.com`.

Important Tools for Buyers and Sellers

One might think that everything is covered by eBay and the services listed up to this point, but there are a few other platforms to make your life easier on the site as a buyer . . . and as a seller.

Sniping with BidRobot

When it comes to buying fixed price items on eBay, there's really no magic formula other than knowing how to use eBay's search. Using some of the tricks I teach on searching can help you ferret out the best of deals.

But what about auctions? There is very little more frustrating than losing an auction by a dollar or so. When I first started writing about eBay, I began to use the word "snipe" — loosely (and generally) defined as "to shoot at individuals as opportunity offers from a concealed or distant position." So to snipe at an auction (metaphorically speaking), you lie in wait and catch the competition off-guard.

As you can tell by reading Chapter 7, I'm a big fan of sniping. It's my favorite way to win an auction. It makes the entire auction experience even more entertaining. When I have the time, I enjoy battling it out for the last few moments of an auction, bidding fiercely, even if (often) unsuccessfully.

There are quite a few auction sniping services on the web. I settled on the one I use now, BidRobot.com (shown in Figure 20-5), because I could quickly get responses to questions and queries.

When I find an auction that I'm serious about, I go to the BidRobot website, log in, and place my future snipe bids. All I have to do is type the item number and my high bid, and that's it. I can shut off my computer knowing that BidRobot will do my bidding for me. Nobody on eBay will know what item I'm desperate to have, because the magical BidRobot doesn't place my bid until a few seconds before the auction closes. If I'm the high bidder, no one will have the chance to bid against me! Mua-ha-haaa!

Figure 20-5:
I use
BidRobot
whenever
I need to
absolutely,
positively
win an item!

It's easy to use BidRobot to snipe single auctions. For single auctions, just type the item number and bid by using only the yellow top section under the BidForm title. You can ignore the entry forms in all other sections.

But what happens when you find that a bunch of sellers have auctions for the same item at low bid amounts? You'd like to take a chance on each item — and only win one? That's where the *BidGroups* feature comes into play. It will allow you to bid on multiple eBay auctions for the same type of item. When you win any one auction that you've put into a BidGroup, BidRobot cancels the remaining bids in that specific group automatically.

BidRobot's services are reasonably priced, based on the amount of time that you want to use the service. As of this writing, BidRobot has placed bids for more than 100,000 eBay users since 1998! You pay a flat rate for all the snipes you can handle. You don't pay any extra charges for the service. For a free trial, visit BidRobot's website at this special URL for my readers `www.bidrobot.com/cool`.

eBay fee calculators

Although eBay has a calculator buried deep in the site, I've found a couple of sites that will do the calculations for you (for eBay sales and other online venues) with a few clicks of your mouse. They are simple to use; `http://salecalc.com/` is shown in Figure 20-6.

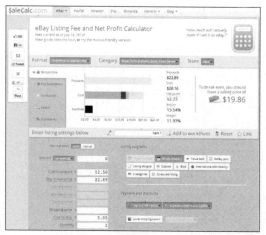

Figure 20-6:
By inputting my data, Salecalc adds in the fees and I see what the net profit will be.

One of the original third-party eBay calculators was developed by Ryan Olbe. Ryan was a programming whiz who keeps his site up to date and had calculators for eBay Canada, Ireland, United Kingdom, and Australia. Ryan has since passed away, and his family is maintaining all the varied calculators: *"All of Ryan's calculators can be found on this site and we will try to keep them up to date as fees change from time to time. We believe this is what Ryan would've wanted and will forever be grateful for the work that he did."* A link to all his calculators can be found at `http://rememberingrolbe.com/`.

The eBay calculator (shown in Figure 20-7) is maintained at `http://www.rememberingrolbe.com/ebay.htm`

Figure 20-7:
An oldie but a goodie for pricing your items.

Kabbage: Working capital

Do you need cash to grow your online business? After you're up and rolling, you might come across a great deal on hot-selling widgets, but find yourself short of cash because they are sold in lots of 50. All businesses need capital to grow. Kabbage provides working capital to online merchants through a short application process that takes under ten minutes (see Figure 20-8).

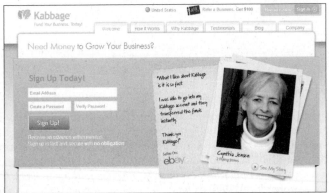

Figure 20-8: The Kabbage home page is your first step toward growing your business.

Kabbage provides funding only to online sellers. Online sellers are generally misunderstood by banks and financial services because traditional underwriting and funding criteria do not account for a virtual commerce business model or the value of recently sold inventory. When you apply, they look at many factors (other than your credit score) to determine how much they can advance, including your seller rating, time in business, transaction volume, and other feedback measurements.

Visit their website at www.kabbage.com for more details.

eBay's Software and Services

When the users call, eBay answers! As eBay grew, the need for additional services and software also grew. eBay answered the need with Turbo Lister software and its Selling Manager products. Read on to see how these services tailored for the eBay user may benefit you.

eBay's free Turbo Lister

Turbo Lister is free software that enables you to upload many auctions simultaneously. I use it regularly to set up my listings. After you prepare your auctions offline, the software uploads your auctions to eBay with just the click of a button. You can edit, preview, and (when you're ready) launch all your auctions at once, or schedule them to launch at different times. Your items can include eBay's templates, and the items will remain archived on your computer for later use. The software is convenient and simple to use, even if you have only a few items at one time — although Turbo Lister will let you launch thousands of listings at a time! The program is free, and you can download it at

```
http://pages.ebay.com/sellerinformation/sellingresources/
turbolister.html
```

I use Turbo Lister myself. I like it because I can store my listings and design my own templates. Listing new items is as easy as making a copy of an older one and filling in new text and photos. Figure 20-9 shows my own Turbo Lister.

Figure 20-9:
Turbo Lister after importing my current listings from eBay.

Selling Manager and Selling Manager Pro

I have used Selling Manager Pro for my eBay sales for many years, and I find it to be a convenient way to quickly relist singly (or in bulk), track the progress of my sales, send bulk e-mails, leave feedback, and keep track of what has and hasn't sold.

You also get a nice selection of reports to help you keep track of how your listings are performing. This way you can tell whether your sales are on target or not. Selling Manager (or Selling Manager Pro) replaces the All Selling page of My eBay. This thorough data is updated automatically from eBay's servers and PayPal, so you have up-to-the-minute info.

Selling Manager is free to all sellers but you must request the feature. The Pro version, which adds inventory management and reporting features, is tailored to high-volume sellers and costs $15.99 a month, but is free for Premium and Anchor eBay Store subscribers. Information on both versions is available at

```
http://pages.ebay.com/sellerinformation/sellingresources/
sellingmanagerpro.html
```

eBay PowerSellers

eBay offers an elite club for PowerSellers, sellers who sell larger quantities of merchandise (as rated by PowerSeller level) on the site. Anyone can become a PowerSeller because you can be qualified not only on the dollar amount of your sales, but also the number of sales. You must first fulfill the following requirements:

- Be an active eBay member for at least 90 days.

- Sell a minimum of $3,000 and 100 items with United States buyers in the past 12 months.

- Maintain at least a 98 feedback percentage.

- Keep your eBay account current.

- Comply with all eBay policies.

- Maintain at least a rating of 4.60 average or higher from U.S. buyers for the past 12 months in all four Detailed Star Ratings (DSRs).

- Have no more than 1 percent of transactions with low DSRs (1s or 2s) with U.S. buyers on item as described, and a maximum of 2 percent of low DSRs on communication, shipping time, and shipping and handling cost.

- No more than 0.30 percent of transactions result in closed cases without seller resolution.

PowerSeller levels include Bronze, Silver, Gold, Platinum, and Titanium, depending on the number of items you've sold or the dollar amount of your sales. You don't need to apply to be a PowerSeller; just check your Seller Dashboard from your My eBay page and eBay will have your status on the page.

Top Rated Sellers

If you go to one of my listings, you will see they have the Top Rated Seller icon on them. A rating of Top Rated Seller is hard to attain, but it gives you distinct advantages over the competition. (I will admit that I've slipped in the past and fallen out of this status. But it's also been well worth reinstating.)

The advantages are clear; you receive

- ✔ Priority customer support
- ✔ A 20-percent discount on Final Value Fees (on item sale price only)
- ✔ Unpaid item protection, which offers credit for certain listing upgrade fees on eligible listing formats
- ✔ Expanded seller protection from PayPal
- ✔ A snappy-looking badge on listing pages and in search results
- ✔ Improved search standing for fixed-price listings in Best Match search results

So how do you get Top Rated Seller status? You must earn PowerSeller status first, and meet the requirements shown in Table 20-1 for Detailed Star Ratings (DSRs). You may also check your status in your Enhanced Seller Dashboard (mine is pictured in Figure 20-10).

Table 20-1 DSR Requirements for Top Rated Seller Status

DSR Category	Percentage of 1 and 2 ratings	Maximum number of occurrences
Item as described	0.50%	2
Communication	0.50%	2
Shipping Time	0.50%	2
Shipping & Handling Charges	0.50%	2

For more information, and any changes in the offerings or requirements, visit `http://pages.ebay.com/help/sell/top-rated.html`.

Figure 20-10:
Click the
link to
Performance
Standards
from your
Seller
Dashboard
to see how
you are
doing.

Appendix

Finding Stuff to Sell

• •

*A*fter you pick clean everything not nailed down in your house, you may want to broaden your horizons. The key to successfully selling items on eBay is to find things people actually want to buy at the right price. I know it seems obvious, but having *stuff to sell* isn't always the same as having *things people want to buy*. Using this concept, you can teach yourself all kinds of effective marketing strategies. Finding the item that may be "the next big thing" takes lots of work, timing, and sometimes a dose of good luck.

As an eBay seller, no doubt you'll receive tons of spam (unsolicited e-mails) guaranteeing that the sender has the hottest-selling items for you to sell on eBay. Think about this for a second. If you had the hot ticket to riches, wouldn't you be selling that product on eBay and making the fortune yourself? These people aren't big-hearted millionaires; they make money by preying on those who think there's a magic way to make money on eBay. There isn't. It takes old-fashioned elbow grease and research.

Knowing the Market

Just as successful stockbrokers know about individual companies, they also need to know about the marketplace as a whole. Sure, I may know about the top designer purses out there, and so do many others. To get a leg up on your competition, you need to know the big picture, taking marketing trends into consideration. Here are some questions you should ask yourself as you contemplate making serious buckets of money (well, I hope) by selling items on eBay:

- ✔ **What items are currently hot?** If you see everyone around you rushing to the store to buy a particular item, chances are good that the item will become more valuable as stocks of it diminish. (iPhone accessories?) The simple rule of supply and demand says that whoever has something everyone else wants stands to gain major profits. Big-box warehouse stores like Costco usually have a full stock of popular items because their (very savvy) buyers purchase by the truckload months in advance — how about visiting a warehouse store to find items at discount?

✓ **Do I see a growing interest in a specific item that might make it a big seller?** If you're starting to hear buzz about a particular item, or even an era ('90s nostalgia? I just found some new-in-the-box copies of Windows 3.1 if you're in the market for tech. '60s aluminum Christmas trees? Who knew?), listen carefully and think of what you already own (or can get your hands on) that can help you catch a piece of the trend's action.

✓ **Should I hold on to this item and wait for its value to increase, or should I sell now?** Knowing when to sell an item that you think people may want is a tricky business. Sometimes you can catch the trend too early and find out that you could have commanded a higher price if only you had waited. Other times, you may invest in a fad that's already passé and find that no one's interested anymore. It's best to test the market with a small quantity, dribbling items individually into the market until you've made back the money you spent to acquire them. When you have your cash back, the rest will be gravy.

I'm a huge fan of the artist George Rodrigue. When building my collection of his famous "Blue Dog" items years ago, I came across a seller who had liberated some early museum exhibition catalogs from a dumpster. Although the old catalogs had been tossed in the trash, they were boxed and bundled — and in perfect condition. Being a true-blue Rodrigue fan, I thought perhaps these catalogs might make good future eBay items. I asked the seller if he had 30 to sell; he said yes, and he sold them to me for $4 each. I resold them over the next five years for between $15 and $35 each. Spotting something evergreen and seeing the future value in items is what it's all about.

✓ **Is a company discontinuing an item I should stockpile now and sell later?** Pay attention to items that are discontinued, especially toys and novelty items. If you find a collectible item that a manufacturer has a limited supply of, you could make a tidy profit. If the manufacturer ends up reissuing the item, don't forget that the original run is still the most coveted — and valuable. I once bought a case of last season's footless pantyhose at a huge discount — I sold them one at a time, at a 400-percent profit, over three years.

✓ **Was there a recall, an error, or a legal proceeding associated with my item?** If so, how it affects the value of the item takes a back seat to eBay policy: An error item, okay. But items that have been recalled for safety reasons can't be sold on eBay (for details, go to pages.ebay.com/ help/policies/recalled.html). For example, a toy recalled for safety reasons may no longer be appropriate for the kids, but even if it's rare and collectible, you *still* can't sell it on eBay.

But here's another angle: Consider that stock shares of (and any paperwork to do with) the now-defunct Enron Corporation became highly prized collectibles after the scandal hit; they still sell on eBay as collectibles.

Some people like to go with their gut feelings about when and what to buy for resale on eBay. By all means, if instinct has worked for you in the past, factor instinct in here, too. If you've done some research that looks optimistic but your gut says, "I'm not sure," listen to it; don't assume that you're just hearing that lunchtime hot dog talking. Try testing the waters by purchasing *one* of the prospective items for resale on eBay. If that sale doesn't work out, you won't have invested a lot of money, and you can credit your gut with saving you some bucks.

Do You Have Talent, Provide a Service?

If you're talented in any way, you can sell your services on eBay. Home artisans, chefs, and even stay-at-home psychics are transacting business daily on the site. (In fact, psychics are doing a land-office business!) What a great way to make money on eBay — make your own product!

Personalized and custom items do well on eBay. There's a demand for personalized invitations, cards, and announcements — and even return address labels (and you thought you had all you needed). Calligraphic work or computer-designed items (customized with Fido's picture, awww) are in big demand today, but no one seems to have the time to make them. Savvy sellers with talent can fill this market niche.

People go to trendy places (when they have the time) like Soho, the Grove, or the Village to find unique custom jewelry. They also go to eBay.

The world is your oyster on eBay, and the sky is the limit. Use your imagination, and you might be surprised at what your new business will be!

Catching Trends in the Media

Catching trends is all about listening and looking. You can find all kinds of inside information from newspapers, magazines, television, and of course, the Internet. Believe it or not, you can even find out what people are interested in these days by bribing a kid. Keep your eyes and ears open. When people say, "That GEICO gecko is *everywhere*," instead of nodding your head vacantly, start getting ideas.

On the web

Newspapers and websites are bombarded by press releases and inside information from companies the world over. Pay close attention to the various sections of the newspaper. Look for stories on celebrities and upcoming movies and see if any old fads are making a resurgence (you can sell items as "retro chic" — Lava Lamps, anyone?).

Trending sites on the web give you up-to-the-second information. Google, for example, has a couple. Take a look at `http://www.google.com/trends/topcharts` for monthly trends and `http://www.google.com/trends/hottrends` that updates by the hour.

Read the stories about retail trade conventions, such as the New York Toy Fair or the Consumer Electronics show. New products are introduced and given the thumbs-up or -down by journalists. This way you can start to think about the direction your area of expertise is heading.

On television

No matter what you think of television, it has an enormous impact on which trends come and go and which ones stick. Why else would advertisers sink billions of dollars into TV commercials? And look at the impact Oprah's Book Club had. Just one Oprah appearance for an author could turn a book into an overnight bestseller. More and more celebrities (even Homer Simpson, who's imaginary) are talking about eBay. The buzz brings people to the site.

Tune in to morning news shows and afternoon talk shows. See what's being featured in the programs. The producers of these shows are on top of pop culture and move fast to be the first to bring you the next big thing. Take what they feature and think of a marketing angle. If you don't, you can be sure somebody else will.

Catch up with youth culture . . .

. . . or at least keep good tabs on it. There seems to be no catching up with it, just as there's no way to say this without sounding over-the-hill: If you remember cranking up The Beatles, New Kids on the Block, or The Partridge Family (say what?) until your parents screamed, "Shut that awful noise off," you may be at that awkward time of life when you hardly see the appeal of what young people are doing or listening to. But if you want tips for hot-selling items, tolerate the awful noise of today's music (how *did* that happen?) and listen to the kids around you. (Try to watch some popular YouTube videos, too.) Children, especially preteens and teens, may be the best trend-spotters on the planet. See what kind of marketing tips you get from your neighborhood hipster when you ask questions like these:

- **What's cool at the moment?** Or "rad" if you want to sound cool — whoops, that was '80s-speak, wasn't it?

- **What's totally uncool that was cool two months ago?** Their world moves at warp speed!

- **What music are you buying?** Kanye West, Kelly Clarkson, Coldplay, and Black-Eyed Peas — yup, all those hot bands with big hits — but maybe *ewww-that's-so-five-minutes-ago* by the time you read this.

- **What could I buy you that would make you really happy?** *Hint:* If the kid says, "a classic red BMW Z-5," or "liposuction," look for a younger kid. (Sorry, iPads are not a useful answer — because almost everyone already has one.)

Check out eBay

An important link on eBay goes to the Popular items. Visit this page and you can find an up-to-date snapshot of the most popular items by category. This is usually pretty eye-opening — you will be surprised at what is listed as a Top Product! Find the link in the eBay navigation links at the bottom of the eBay home page, or you can also reach this page by going directly to `http://popular.ebay.com/`.

Check out magazines

Magazines geared to the 18–to–34 age group (and sometimes to younger teens — they call them *tweens*) can help you stay on top of what's hot. See what the big companies are pitching to this target audience and whether they're succeeding. If a celebrity's suddenly visible in every other headline or magazine, be on the lookout for merchandise relating to that person. (Are we talking hysteria-plus-cash-flow here, or just hysteria?)

Collecting magazines

Although not quite a plethora, the number of magazines geared to collectors is definitely approaching a slew. Although these magazines won't help you catch a trend (by the time it gets into one of these magazines, somebody's already caught it), they can give you great information on pricing, availability, and general collecting information. And you can follow the course of a trend for a real-life example of how it works. Many are available on the web; here's a list of collectors' magazines that I like:

✔ *Antique Trader* has been the bible of the antique collecting industry for over 40 years. Visit its online home at www.antiquetrader.com for more articles and other information.

✔ *Dolls Magazine* has info on everything related to dolls of all types. Go to www.dollsmagazine.com.

✔ *Numismatic News* is an old standard that has been around for more than 50 years. The first issue each month includes a pull-out guide to retail U.S. coin prices. Every three months, it also includes a U.S. paper-money price guide at http://www.numismaticnews.net.

The Hunt for eBay Inventory

If you're not sure what you want to sell for profit on eBay — but you're a shop-till-you-drop person by nature — you have an edge. Incorporate your advanced shopping techniques into your daily routine. If you find a bargain that interests you, chances are you have a knack for spotting stuff that other shoppers would love to get their hands on.

The goods are out there

When you shop to sell on eBay, don't rule out any shopping venue. From the trendiest boutique to the smallest second-hand store, from garage sales to Saks Outlet, keep your eye out for eBay inventory. The items people look for on eBay are out there; you just have to find them.

Check your favorite eBay category and see what the hot-selling items are. Better yet, go to your favorite store and make friends with the manager. Store managers are often privy to this type of information a couple of months in advance of a product release. If you ask, they'll tell you what's going to be the hot new item next month. After you're armed with the information you need, seek out that item for the lowest price you can, and then you can give it a shot on eBay.

Keep these shopping locales in mind when you go on the eBay hunt:

- ✔ Upscale department stores, trendy boutiques, outlet stores, or flagship designer stores are good places to do some market research. Check out the newest items — and then head to the clearance area or outlet store and scrutinize the bargain racks for brand-name items.

- ✔ Tour some of the discount and dollar stores in your area. Many of the items these places carry are *overruns* (too many of something that didn't sell), *small runs* (too little of something that the big guys weren't interested in stocking), or out-of-date fad items that need a good home on eBay.

- ✔ Garage sales, tag sales, and moving sales offer some of the biggest bargains you'll ever come across. Check for vintage kitchen pieces, designer goods, and old toys, and make 'em an offer they can't refuse.

- ✔ Thrift stores are packed with used but usually good-quality items. And you can feel good knowing that the money you spend in a nonprofit thrift shop is going to a good cause. (Look out for vintage Hawaiian shirts.)

- ✔ Find going-out-of-business sales. You can pick up bargains by the case if a shopkeeper just wants to empty the shelves so the store can close.

- ✔ Take advantage of any flea markets or swap meets in your area.

- ✔ Gift shops at museums, monuments, national parks, and theme parks can provide eBay inventory — but think about where to sell the items. Part of your selling success on eBay is *access.* People who can't get to the Kennedy Space Center may pay handsomely for a baseball cap with the official NASA logo on the box. Consider sports venues and theme parks as well.

- ✔ Hang on to the freebies you get. If you receive handouts (lapel pins, pencils, pamphlets, books, interesting napkins, flashlights, towels, stuffed toys) from a sporting event, premiere, or historic event — or even a collectible freebie from a fast-food restaurant — any of them could be your ticket to some eBay sales.

Tips for the modest investor

If you're interested in making money in your eBay ventures but you're starting with limited cash, follow this list of eBay inventory do's and don'ts:

- ✔ **Don't** spend more than you can afford to lose. If you shop at boutiques and expensive department stores, buy things that you like to wear yourself (or give as gifts) in case they don't sell.

✔ **Do** try to find something local that's unavailable in a wider area. For example, if you live in an out-of-the-way place that has a local specialty, try selling that on eBay.

✔ **Don't** go overboard and buy something really cheap just because it's cheap. Figure out who would *want* the item first.

✔ **Do** consider buying in bulk, especially if you know that the item sells well on eBay or if the item is inexpensive. Chances are good that if you buy one and it sells well on eBay, by the time you try to buy more, the item's sold out. If an item is inexpensive (say, 99 cents), I always buy at least five. If no one bids on the item when you hold your auction, you're only out $5. (Anyone out there need any Bicentennial Commemorative coffee mugs?)

Index

• *C* •

• D •

• J •

• K •

Math & Science

Algebra I For Dummies,
2nd Edition
978-0-470-55964-2

Anatomy and Physiology
For Dummies,
2nd Edition
978-0-470-92326-9

Astronomy For Dummies,
3rd Edition
978-1-118-37697-3

Biology For Dummies,
2nd Edition
978-0-470-59875-7

Chemistry For Dummies,
2nd Edition
978-1-1180-0730-3

Pre-Algebra Essentials
For Dummies
978-0-470-61838-7

Microsoft Office

Excel 2013 For Dummies
978-1-118-51012-4

Office 2013 All-in-One
For Dummies
978-1-118-51636-2

PowerPoint 2013
For Dummies
978-1-118-50253-2

Word 2013 For Dummies
978-1-118-49123-2

Music

Blues Harmonica
For Dummies
978-1-118-25269-7

Guitar For Dummies,
3rd Edition
978-1-118-11554-1

iPod & iTunes
For Dummies,
10th Edition
978-1-118-50864-0

Programming

Android Application
Development For
Dummies, 2nd Edition
978-1-118-38710-8

iOS 6 Application
Development For Dummies
978-1-118-50880-0

Java For Dummies,
5th Edition
978-0-470-37173-2

Religion & Inspiration

The Bible For Dummies
978-0-7645-5296-0

Buddhism For Dummies,
2nd Edition
978-1-118-02379-2

Catholicism For Dummies,
2nd Edition
978-1-118-07778-8

Self-Help & Relationships

Bipolar Disorder
For Dummies,
2nd Edition
978-1-118-33882-7

Meditation For Dummies,
3rd Edition
978-1-118-29144-3

Seniors

Computers For Seniors
For Dummies,
3rd Edition
978-1-118-11553-4

iPad For Seniors
For Dummies,
5th Edition
978-1-118-49708-1

Social Security
For Dummies
978-1-118-20573-0

Smartphones & Tablets

Android Phones
For Dummies
978-1-118-16952-0

Kindle Fire HD
For Dummies
978-1-118-42223-6

NOOK HD For Dummies,
Portable Edition
978-1-118-39498-4

Surface For Dummies
978-1-118-49634-3

Test Prep

ACT For Dummies,
5th Edition
978-1-118-01259-8

ASVAB For Dummies,
3rd Edition
978-0-470-63760-9

GRE For Dummies,
7th Edition
978-0-470-88921-3

Officer Candidate Tests,
For Dummies
978-0-470-59876-4

Physician's Assistant Exam
For Dummies
978-1-118-11556-5

Series 7 Exam
For Dummies
978-0-470-09932-2

Windows 8

Windows 8 For Dummies
978-1-118-13461-0

Windows 8 For Dummies,
Book + DVD Bundle
978-1-118-27167-4

Windows 8 All-in-One
For Dummies
978-1-118-11920-4

e Available in print and e-book formats.

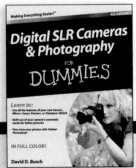

Available wherever books are sold. For more information or to order direct: U.S. customers visit www.Dummies.com or call 1-877-762-2974.
U.K. customers visit www.Wileyeurope.com or call (0) 1243 843291. Canadian customers visit www.Wiley.ca or call 1-800-567-4797.

Connect with us online at www.facebook.com/fordummies or @fordummies

Take Dummies with you everywhere you go!

Whether you're excited about e-books, want more from the web, must have your mobile apps, or swept up in social media, Dummies makes everything easier .